A
POLE APART

A POLE

The Emerging Issue

A TWENTIETH CENTURY FUND REPORT

APART

of Antarctica

PHILIP W. QUIGG

New Press

McGRAW-HILL BOOK COMPANY
*New York   St. Louis   San Francisco   Auckland   Bogota   Guatemala
Hamburg   Johannesburg   Lisbon   London   Madrid   Mexico   Montreal
New Delhi   Panama   Paris   San Juan   São Paulo   Singapore
Sydney   Tokyo   Toronto*

1 2 3 4 5 6 7 8 9 D O C D O C 8 7 6 5 4 3 2

ISBN 0-07-051053-9

LIBRARY OF CONGRESS CATALOGING IN PUBLICATION DATA

Quigg, Philip W.
A pole apart.
1. Antarctic Regions—International status.
I. Title.
JX4084.A5Q53   341.2'9'09989   82–7733
ISBN 0–07–051053–9   AACR2

Book design by A. Christopher Simon

To Ada

The Twentieth Century Fund is an independent research foundation which undertakes policy studies of economic, political, and social institutions and issues. The Fund was founded in 1919 and endowed by Edward A. Filene.

Acknowledgments

An author's warmest thanks must be to those who were willing to read and comment on his manuscript. Ernest A. Gross, Thomas O. Jones, A. P. Crary, James E. Heg, and Lawrence J. Baack, none of whom (it must be ritually affirmed) bears any responsibility for the outcome, have my deep gratitude for their criticisms and suggestions. Of the many people who were interviewed, those who made a particular contribution to my understanding were Paul Daniels, principal U.S. negotiator of the Antarctic Treaty; the aforementioned Tom Jones, who was the first director of the U.S. Antarctic Research Program; John A. Heap, head of the Polar Regions Section, and David J. Edwards, legal counselor, in the British Foreign and Commonwealth Office; Ian W. D. Dalziel of the Lamont Geological Observatory; and R. Tucker Scully, the most knowledgeable Antarctic hand in the Department of State.

In Rome, John A. Gulland, chief of the Marine Resources Service of the U.S. Food and Agricultural Organization, and his colleagues, J. E. Carroz, director of the Fishing Policy and Planning Division, L. P. D. Gertenbach, Zbigniew Karnicki, and Michel Savini, were extremely helpful. At the British Antarctic Service in Cambridge, Richard M. Laws, Raymond J. Adie, Charles Swithinbank, and especially Inigo Everson gave generously of their time and expertise. Also in Cambridge, H. G. R. King, librarian at the Scott Polar Research Institute, was unstinting in providing assistance, while, in Washington, Franklin W. Burch of the Center for Polar Archives was equally helpful. Library staffs at the Council on Foreign Relations, New York Public Library, Princeton University Library, the George Arents Research Library at Syracuse University, the Explorers' Club, Hunter College, and the Department of State all helped me with good grace to find my way.

For the opportunity to converse at some length, I am grateful to Ambassadors Keith G. Brennan of Australia, Alfred van der Essen of Belgium, and M. C. W. Pinto of Sri Lanka. Others who were generous to me with their time were Jean Vaugelade, director of Expeditions Polaires Françaises, and George Hemmen, secretary of SCOR/SCAR, and his assistant Jane Whiting, as well as Martin Holdgate, Philip C. Jessup, Robert D. Hayton, and Charles Neider.

I am especially grateful for the counsel of John R. Twiss, Jr., and Robert J. Hofman of the Marine Mammal Commission, and of John A. Dugger of the Department of Energy. At the Department of State, Thomas R. Pickering, George H. Aldrich, David Colson, Norman Wulf, and Lisle A. Rose each added something to my comprehension. At the National Science Foundation's Division of Polar Programs, Edward P. Todd, Francis Williamson, Joseph E. Bennett, Walter Seelig, and Guy Guthridge made themselves easily accessible. At the National Oceanic and Atmospheric Administration, Martin Belsky, Alan F. Ryan, and Robert Stockman were most helpful.

Jaime Bazan of the Chilean embassy, Colin R. Keating of the New Zealand embassy, and Ricardo Quadri and Jorge J. Matas of the Argentine embassy, all in Washington, did me kindnesses that were much appreciated. Others to whom I am indebted are David Keeney of the Senate Foreign Relations Committee; Louis DeGoes of the Polar Research Board; Donald R. Wiesnet and Craig Berg of the National Oceanic and Atmospheric Administration's National Earth Satellite Service; Gerald S. Schatz of the National Academy of Sciences; James N. Barnes of the Center for Law and Social Policy; Miriam Levering of the United Methodist Law of the Sea Project; Patricia Scharlin, a member of the Antarctic Section of the Department of State's Public Advisory Committee on Ocean Affairs; Alan Seilen of the Environmental Protection Agency; John Lawrence Hargrove of the American Society of International Law; John Behrendt of the U.S. Geological Survey (Denver); and John N. Garrett of the Gulf Oil Exploration and Production Company (Houston). Finally, I am enormously grateful to the Twentieth Century Fund for giving me the opportunity to write this book.

Contents

Foreword

Because the Trustees and staff of the Twentieth Century Fund have for some time been concerned about the problems posed by increasing world demand for and slowly growing—or even declining—supplies of natural resources, they had been examining the possibility of international cooperation as a means of resolving them. In the course of considering how to proceed, we learned of one international institution that was beginning to deal imaginatively with these issues. This was the Antarctic Treaty, which, it turned out, was an unusually effective experiment in international cooperation.

Signed in 1959 by twelve nations who had established claims or bases in the region, the treaty was designed to promote scientific research and prevent militarization of the region. This arrangement had been working very well, but then severe internal and external pressures arising from the expectation of finding valuable resources in Antarctica seemed to be threatening its stability. Since the Fund has a long history of involvement in analyzing the U.S. role in international affairs, it seemed an appropriate time to study the complicated mix of economic, political, scientific, and environmental factors involving the array of nations who were either participants or seeking participation in the Antarctic Treaty.

Moreover, in Philip Quigg, former managing editor of *Foreign Affairs*, author and editor of books on American foreign policy and developing countries, the Fund found an ideal candidate for such a project. Mr. Quigg, who also is an authority on environmental issues, has succeeded in producing a clearly reasoned and well-reported book, which examines the future of the treaty and the options available for resolving the territorial and resource issues that are threatening it. He has studied similar issues that are currently the focus of much attention—the Law of the Sea treaty and the theory of the "common heritage of mankind," promoted by many nations who fear they will not receive their fair share of the world's resources—a theory that is likely to be at issue whenever man's frontiers, from the Amazon to the moon, are discussed.

The treaty allows for review and revision in 1991. This contributes to uncertainty as to whether the treaty system can survive Antarctica's transition from pure science laboratory to an arena where significant wealth and expanded contention are serious possibilities. Mr. Quigg has provided extensive background and many recommendations to guide both those who will be making critical decisions and those who would like to understand the issues and influence the outcome. The Fund is grateful for his effort.

M.J. Rossant, Director
The Twentieth Century Fund
March 1982

Abbreviations and Acronyms Used in the Text

ACMRR	*Advisory Committee on Marine Resources Research*
BANZARE	*British, Australian, New Zealand Antarctic Research Expedition*
BIOMASS	*Biological Investigation of Marine Antarctic Systems and Stocks*
COFI	*(FAO) Committee on Fisheries*
DPP	*Division of Polar Programs (in NSF)*
EC	*European Community*
EEZ	*Exclusive Economic Zone*
FAO	*Food and Agriculture Organization of the United Nations*
FIBEX	*First International BIOMASS Experiment*
IABO	*International Association for Biological Oceanography*
ICSU	*International Council of Scientific Unions*
IGY	*International Geophysical Year*
IIED	*International Institute for Environment and Development*
IOC	*Intergovernmental Oceanographic Commission*
IUCN	*International Union for Conservation of Nature and Natural Resources*
IUGG	*International Union of Geodesy and Geophysics*
IWC	*International Whaling Commission*
MMC	*Marine Mammal Commission*
MMT	*Million Metric Tons*
MSY	*Maximum Sustainable Yield*
NIEO	*New International Economic Order*
NOAA	*National Oceanic and Atmospheric Administration*
NSF	*National Science Foundation*
OES	*Office of Oceans and International Environmental and Scientific Affairs (U.S. Department of State)*

SCAR	*Scientific Committee on Antarctic Research*
SCOR	*Scientific Committee on Oceanic Research*
UNCLOS	*United Nations Conference on the Law of the Sea*
UNDP	*United Nations Development Program*
UNEP	*United Nations Environment Program*
USARP	*United States Antarctic Research Program*
VLF	*Very Low Frequency*
WMO	*World Meteorological Organization*

List of Maps

THE SOUTHERN OCEAN
AND ANTARCTICA'S RELATION TO OTHER CONTINENTS

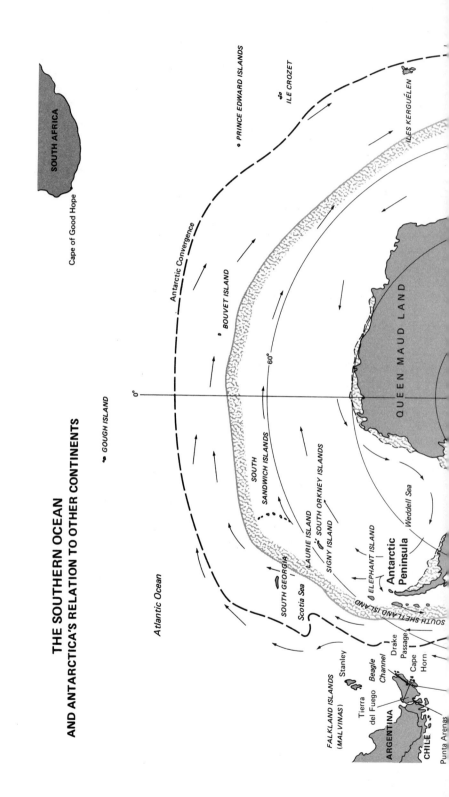

SOUTH AFRICA

Cape of Good Hope

• GOUGH ISLAND

Atlantic Ocean

Antarctic Convergence

• PRINCE EDWARD ISLANDS

ILE CROZET

• BOUVET ISLAND

ILES KERGUÉLEN

60°

0°

QUEEN MAUD LAND

SOUTH
SANDWICH ISLANDS

SOUTH GEORGIA

Scotia Sea

LAURIE ISLAND

SOUTH ORKNEY ISLANDS

SIGNY ISLAND

ELEPHANT ISLAND

Antarctic
Peninsula

Weddell Sea

SOUTH SHETLAND ISLANDS

FALKLAND ISLANDS
(MALVINAS)

Stanley

Tierra
del Fuego

Beagle
Channel

Drake
Passage

Cape
Horn

ARGENTINA

CHILE

Punta Arenas

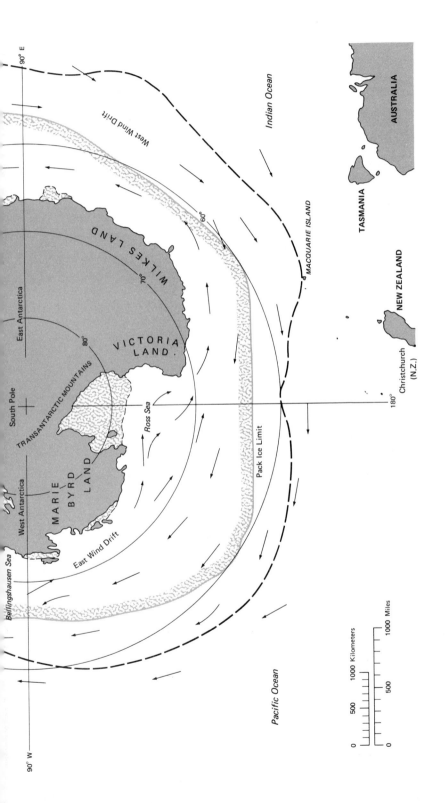

90° E

West Wind Drift

Indian Ocean

AUSTRALIA

TASMANIA

MACQUARIE ISLAND

60°

WILKES LAND

East Antarctica

70°

NEW ZEALAND

South Pole

80°

VICTORIA LAND

TRANSANTARCTIC MOUNTAINS

Christchurch (N.Z.)

180°

Ross Sea

MARIE BYRD LAND

West Antarctica

East Wind Drift

Pack Ice Limit

Bellingshausen Sea

Pacific Ocean

90° W

0   500   1000 Kilometers

0   500   1000 Miles

Introduction

The polar ice cap is a deep freeze of cosmic dimensions,
where yesterday is forever.

—Roger Tory Peterson

Because Antarctica is a continent without indigenous population, it attracts attention only spasmodically. Because its climate is
uniquely inhospitable, it has so far drawn only explorers, scientists, and a relative handful of tourists in the secure comfort of
luxury cruise ships. Public interest has focused on Antarctica only
for brief periods: when fortunes were made slaughtering fur seals
to the point of extinction in the early nineteenth century; when
brave men such as Ernest Shackleton, Robert Scott, and Roald
Amundsen were struggling to be first at the South Pole; or when,
half a century ago, Richard Byrd mounted a series of large,
complex expeditions exploiting radio and the airplane.

The last flurry of interest in Antarctica was in the late 1950s,
when, as part of the International Geophysical Year (IGY), scientists learned more about the region in a relatively few months than
all the knowlege acquired since the circumnavigation of Antarctica by Captain James Cook. This explosion of scientific interest was
followed almost immediately by a treaty, which drew wide attention because, at the height of the Cold War, it involved the United
States and the Soviet Union in unprecedented agreement. The

Antarctic Treaty, negotiated by twelve nations in 1959, ensured that the continent would not be militarized and that continuing scientific research would be characterized by cooperation, freedom of access to all, and exchange of information and scientists. Each of the twelve nations—those that had been active in Antarctica during the IGY—had unqualified right of inspection to ensure that the treaty was being observed.

Seven of the original signatories had long asserted territorial sovereignty over portions of the continent. These pie-shaped claims—by Argentina, Australia, Chile, France, New Zealand, Norway, and the United Kingdom—were not recognized by the other treaty powers—namely Belgium, Japan, South Africa, the Soviet Union, and the United States. This issue is still a cause of tension among the parties. The treaty dealt with it simply by postponing it, saying that nothing in the treaty should affect the claims in any way: During the life of the treaty they could not be strengthened, diminished, or expanded. Since several of the claimants had previously been pointing weapons at one another and occasionally pulling the trigger, this was more of an achievement than it might appear.

Antarctica is a continent representing nearly one-tenth of the terrestrial world. But in common usage, it is also a region embracing the Southern Ocean, which is hardly separable from the icelocked land that appears to expand and contract with the seasons. The treaty recognizes this by extending its purview to 60° south latitude, thus covering one-sixteenth of the surface of the globe. The treaty does not say anything about the possible resources of Antarctica—not because the matter was overlooked but because it was too entangled with the problem of territorial claims to permit solution. Now, after more than two decades of relative obscurity, Antarctica is reentering public consciousness largely because of the expectation that its resources may soon be exploited. The expectation of riches is supported primarily by the shrimplike krill that swarm in profusion in the Southern Ocean —possibly enough to double the harvest of fish from the sea—and by the probability that the continental shelves of Antarctica contain oil and gas. There is also the possibility that icebergs may someday water arid lands and that tourism will expand substantially. Whether the protein-rich krill can in fact add hugely to the world's food supply without irreparably disrupting the marine ecosystem is uncertain. Whether large deposits of oil will be found and whether, if found, they can be economically extracted without severe damage to the environment are even more speculative. Nevertheless, the anticipation of such developments is sufficient to put additional pressures on the treaty parties, to arouse new interest among outsiders who want a share of the spoils (if any), and to require the creation of new institutions to make up for the limitations of the Antarctic Treaty. Ground rules for exploration and exploitation must be agreed upon in order to protect the environment and to determine how the benefits will be divided. Ways must be found to ensure that the harvesting of krill does not endanger the great whales and other species dependent on krill for food.

Some people hope that krill fishing will remain uneconomic and that oil and other minerals will not prove exploitable. They would like to see Antarctica remain an unspoiled preserve, a laboratory for science, a benchmark for measuring changes in the global environment. They wish for the fulfillment of Captain Cook's prophecy, when he adduced the existence of a desolate and ice-encrusted continent that he had not seen: "I make bold to declare that the world will derive no benefit from it."

Through the foresight of its drafters, the Antarctic Treaty possesses the capacity for change, and it has in fact evolved into a system of governance without an executive and without a bureaucracy. Depending on one's perspective, this treaty system may be regarded as the last stand of colonialism, an association of the world's largest real estate operators, a political anachronism whose days are numbered, or an astonishingly successful experiment in international cooperation among antagonistic nations.

One of the primary objectives of the Antarctic Treaty was to prolong the peaceful, cooperative environment in which science had been conducted during the IGY. Since the treaty was ratified in 1961, the business of Antarctica has been science and its only export, knowledge. By and large, the treaty entails more obligations than privileges. If this situation is now to change, if valuable resources are to be found and exploited, then obviously much will be altered. The exclusiveness of the treaty nations—now numbering fourteen with the addition of Poland and West Germany— becomes less acceptable to other countries. Legal, political, and ethical questions arise as to whether Antarctica belongs to everyone or no one or the Club of Fourteen or some combination of these.

The treaty nations are far less representative of the international community than they were in the late 1950s. Since then, the United Nations has doubled in size, and a New International Economic Order implicitly calls for an end to what the treaty members appear to represent. The seemingly endless Law of the Sea Conference strengthened the conviction of the treaty members that they should not share decision-making and, at the same time, set a precedent for declaring Antarctica the common heritage of mankind. By creating exclusive economic zones extending two hundred miles to sea, the convention has also inferentially enlarged existing Antarctic claims.

The next decade may be critical for Antarctica. Between now and 1991, when the terms of the Antarctic Treaty may be reviewed, the long-term future of the continent may be decided: whether the Antarctic will yield significant resources and for whose benefit; whether decision-making will remain concentrated in a few experienced nations or be dispersed, with enhanced danger of irresponsibility; whether the Antarctic environment will be adequately protected; whether the Antarctic Treaty system will survive the internal and external pressures arising from the expectations of finding mineral resources; whether the process of cooperation can surmount a war between two charter members of the treaty; and whether nations can, "in the interest of all mankind"—as the treaty states—ensure "that Antarctica shall continue forever to be used exclusively for peaceful purposes and shall not become the scene or object of international discord."

CHAPTER

[

Discovery and Exploration

Exploration is the physical expression of the Intellectual Passion.

—*Apsley Cherry-Garrard*

The Antarctic existed in theory and imagination long before its reality was established. The theory was created by the wild surmise of the Greeks, who, having reasoned that the world was round, hypothesized that the Southern Hemisphere must mirror the tropical, temperate, and frigid zones of the North; and further, that there must be a vast continent near the southern pole to balance the great weight of the land masses of the Northern Hemisphere. The earliest maps of the Southern Hemisphere, by Orontius and Mercator in the sixteenth century, show a gigantic *Terra Australis* (southern land) virtually filling the Southern Ocean. After each successive voyage of exploration, this *terra incognita* shrank, but it was not until the middle of the past century that we had even an approximate idea of the continent's size. And it was another century before we comprehended its essential geography and geology.[1]

The land existed in imagination because the unknown always excites fantasies. The ancient world thought of the tropics as an impenetrable barrier, where seas boiled and deserts sizzled. Early Christianity found no reason to disagree. Man was created only once, according to Genesis; so if there were creatures within or beyond the torrid zone, they could not be human. Even those who accepted the concept of a spherical world peopled the Southern Hemisphere with monsters—half man, half beast.

The first to prove that one could survive passage across the equator were the seamen of Prince Henry the Navigator who pressed down the coast of Africa in the mid-fifteenth century and found a green and pleasant land. In 1488, Bartholomew Diaz rounded the Cape of Good Hope, thereby disproving Ptolemy's theory that *Terra Australis* was attached to Africa. Ferdinand Magellan's even more remarkable feat of finding a passage from the Atlantic to the Pacific both illuminated and clouded the question of a southern continent: It proved that South America was not strictly part of *Terra Australis*, but suggested that the southern land mass extended as far northward as Tierra del Fuego.

Despite the subsequent discoveries of Drake, who found the passage that bears his name; of Tasman, who lopped what is now Australia from the hypothetical southern continent; and of Halley (he of the comet), who in 1700 became the first scientist to enter the Southern Ocean and the first to describe pack ice, the frozen sea surrounding Antarctica—despite three centuries of exploration of the Southern Hemisphere, the most extraordinary myths persisted. On the basis of one of these, Bouvet de Lozier set sail in 1737 with the support of the French East India Company to find the illusory Gonneville Land or South India, which had been described in glowing terms more than two centuries earlier, but whose even approximate location had been lost.[2]

What Bouvet discovered was the most isolated island on earth— one that was subsequently "lost" for nearly two hundred years but that now bears his name. He was the first to venture as far south as latitude 57°. He then sailed in an easterly direction for many hundreds of miles along the edge of the pack ice. After studying the huge, flat-topped icebergs he encountered, he speculated— and was the first to do so—that they could have been produced only by a large land mass farther to the south.

Despite Bouvet's discouraging report, another Frenchman, Charles de Brosses, produced a five-volume study in which he insisted that there was indeed a gigantic continent to the south, with lands to be colonized, wealth to be exploited, and natives to be uplifted—expressly by the French. He ingeniously used the explorers' reports of ice to strengthen his case: He reasoned that, since the open sea does not freeze, the great fields of ice must come from great rivers that only a great continent could spawn.

De Brosses not only created illusions at home and abroad; he seemed to encourage visions in others. In 1772, Yves-Joseph de Kerguélen-Trémarec set sail in one final attempt to find and claim the elusive continent for France. He believed he found what he was looking for in the Indian Ocean, and since foul weather prevented further investigation, he hurried back to Paris with an ecstatic account of what he had named South France:

> The lands which I have had the happiness to discover appear to form the central mass of the Antarctic continent. . . . This land which I have called South France is so situated as to command the route to India, China and the South Seas. . . . The latitude in which it lies promises all the crops of the Mother Country. . . . No doubt wood, minerals, diamonds, rubies and precious stones and marble will be found. . . . If men of a different species were not discovered at least there will be people living in a state of nature, knowing nothing of the artifices of civilized society. In short South France will furnish marvellous physical and moral spectacles.[3]

The next year, Kerguélen returned to South France with instructions to establish trade relations with the natives and, if possible, to explore the coast of the southern continent as far as 60°S. On this second visit, he discovered that what he had named South France was a barren island (actually an archipelago), virtually without vegetation, and with an incalculable expanse of ocean to the south of it. Although he renamed it Land of Desolation, it is known today as Iles Kerguélen. In those experiences of the French, there may lie a lesson for those who today have limitless expectations of Antarctica.

Britain had its equivalent of de Brosses in Alexander Dalrymple. More highly educated and widely traveled than de Brosses, he nevertheless contended as late as 1772 that the southern continent must "extend over 100° of longitude and be larger than Asia and probably have a population of 50 millions."[4] Hoping to capitalize on the interest he had stirred, Dalrymple himself wanted to command an expedition to prove his theory once and for all. Instead, the Royal Society and the Navy agreed on James Cook, who had already made one long voyage of discovery in the South

Pacific. This extraordinary man of humble birth, self-taught and a master surveyor, was for all time to dispose of the dream of a large, rich, temperate, inhabited continent.

Sailing from Plymouth in 1772, Cook spent the next three years circumnavigating Antarctica. He "followed the guardian ice all around the world, trying repeatedly to penetrate it like a dog looking for a hole in a fence."[5] In his journal, Cook admits that he and his crew were in almost constant fear of ice—not so much of being entrapped or crushed by sea ice as of having ice fall on them from the perpendicular faces of the icebergs that towered above their fragile ships. When the ice became too fearsome or impenetrable, Cook would retreat northward and then move east again. When the austral autumn came, he withdrew to more temperate climes to rest and reprovision.[6]

In the second season of stabbing beyond the Antarctic Circle, Cook reached latitude 71°10', incomparably farther south than any man had been. Despite this and other occasions when he might have sighted land, Cook never claimed to have seen Antarctica, although later he conceded in his journal: "It is probable we have seen a part of it."[7] Two of his officers were sure they had seen the continent, and two explorers who followed seven decades later— Dumont D'Urville and James Clark Ross—concurred.[8]

Toward the close of the third season, as he was about to head north, ending a voyage of more than seventy thousand miles, Cook wrote:

> I firmly believe that there is a track of land near the pole which is the source of most of the ice that is spread over this vast Southern Ocean. . . . The risque one runs in exploring a coast, in these unknown and icey seas, is so very great that I can be bold enough to say that no man will ever venture farther than I have done; and that the lands which may lie to the South will never be explored.[9]

Cook reported at length on the profusion of wildlife in the south polar seas. Using these accounts and his published charts, which were prepared with unparalleled accuracy, an armada of sealers descended on the subantarctic islands—generally those north of 60°S. Beginning in 1784, the sealers methodically stripped each breeding ground, then pressed farther south until, by 1830, species of commercial value were virtually extinct. No one knows how many seals were killed, but unquestionably scores of millions perished. An experienced man could kill and skin fifty seals an hour. By one account, sixty men on two ships killed forty-five thousand seals in one season,[10] and in the decade after 1815, there were about two hundred English and American sealers in Antarctic waters. The most sought-after species were the fur seal for its pelt and the elephant seal for its oil. Pelts were by far the more valuable. Although they brought only fifty cents apiece in New York, transshipped to Canton the price was five dollars.[11] When the seals were exterminated, the hunters turned for oil to the king and royal penguins and decimated them as well.[12] After 1830, they turned once again to the more dangerous and difficult pursuit of whales.

Thus, for a couple of decades, sealers looking for more profitable harvests were the principal Antarctic explorers. Most were secretive, for a newfound breeding ground was the equivalent of a gold mine. The best-known sealers were a Scotsman, James Weddell, who sailed boldly into the sea now bearing his name and, in what must have been an exceptionally warm summer, reached 214 miles closer to the South Pole than had Captain Cook; John Biscoe, whaling skipper for the London firm of Enderby Brothers, who made the second circumnavigation of Antarctica; and an American, Edmund Fanning, who began seal hunting in southern waters in 1800 and who might have led the first official U.S. expedition to Antarctica but for the War of 1812. The Americans were the most numerous. In the 1820-21 season, when the first sighting of the continent is said to have occurred, there were thirty American sealing vessels at the South Shetland Islands, almost within sight of the Antarctic Peninsula.[13] There were also twenty-four British vessels.

THE DISCOVERY OF THE CONTINENT

Britain, the Soviet Union, and the United States each claim to have discovered Antarctica. In this contest, sighting offshore islands did not count, although in a land where islands were frequently lashed to the mainland by solid ice, more than a century would elapse before all the necessary distinctions were made. The debate as to who was first has been unconscionably long and sterile, especially because it is quite possible that all the principal candidates were preceded by sealers, who considered their discoveries proprietary information and kept their mouths and their logs closed. However unserious their relevance, the events of 1820–21 in Antarctica must be told, if briefly, because they have a bearing on later history and contemporary politics.

In 1819, an English sea captain, William Smith, in command of a merchant ship, sighted what are now known as the South Shetland Islands as he swung far to the south of the Horn to escape severe headwinds. After claiming the islands for the British Crown, Smith proceeded to Valparaiso, where he reported his discovery to an officer of the Royal Navy. As a good empire builder should, Captain William Shirref saw the strategic value of possessing the southern flank of the Drake Passage. On the spot, he chartered Smith's ship, retaining Smith as skipper and pilot, and put on board as commanding officer his own master, Edward Bransfield. His orders were to survey the coast and harbors of the new land and "to observe, collect and preserve every object of natural science."[14] Further, his instructions read, "You will ascertain the natural resources for supporting a colony and maintaining a population, or if it be already inhabited, will minutely observe the character, habits, dresses and customs of the inhabitants, to whom you will display every friendly disposition."[15]

Bransfield landed on one of the largest of the South Shetland Islands in January 1820 and named it King George Island. Late in the same month, he sighted what he called Trinity Land, which Americans believe was an island and which the British are convinced was the northern tip of the Antarctic Peninsula. Bransfield remained in the area until March 21, and traveled well south of the Shetlands to latitude 64°30'.[16]

The British claim for Bransfield's primacy has been weakened by the embarrassing fact that his report to the Admiralty was promptly lost and has never been found. However, the charts of his ship, the *William*, survive, and from these, as well as accounts by two of the crew, it seems probable that Bransfield did indeed sight the Antarctic mainland, not in January, but early in February.[17]

The Russian contender for discoverer of Antarctica was Thaddeus Fabian Gottlieb von Bellingshausen, a naval officer and profound admirer of Captain Cook. He was sent to the Southern

Ocean by Czar Alexander I, ostensibly to find unclaimed harbors and potential staging areas to facilitate transportation by sea between Russia's European ports and its Pacific coast.[18] Bellingshausen was well equipped with two stout ships. the *Mirnyi* and the *Vostok* (for which major Soviet bases in Antarctica today are named). After some preliminary charting of several subantarctic islands, Bellingshausen entered Antarctic waters at almost the same time as Bransfield.

On January 27, 1820, Bellingshausen's ships crossed the Antarctic Circle and, over two seasons, circumnavigated Antarctica in a much tighter circle than had Captain Cook. The Russian must have had many opportunities to see the mainland, even as early as January 1820, but he never claimed to have done so in that year. However, the descriptions in his diary and the ship's positions as recorded in his log now suggest that he may well have seen distant mountains on the continent.[19]

The following January, as Bellingshausen approached the base of the Antarctic Peninsula from the west, he saw what was unmistakably land, for bare rocks and cliffs were visible. He named it Peter I Island and then sailed on to the southeast, where, at 69°S, there loomed a high, rugged terrain of vast dimensions. Bellingshausen named this Alexander I Land, believing it to be part of the Antarctic continent. It was not until 1940 that a sledge journey by two Americans, Finn Ronne and Carl Eklund, proved it to be an island.

For more than a century, Americans were firm in the belief that the discoverer of Antarctica was Nathaniel Palmer, twenty-one-year-old skipper of the sloop *Hero*, part of a sealing fleet out of Stonington, Connecticut. In November 1820, Palmer made an exploratory cruise that carried him close to the peninsula. Kenneth J. Bertrand, who has written the authoritative history of Americans in Antarctica, stated, "[T]here can be no doubt that Palmer was able to see from his position, off the southeast coast of Deception Island, the Antarctic mainland toward which he was setting his course."[20]

Palmer has been the American candidate for discoverer of Antarctica primarily because his exploits were widely publicized by his mentor, Edmund Fanning. The whereabouts of the many other American sealers in the Shetlands that season were little known. In the early 1950s, two logbooks were found, adding appreciably to our knowledge of Antarctic sealing in that period. The logbooks are for the ship *Huron* under Captain John Davis and the schooner *Huntress* under Captain Christopher Burdick. The two men met during a stop at the Falkland Islands and decided to join forces. Not only did they both probably see the Antarctic continent, but Captain Davis went ashore on the peninsula, February 7, 1821, at a point slightly to the south of the area seen by Palmer. This landing is the first to be documented.[21] Although other American sealers probably saw the Antarctic continent that season, most American authorities still credit Palmer with being first.

In one of those extraordinary meetings that have marked the history of Antarctic exploration, Palmer in his 47-foot sloop encountered Bellingshausen in his 130-foot warship off Deception Island. Except for their mutual surprise, the meeting appears to have been an unmemorable occasion, the conversation being largely about sealing. Bellingshausen's account of this meeting, which is now generally accepted as accurate, was not published for some years. His heavily expurgated writings were not translated into English until 1945, when historical scholarship was not the only Soviet motivation. But on the American side, in the absence of any written account by Palmer, the meeting was romanticized out of all credence, until Bellingshausen was said to have conceded all rights of discovery to the young American and to have spoken in words of profound admiration.

The accomplishments of Bellingshausen were largely ignored by the government that sent him, while Palmer became something of a hero. Within five months of his return to Stonington, a chart was published designating the area south of the Shetlands as "Palmer's Land." Later, on official U.S. maps, the entire peninsula was named for Palmer.[22] Strangely, the British called the peninsula Graham Land, a name applied in 1833 by Biscoe, skipper for Enderby Brothers, in a not very subtle gesture honoring Sir James R. G. Graham, an unpopular politician with no connection to Antarctica, but nevertheless First Lord of the Admiralty.[23] Bransfield, the simple master in His Majesty's Navy, was thus bypassed (although the strait between the peninsula and the South Shetland Islands was later named for him). To complicate the situation further, the Chileans call the peninsula O'Higgins Land and the Argentines call it San Martin Land, each honoring its national hero. After years of haggling, the English-speaking nations involved in Antarctica finally reached a compromise in 1964: The panhandle is officially the Antarctic Peninsula; the slimmer northern portion is Graham Land, and the wider southern portion is Palmer Land.[24]

SEARCH FOR THE SOUTH MAGNETIC POLE

The remarkable events of 1820–21 were exceeded in 1838-41, when three substantial expeditions explored the Pacific coast of Antarctica at the same time. Each was government sponsored, each was motivated at least in part by an intense interest in studying the earth's magnetic force, and each survived through miracles of luck and fortitude.

The first to enter Antarctic waters was the United States Exploring Expedition of 1838-42, led by Lieutenant Charles Wilkes. Congress had had the project in mind since 1821, and in 1825, in his first annual message to Congress, President John Quincy Adams called for exertions in Antarctic exploration "equal or proportionate" to those of Britain, France, and Russia. But it was not until 1838 that an expedition—ill-equipped, ill-manned, and ill-tempered— departed on a mission embracing much more than the Antarctic alone. The 440 men chosen for the expedition included seven scientists. Missing was one of the most experienced and able: James Eights, the first American scientist to have worked in Antarctica (in 1829-30), was dropped at the last moment without explanation.[25]

Wilkes's ramshackle flotilla was rotten and leaking; one vessel was lost with all hands. Nevertheless, in the first season Wilkes reached 70°S off what is considered the most impenetrable part of the entire Antarctic coastline, Marie Byrd Land. The next season he cruised along the Antarctic ice pack opposite Australia for fifteen hundred miles, seldom out of sight of land when visibility was tolerable. His expedition is thus credited with being the first to provide proof of the existence of an Antarctic continent.[26] He made two landings, although on islands, planted the flag, and collected rock specimens. On his return to the United States, Wilkes was welcomed not with honors but with a court martial; he was accused of "oppression, injustice, administering illegal punishments, falsehood and scandalous conduct."[27] At least some of the charges were probably true, for Wilkes drove his crew mercilessly. But in Europe, his accomplishments were immediately recognized. The Royal Geographical Society awarded him its gold medal, and the area he explored remains generally known among all countries as Wilkes Land. Today, Bertrand has written, "[T]here can no longer be any doubt of the greatness of his achievements."[28]

In the same waters at the same time was Jules Sébastien César Dumont D'Urville, leader of the French expedition, smaller in size and far less contentious. With somewhat greater accuracy than Wilkes,[29] D'Urville determined that the South Magnetic Pole was some 350 miles inland from a coast that was unapproachable because of ice, but D'Urville did land on an offshore island and claimed the adjacent coast for France, naming it, after his wife, Adélie Land.

D'Urville was a man of culture (he discovered the Venus de Milo and was largely responsible for getting it to France), and his ten-volume account of his two seasons in Antarctic waters—never translated into English—is said to be one of the most literate descriptions of Antarctica ever published.

The third and best-prepared expedition was that of the British under James Clark Ross, discoverer of the North Magnetic Pole and a naval officer with eighteen years' experience in polar exploration. His two stout ships, *Erebus* and *Terror*, were the first in Antarctic waters to be reinforced and double sheathed in copper for work in ice. Ross was free to pick his own crews, choose his own supplies, and adapt his very flexible orders, which emphasized establishing weather stations and studying magnetic variations.

Only after Ross had spent a season in the subantarctic did he hear that Wilkes and D'Urville had preceded him in the coastal zone nearest to the South Magnetic Pole. Therefore, he dropped that objective and headed south on a more easterly meridian, where sealers had told him there was often a large expanse of open water beyond the pack ice. It was a fortunate change in plan, for Ross's discoveries proved incomparably the most interesting. After literally smashing through the ice, something never done before because no ship was strong enough, Ross did indeed emerge in open water, his vessels badly damaged by a storm but intact. He sailed into the sea that now bears his name and, landing on an island at the westward end, named a large slice of land for Queen Victoria. He discovered the Transantarctic Mountains where they run due south from Cape Adare at elevations of ten thousand feet or more. Ross followed them, often only a few hundred yards offshore. By the time he reached 77°S, much farther south than anyone had been, he could see a towering volcano belching flame and smoke. He named it Mount Erebus and a neighboring mountain, Terror; what appeared to be a bay to the west he named McMurdo for one of his officers.

But Ross's further penetration southward was blocked by his most astonishing discovery: an ice cliff that reached up to two hundred feet in height above the sea and that extended seemingly forever to the east. Ross followed the ice barrier for 250 miles (of its more than 600 miles) before the season became perilously late and he had to depart, wintering in Tasmania. Ross spent two more seasons in Antarctic waters, extending his knowledge of the continent's geography. But his only further discovery of note was an indentation in the ice barrier, later called the Bay of Whales. This was to serve as both a harbor and a ramp up the ice shelf for Roald Amundsen on his dash to the Pole and for Admiral Byrd's base, Little America, over many years.

We now know that the Ross Ice Shelf fills a bay the size of France, that most of it is floating, and that it is between eight hundred and a thousand feet thick (more toward the southern head of the bay). Periodically, large chunks of it break off and drift north as giant, tabular icebergs. The largest ever measured was 208 miles long and 60 miles wide—larger than the State of Massachusetts.[30] It had "calved" from the Ross Ice Shelf, which is merely the largest of many more or less permanent ice shelves that fill indentations in the coastline of Antarctica.

Ross's tough little ships got back to England in good shape after an absence of four and a half years. No further exploration of the Antarctic continent was undertaken for the next fifty-two years. However, there was one oceanographic expedition of some significance in 1874; and in 1882–83, during the First International Polar Year, scientists of several nations made limited observations in subantarctic waters.[31] The oceanographic expedition was conducted by Britain in H.M.S. *Challenger*. While the Antarctic phase was only a small part of a global program of maritime research and exploration, it is worthy of mention because, although *Challenger* was never within sight of Antarctica, it obtained important new knowledge of the continent. Seafarers and scientists, including

American geologist James Eights and, later, Charles Darwin, had noted rocks imbedded in north-drifting icebergs. The *Challenger* expedition therefore dredged the ocean bottom along the geographic melt-line of Antarctic icebergs and found rocks of granite, quartz, sandstone, and limestone, in contrast to rocks of volcanic origin found on seabeds to the north. If any doubt remained that a great continent existed near the pole, it was now removed.[32]

Nevertheless, two more decades elapsed before interest in Antarctica intensified to the point of sending expeditions. Although whaling interests had something to do with this renaissance, it could not have developed as it did without the efforts of three men, Maury, Murray, and Markham, none of whom ever traveled to Antarctica.

Commander Matthew Fontaine Maury was superintendent of the U.S. Naval Observatory and Hydrographical Office. He was internationally known for his *Wind and Current Charts* and *Sailing Directions,* which saved many days at sea through the rerouting of sailing ships. He also played a leading part in the first International Maritime Meteorological Conference, which he had proposed, held in Brussels in 1853. Since Maury could gather his data only with wide international cooperation, and since data from the Southern Ocean were inadequate for his purposes, in April 1861, he sent identical letters to nine governments pleading for an international, cost-sharing assault on Antarctica.[33] The previous November, he had been in London addressing the Royal Geographical Society on the same theme, stating that Britain had a particular responsibility for Antarctic research because its great empire surrounded Antarctica and its possessions were only eight to ten days away by steamboat. Although the society members reacted rather coldly to this lecture, Maury was later credited with arousing interest that led to the *Challenger* expedition. In the United States, the outbreak of the Civil War prevented even consideration of Maury's proposal, and for decades thereafter the country was too preoccupied with internal expansion to find interest in Antarctica. But long afterward, Maury was cited by those favoring Antarctic exploration,[34] and a British historian of science has referred to him as "probably the true father of international cooperation."[35]

John Murray, a Canadian biologist and oceanographer, was given the task of collating the data collected by the *Challenger* expedition; the material was ultimately published in fifty volumes. Having completed this gigantic task, he addressed the Royal Geographical Society in late 1893 and there gave a most astonishingly accurate description of Antarctica deduced from the scientific literature published up to that time. Murray concluded with an impassioned plea for a rebirth of Antarctic exploration. This time the audience was both impressed and receptive. Later, Murray represented the Royal Society[36] in planning the British Antarctic expedition that departed in 1901.[37]

Clements Markham was president of the Royal Geographic Society from 1893 to 1905. A skilled and persuasive establishmentarian, he was responsible for the declaration of the Sixth International Geographic Congress (held in London in 1895) that "the exploration of the Antarctic regions is the greatest piece of geographical exploration yet to be undertaken."[38] Scientific societies were urged to send expeditions, and they did. Moreover, Markham himself coordinated the expeditions of Sweden and Germany with that of Britain so that they would be geographically complementary. But Markham was best known as the chief instigator, fundraiser, and shaper of Britain's first Antarctic expedition in almost sixty years.

A romantic in his perception both of exploration and of the Royal Navy, in which he had briefly served as a youth, Markham quarreled with scientists, and in particular with Murray, over the objectives and leadership of the expedition. Markham had his way in having a young naval officer, Robert Falcon Scott, placed in total command.[39] What Markham failed to note, history has now made clear: Naval training and experience are not transferable to polar exploration on land; and the triumphs of Cook and Ross, the finest products of a great seapower, were not to be repeated. Although the two Scott expeditions made substantial contributions to science, it was the snow-wise Scandinavians who swept across Antarctica with unrivaled efficiency.[40]

AN EXPLOSION OF EXPLORATION

To Markham's chagrin, Scott's Discovery Expedition (named for his ship) was by no means the first to depart, and indeed, there were so many expeditions within a decade that only the most important can be touched on here. The summary treatment cannot

MAJOR GEOGRAPHICAL FEATURES

Atka Bay

SOUTH
SHETLAND ISLANDS
PAULET ISLAND
Hope Bay
SNOW HILL ISLAND
**Antarctic
Peninsula**
Bransfield Strait
DECEPTION
ISLAND
GRAHAM
LAND

COATS
LAND

Weddell Sea

Vahsel
Bay

Gerlache Strait
Cape Anna

PALMER LAND

Filchner Ice
Shelf

ALEXANDER
ISLAND

Ronne Ice Shelf

Dufek
Massif

PENS
MOU

Bellingshausen Sea

ELLSWORTH
LAND

90° W

Eights Coast

PETER I ISLAND

THURSTON
ISLAND

MARIE
BYRD
LAND

Amundsen Sea

EDSEL FORD
RANGES

Ruppert Coast

ROCKEFELLER MOUNTAINS

Kainan
Bay

0		500		1000 Kilometers

0		500		1000 Miles

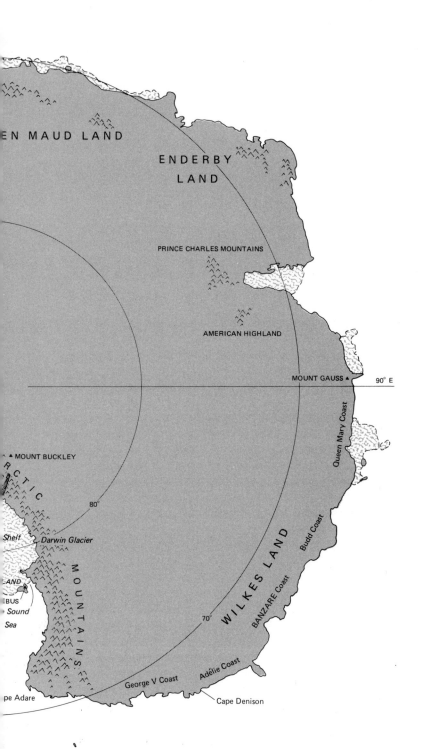

EN MAUD LAND

ENDERBY
LAND

PRINCE CHARLES MOUNTAINS

AMERICAN HIGHLAND

MOUNT GAUSS ▲   90° E

▲ MOUNT BUCKLEY

RCTIC

Queen Mary Coast

80°

Shelf   Darwin Glacier

Budd Coast

LAND ▲

EBUS

Sound

Sea

M
O
U
N
T
A
I
N
S

BANZARE Coast

W I L K E S   L A N D

70°

Adélie Coast

pe Adare

George V Coast

Cape Denison

convey the courage, the suffering, the disasters, and the sheer theater of these extraordinary events.

The first to sail, in 1897, was a Belgian expedition under Adrien de Gerlache de Gomery, a naval officer with a genuine interest in science. His ship was a small but heavily reinforced Norwegian sealer, renamed the *Belgica,* and his cosmopolitan company of nineteen men included the young Roald Amundsen as first mate, a Russian geologist, a Rumanian naturalist, an American doctor, and a Polish meteorologist—Henryk Arctowski, for whom the first Polish station in Antarctica would be named. After several months observing now extinct tribes in Tierra del Fuego, the expedition reached the South Shetland Islands in late January 1898. For the next two months, the *Belgica* sailed southward along the west coast of the Antarctic Peninsula. Nineteen landings were made and six nights were spent ashore at Cape Anna, where a party of five struggled to an elevation of fifteen hundred feet to get a better perspective on the strait that now bears Gerlache's name. The expedition's scientists found quantities of moss and lichens and were the discoverers of the mites and wingless flies that are Antarctica's only form of terrestrial fauna. Recklessly continuing southward beyond 71°S well into March, the *Belgica* became trapped in ice in the middle of the Bellingshausen Sea. There it remained for 347 days, of which 68 were without sun above the horizon. One man died of heart failure, two went mad, and all suffered from anemia, lethargy, and acute depression or paranoia. When summer came, and efforts to break up the ice with explosives failed, the men used ice saws to cut their way out, clearing a path for their ship through ice four feet thick for a distance upwards of a mile (accounts differ). It was March 28, 1899, before the *Belgica* was entirely free of ice and sailing home, a battered ship with a battered crew.

The next to depart was a Norwegian-born resident of Australia, Carsten Borchgrevink, who obtained financial support from a British magazine publisher, Sir George Newnes. Borchgrevink sailed down the Thames in August 1898 with three highly qualified scientists and a determination to be the first party to winter over on the Antarctic continent. In the course of a whaling expedition three years earlier, Borchgrevink had gone ashore at Cape Adare at the western entrance to the Ross Sea, and it was to this relatively sheltered beach that he headed his ship *Southern Cross.* The endless winter was made more bitter by the death of the expedition's zoologist, Nicolai Hanson, from an intestinal disease. Hemmed in by mountains and uncertain ice, the party of ten was confined in its exploring, but the following season, the expedition sailed south and successfully mounted the Barrier (the Ross Ice Shelf). Using dogs for the first time in Antarctica, Borchgrevink and two companions sledged to 78°S, farther south than anyone had yet been. Among the expedition's discoveries was the fact that the ice shelf had receded thirty miles since it had been charted by Ross.

In 1901, three coordinated expeditions set out for Antarctica— German, Swedish, and British. Erich von Drygalski, a professor of geography, led the German expedition with five other scientists and a ship especially built for Antarctic waters, the *Gauss* (named for the world-famous German mathematician who had earlier aroused so much interest in the South Magnetic Pole). They were the first to explore the Indian Ocean sector of the Antarctic coast in the region of 90°E. Almost immediately locked in ice, they were forced to winter over, but a ring of grounded icebergs protected their ship from the danger of being crushed. Magnetic and astronomical observatories were built on the floes, using ice blocks. When spring came, the Germans sledged the fifty miles to the coast, which they named for Kaiser Wilhelm; an extinct volcano was named Mount Gauss. To obtain a view of the interior, Drygalski rose fifteen hundred feet in a captive balloon. To make their escape from the ice, the men laid a pathway of ashes that absorbed enough of the sun's heat to open a channel through the floes. Although the expedition's achievements were modest, German interest in Antarctica was established and has continued at intervals to this day.

The Swedish expedition was led by Otto Nordenskjold, with Carl Larsen (a famous seagoing explorer in his own right) as master of the *Antarctic*. Their aim was to explore the east coast of the Antarctic Peninsula, where the prevailing winds and currents drive the sea ice against the shore, summer and winter. The *Antarctic* made little progress into the Weddell Sea before it was stopped by solid ice. According to plan, Nordenskjold and five companions were put ashore on Snow Hill Island to winter over, while the *Antarctic* conducted research in the Drake Passage before returning the following spring to pick them up. But the ice was so impenetrable throughout the next warm season that the ship did not even get close to the island, and it became briefly entrapped near Paulet Island. From there, three men set out across the ice to Nordenskjold's camp, two hundred miles to the south, but open water blocked their way, and they were forced to return to Paulet Island, where they remained isolated for nine months. Meanwhile, after several times breaking free, the *Antarctic* was permanently locked in ice and her hull finally crushed. On February 12, 1903, exactly one year after Nordenskjold was put ashore, the *Antarctic* sank, and her crew struggled for two weeks across the ice floes to reach a desolate shore midway between Snow Hill and Paulet Island. Thus the expedition, divided by mischance into three parties, had to spend a second winter in Antarctica, surviving almost entirely on penguin meat for eating and blubber for heating. One member of the ship's company died in midwinter of consumption. All others survived. By what seemed miracles of coincidence, the three groups were reunited and rescued by the first Argentine ship ever to venture into Antarctic waters. Throughout this extraordinary saga, the participants showed as much tenacity in preserving their scientific samples as in saving their own lives. Notably, the expedition obtained evidence of the extraordinary biological richness of the Antarctic's marginal sea and was the first to find fossil proof that the continent had once been a luxuriant land. Nordenskjold, a geologist, also was the first to surmise that the peninsula was a geological extension of South America.

While Drygalski explored an Indian Ocean segment of the Antarctic coast and Nordenskjold an Atlantic shore, Scott's Discovery Expedition made a systematic effort to push inland from the better-known and more accessible coast facing the Pacific. In his ship *Discovery*, Scott first sailed the entire seaward length of the Ross Ice Shelf to its mountainous anchor in the east, which he called King Edward VII Land. When autumn came, he set up his base at the opposite corner of the Ross Sea, in McMurdo Sound, where two winters were spent aboard ship, although huts were built ashore on Ross Island for scientific observations and for emergency stores. The following summer, 1902–03, Scott and two companions set out across the ice shelf with three sledges and nineteen dogs, all of which perished. The party reached 82°17′S, 380 miles farther south than the point Borchgrevink had attained and within sight of a great mountain range, later to be known as the Transantarctic Mountains. Suffering from malnutrition, scurvy, and snow blindness, the three men barely made it back. Meanwhile, a party of two climbed one of the many glaciers that pour out of the mountain range across McMurdo Sound from Ross Island. As Scott confirmed on a similar expedition the following summer, these mountains rim a seemingly endless plateau at an elevation of nine thousand feet.

The *Discovery*, which had remained trapped in ice throughout the summer of 1903, finally broke free in mid-February 1904, and after twenty-six months on the continent, the expedition sailed for home. Its six scientists had gathered masses of data—meteorological, magnetic, biological, and geological. The expedition had discovered the first of the snowless "dry" valleys, which remain of intense interest to scientists to this day. It also had established the high probability that what had been known as the "Barrier" was indeed a huge expanse of floating ice and that the mountains of Victoria Land continued in an unbroken chain for more than a thousand miles to the south and east.

While the Discovery Expedition was still in progress, a Scotsman was exploring the eastern reaches of the Weddell Sea and a Frenchman was carefully charting the islands off the west coast of the Antarctic Peninsula. In the second of two seasons of exploration, 1903–04, William S. Bruce was the first to sight the eastern limit of the Weddell Sea, which he named Coats Land for his sponsor. But Bruce is best remembered for turning over to Argentina the meteorological station he had established, after failing to obtain continuing support from his own government. This station on Laurie Island in the South Orkneys provided Argentina with its first foothold in Antarctica and a future of conflicts with Britain.

Jean-Baptiste Charcot, director of the French Laboratory of Maritime Research, led two expeditions, first in the *Français* (1903–05) and then in the *Pourquoi Pas?* (1908–10). He initially was drawn to Antarctica on a mission of mercy—to rescue the Nordenskjold expedition. When this proved to have been already accomplished, Charcot remained in Antarctic waters to explore and make charts of such excellence that they were copied by the British for years. Although he renewed French interest in Antarctica, Charcot never visited Adélie Land, which had been claimed for France seventy years earlier.

Ernest Shackleton, one of Scott's companions on the sledging journey across the Ross Ice Shelf in 1903, was invalided home on

Scott's orders after the first season. Feeling humiliated and indignant, Shackleton resolved to return. Having obtained modest financing from private sources, he arrived back in Antarctica in 1907 in a pitifully small ship, the *Nimrod*, with a contingent of able scientists and ten Siberian ponies that he hoped would haul his sledges to the South Pole. As Scott had denied him use of the Discovery base at Hut Point on the west end of Ross Island, Shackleton wasted precious time searching unsuccessfully for a sheltered site along the front of the ice shelf. By the time he concluded that there was no alternative but to use Ross Island (although he camped at the east end, two days' march farther from the pole and far less accessible to the ice shelf), the season was too far advanced to permit the laying of supply depots, essential to a race for the pole the following summer. Moreover, by the time Shackleton and three companions were ready to depart, only four ponies survived; of these, three expired before the ice shelf was crossed and the fourth fell down a crevasse on Beardmore Glacier. Nevertheless, on Christmas Day 1908, the four men reached an elevation of ninety-five hundred feet at the edge of the high plateau that covers the greater part of the continent. They had been on the march for two months and were exhausted, having man-hauled their sledges most of the way. But they pressed on to within ninety-seven miles of the pole. There, on January 9, Shackleton made the wise but excruciatingly difficult decision to turn back. The four men got back to camp by the narrowest of margins, having traveled fifteen hundred miles in four months. With them they brought samples of coal, fossilized wood, and plant impressions in boulders, indicating that even the interior of the continent had once been forested.

While Shackleton was pushing south, another party, of three men, led by a fifty-one-year-old geologist, Edgeworth David, was exploring westward across the mountains of Victoria Land. On January 16, 1909, they planted the British flag on the South Magnetic Pole. By the time they returned, they had traveled 1,260 miles over previously unexplored and particularly difficult terrain. Meanwhile, scientists at the base were adding to the observations begun by the Discovery Expedition.

Had Shackleton been able to make better preparations, he almost certainly would have been the first to reach the South Pole. As it was, his achievement was extraordinary. On his return to

England, he was lionized for his accomplishments, and a grateful government paid off the considerable debts he had incurred to finance the expedition.

Douglas Mawson, who had been with David when he reached the South Magnetic Pole, was the first and greatest of Australia's Antarctic explorers. On his most celebrated expedition, that of 1911-14, he was the first to maintain a radio link to the outside world (to Australia via a relay station on Macquarie Island) and the first to explore the inland coast between Victoria Land and Adélie Land, which he named King George V Land. In the most harrowing journey ever made in Antarctica, Mawson lost both of his sledging companions—Belgrave Ninnis in a fall down a crevasse along with almost all their food; Xavier Mertz from Vitamin A toxification as a result of eating the liver of their expired dogs.[41] Mawson, too, was poisoned, although he believed he was merely suffering from malnutrition. Crossing one of the most heavily crevassed glaciers on the continent, he dragged himself the last hundred miles back to Commonwealth Bay in thirty days, alone and virtually without food. His ship *Aurora* had already departed to pick up another party exploring more than a thousand miles to the west in a new territory they named Queen Mary Land.[42] In very poor health, Mawson had to spend an unscheduled second winter in Antarctica.

The conquest of the South Pole by Amundsen and Scott in 1911-12 is not the most heroic or remarkable story of Antarctic adventure, but it has captured the imagination of generations. For the British, especially, there is powerful symbolism in Scott's tale of valor and failure—for the event constituted a hinge between an era of epic grandeur for the British Empire and decline to a second-ranked island nation. When the remnants of Commander Scott's expedition returned to England, World War I was only months away.

Norwegian Roald Amundsen was one of the few Antarctic expedition leaders who was a professional explorer. He had no other vocation, and he trained himself with the single-mindedness that characterized everything he did. He had been the first to negotiate the Northwest Passage and was planning a well-provisioned assault on the North Pole when the world learned that Admiral Robert Edwin Peary had beaten him to the long-sought goal. Not one to brood, Amundsen sailed anyway as scheduled, in early June 1910, with nineteen men, ninety-seven dogs, and supplies for three years packed into the small, well-built *Fram*, but he traveled south instead of north. When Scott reached Melbourne in October 1910, he was greeted with a jolting cable from Madeira: "Beg leave to inform you proceeding Antarctica. Amundsen."

The Norwegian set up winter quarters on the Ross Ice Shelf at the head of the Bay of Whales, a site that Shackleton and others had considered too unstable. Amundsen reasoned that the area was anchored on solid bottom and would survive long enough. The decision put him sixty miles nearer the South Pole than was Scott at McMurdo Sound. Still, Scott's route through the Transantarctic Mountains via the Beardmore Glacier had been scouted by Shackleton, whereas Amundsen had no idea how he was going to reach the high plateau. Before winter set in, Amundsen distributed four tons of supplies at three depots across the Ross Ice Shelf. During the four-month night, the men kept busy honing their equipment to perfection; for example, the weight of their sledges was reduced by a third without loss of strength.

After one false start, Amundsen set out on October 19, 1911, with four companions and fifty-two of the strongest huskies. They fairly flew over the ice shelf and encountered only minor difficulty in finding a route up into the mountains. When they reached nearly eleven thousand feet, they adhered precisely to plan and slaughtered twenty-four dogs (ten had already died) to provide fresh meat for men and dogs alike. For the next two weeks, the terrain was unexpectedly difficult, but thereafter they practically galloped, arriving at the South Pole a week before the summer solstice and eight weeks after leaving their base. They spent three days circling the pole to make sure they had not miscalculated its position. Having planted the Norwegian flag, written messages for Scott, and deposited some excess supplies, they headed back to their base camp, arriving on January 25. They had covered 1,860 miles in ninety-nine days. Everything had gone as scheduled, the men had ridden much of the way, and the eleven surviving dogs were in the best of shape.[43]

Meanwhile, Scott, in the *Terra Nova*, had arrived at McMurdo Sound on January 4, 1911, with sixty-five men, thirty-three dogs, nineteen Manchurian ponies, three tracked motor sledges, and ambitious plans for scientific investigation. The Royal Geographic

Society was again one of Scott's most generous backers (although not an official sponsor as before), and its president had written: "So far as attainment of the Pole is concerned, it is well known that only about a hundred miles remain to be covered. . . . This spot may not exhibit any features of exceptional scientific interest, and the Royal Geographic Society could hardly advocate an expedition with the South Pole as its sole objective."[44]

Everyone on the expedition worked with impressive dedication year-round, and the scientists produced reports that would fill twenty volumes.[45] But by the time Scott was ready to leave for the pole, the motorized sledges had proven almost useless; more than half the ponies had perished, and the remainder expired on the first leg of the journey. The dogs (some of which had also died) were almost unmanageable. Three support parties of four men each helped Scott to man-haul supplies a part of the way; the last of the supply teams did not turn back until it was within 178 miles of the pole and very nearly did not make it back to McMurdo. From there, Scott and four companions proceeded southward and reached the pole on January 17, 1912—exhausted, in poor health, and dejected by the discovery that Amundsen had been there more than a month earlier. The harrowing return trip was not completed. After two of his men had perished from cold, hunger, and exhaustion, Scott made his last camp in a blizzard 176 miles from the base at Hut Point. The bodies were found the following season.

What made this tragic event especially moving and gave it stature in British heritage was the character of the men as reflected in Scott's diary and in the letters he wrote to friends and to the kin of his comrades even as they were dying. Their courage and cheerfulness in the face of death excite admiration and have been an inspiration to succeeding generations.[46]

Yet for inexhaustible determination and glorious failure on an epic scale, Scott was again to be bested, by Shackleton. The idea that Antarctica might be two continents divided by a narrow strait running between the Ross and Weddell seas had been mooted for some years. Bruce was the first to try, in 1910, to mount a transantarctic expedition that might decide the issue, but he failed to obtain funds. He was followed by a German, Wilhelm Filchner, who also explored the Weddell Sea and discovered the ice shelf named for him. But his ship, the *Deutschland*, was beset by ice in the winter of 1912 and for nine months drifted wherever the entrapping ice took it, a distance of six hundred miles—its scientists at work all the while. Filchner escaped, but for lack of funds his plan to cross the continent had to be abandoned.

Shackleton succeeded with the fundraising if little else. The plan was for a support party to lay supply depots inland from the Ross Ice Shelf, while Shackleton, with the main party in the *Endurance*, struck inland from the head of the Weddell Sea. But Shackleton never reached his destination. His ship became locked in ice on January 19, 1915 (unusually early in the season), and for nine months it drifted at the mercy of the sea's powerful current. Then *Endurance* was slowly crushed to kindling, and Shackleton with twenty-seven men took to the ice floes. The nearest land was four hundred miles away. They would need whaleboats later in the season when the ice broke up, but these proved too heavy and cumbersome to drag over the broken pack. Therefore, from October 26, when the ship went down, to early April, when they took to their boats, the men were immobilized on a melting ice floe— miserably wet and nearly out of their minds with boredom. On April 15, they reached Elephant Island, off the tip of the Antarctic Peninsula, twelve hundred miles from Vahsel Bay, where Shackleton hoped to land.

Since chance rescue from Elephant Island was virtually impossible, Shackleton set off for help with five men in a twenty-two-foot boat. Sailing 870 miles through the world's roughest seas in early winter, they reached South Georgia, where there was a whaling station. Landing on the opposite shore, they still had to negotiate a six-thousand-foot range never before crossed. In this final epic battle with nature, Shackleton and his companions survived. Because winter was now well advanced, all hands at Elephant Island were rescued only with the greatest difficulty. Meanwhile, even worse horrors and ill fortune had befallen the ten-man support party that had been put ashore at McMurdo. With monumental effort, they had laid four supply depots—two of them well up the Beardmore Glacier—for an expedition that would never come. Then, as winter set in, their ship, intentionally icebound in the shelter of McMurdo Sound, was driven out to sea in a gale, leaving them poorly equipped. By the time Shackleton reached them, three men had died.[47]

BYRD AND THE AMERICAN DECADE

With these tragic adventures, the heroic era of exploration came to an end. World War I picked up the tempo of technological advance, especially in transportation and communication. The radio and the airplane altogether changed the style and scope of Antarctic expeditions, although the physical and emotional demands were not altered as much as might have been expected. Flying was dangerous, tracked vehicles no less than sledges could fall down crevasses, and the long winter nights were still full of stress. But an airplane with cameras could explore four thousand square miles per hour—the equivalent of an entire season's reconnaissance by dogteam.[48] Expeditions were now in instantaneous communication with their national capitals as well as with their scientific parties crisscrossing the continent.

Although Richard E. Byrd was not the first to use either the airplane, the radio, or the tracked vehicle in Antarctica, he expanded their uses and improved their efficiencies in the course of four expeditions, starting in 1928. The new techniques he developed are today considered as important as the work of his explorers and scientists. On the advice of Amundsen, he also had an ample supply of sled dogs that proved invaluable, and his first flagship was a square-rigger with a thirty-four-inch wooden hull. He also kept Antarctica in the public eye—especially the American eye—as it has not been since. After an absence of ninety years, the United States was back in Antarctica.

The first Byrd expedition was the most dramatic. Setting up his base, Little America, near the edge of the Ross Ice Shelf, Byrd flew east to discover and name the Rockefeller Mountains and the Edsel Ford Range for his two principal backers. His chief scientist and second in command, Laurence M. Gould, traveling by dog sledge due south to the Queen Maud Range, proved that these mountains are geologically similar to those studied by the Scott expeditions in Victoria Land and therefore part of what Gould later called "the most stupendous fault block mountain system in the world."[49] Then the geological party turned eastward, passing out of the territory claimed by New Zealand and into Marie Byrd Land (previously only overflown), which Gould claimed as "a dependency or possession of the United States."[50] Meanwhile, Byrd was fulfilling his greatest ambition in Antarctica—to fly over the South

Pole, as he had previously been first to fly over the North Pole.

With pilot, radio operator, cameraman, and Byrd himself as navigator, the trimotor *Floyd Bennett* (named for Byrd's recently deceased flying companion) crossed the Ross Ice Shelf, stopped for fuel at a supply depot, and started up the uncharted Liv Glacier to the high central plateau. The plane was calculated to have a maximum altitude of eleven thousand feet—just about the height of the pass. But weighed down with emergency provisions, the plane stopped climbing at ten thousand feet and wobbled in the thin, turbulent air. Two bags of food weighing four hundred pounds—their entire emergency ration—were dropped overboard. The desperate measure worked; the Great Antarctic Horst was crossed. Over the pole, Byrd dropped flags of the United States, Great Britain, France, and Norway, and nineteen hours after their departure, Byrd and his companions were back in Little America. Byrd returned to the United States a hero, rewarded by special act of Congress with a jump in rank from Commander to Rear Admiral.[51]

What added a new dimension to these events was that they were known instantly in all the capitals of the world. The radio message from the *Floyd Bennett* over the South Pole was picked up directly in New York. *The New York Times* had its own correspondent, Russell Owen, at Little America. On the first expedition, Little America could send only by Morse code, although it could receive voice radio. The second expedition, 1933–35, included a professional CBS radio announcer to preside over the licensed station at Little America, KFZ. Regular broadcasts to the United States contained commercials sponsored by General Foods and amateur entertainment to pad out the news.[52] At the depth of the Depression, these shortwave programs conveyed a spirit of adventure and enterprise and American grit to cheer the downhearted and to make the nation keenly aware of Antarctica, which then held the same fascination that the moon landings would have for a later generation.

The growth of shortwave radio in Antarctica gradually altered the Antarctic ambiance beyond reckoning. As early as 1929, two radio stations in the United States were beaming broadcasts to Little America with messages from relatives, friends, and politicians, as well as music and entertainment.[53] The sense of total, prolonged isolation was gone forever. For the expedition leader and his chief lieutenants, there was now no escape from the demands of communicating by radio—with sponsors and the public in the United States, with supply bases in New Zealand, and with their own polar parties on the continent.

On his second expedition, Byrd made the rash decision to winter over alone in an advance base 123 miles south of Little America. The admiral's stated reason for wintering alone was that provisions were not adequate for three men, as planned, and two men would get seriously on each other's nerves. Apart from whether Byrd's psychology was faulty, there is the question whether as commander of a large expedition he should have isolated himself in this fashion. Frank Debenham, writing from his experience as a geologist with Scott, describes "the unhappy picture of a great organizer and planner struggling with the details of how to cook, how to mend leaky chimneys, how to send Morse messages. It was a rather critical case of a square peg trying to fit into a round hole."[54] Byrd very nearly died of carbon-monoxide poisoning from a faulty stove and the motor that powered the radio. He was rescued early the next spring after five months of what he thought would be a marvelous opportunity to "live in utter simplicity . . . and think things over."[55]

Unfortunately, the publicity accorded this bit of dramatics overshadowed the considerable scientific and technological achievements of the expedition, which did the first seismic work to determine the depth of the ice on the Ross Shelf; proved almost beyond doubt that no strait existed between the Ross and Weddell seas; advanced cosmic research; collected many samples of rock, moss, and lichen; and experimented with new transport—two light snowmobiles, three heavy snowmobiles, one six-ton tractor, and four airplanes—with mixed results. Bertrand identifies no fewer than twenty-one objectives that were successfully accomplished—no small achievement for a privately financed expedition mounted in the depths of the Depression.[56]

Byrd's flight to the pole had been over terrain that was generally known. Lincoln Ellsworth, a millionaire aviator/explorer, took off with one companion from an island off the tip of the Antarctic Peninsula with the aim of making a transcontinental flight to Little America twenty-three hundred miles away. Although for much of the way he would be flying over totally unknown territory, he gambled that when the weather turned foul he would find a place to set down his specially built monoplane, the *Polar Star*. He and his fellow-pilot, Herbert Hollick-Kenyon, successfully made five landings, the last without fuel, twelve miles from their goal. They nearly perished on that last leg, for Little America was unoccupied that season (1935–36), and in any case, their radio transmitter had long since gone dead. After ten days on the ice shelf, where their navigation proved vastly inferior to that in the air, they reached Little America. They were picked up by ship a month later.

The land at the base of the Antarctic Peninsula and the mountains at the head of the Weddell Sea were seen for the first time by Ellsworth, and both were named for his father, while the plateau to the southwest, abutting Marie Byrd Land, is named for Hollick-Kenyon. On this plateau, at the site of their first landing, Ellsworth raised the American flag and claimed, "so far as that act would allow," all land between 80°W and 120°W for the United States.[57] Three years later, on an expedition hounded by bad luck, Ellsworth made a series of flights over what became known as the American Highland in the Indian Ocean sector.[58]

Although the United States dominated Antarctic exploration and research in this period, it was by no means alone. In the late 1920s, Lars Christensen of the Norwegian whaling dynasty explored extensively off the coast of Queen Maud Land and Enderby Land and sponsored inland flights by a skilled aviator, Hjalmar Riiser-Larsen. In 1929–31, Sir Douglas Mawson was back in East Antarctica, heading the British, Australian, New Zealand Antarctic Research Expedition, today commemorated in the BANZARE Coast. Between 1925 and 1939, the British Discovery Committee (using Scott's old ship *Discovery*) conducted the first sustained research in Antarctic oceanography and marine biology, motivated largely by a desire to preserve the flourishing whaling industry. Thirteen separate cruises were financed through lease of harbor rights and shore stations to whaling companies. And finally, Germany conducted an expedition just before World War II. Under direct orders from Hermann Goering the eight-thousand-ton *Schwabenland* stood off Queen Maud Land in 1938–39, catapulting seaplanes into the air. They systematically surveyed the coast as much as three hundred miles inland. Some 11,600 aerial photographs were taken, although none of the negatives survived the war. At intervals of fifteen to twenty miles, the planes dropped spearlike markers bearing the swastika, which was also planted by small landing parties. The Germans named the area Neu-Schwabenland, a name that did not stick.[59]

Although the Germans made a significant contribution to Antarctic geography and pioneered new techniques of photomapping, the world was warrantably skeptical of German purposes. Before the *Schwabenland* reached Antarctica, Norway preclusively laid claim to that part of the continent, in which it had so long demonstrated an interest. The German presence in Antarctica made it easier for President Franklin D. Roosevelt to obtain support for a new government agency, the United States Antarctic Service, to conduct yet another Byrd expedition, in 1939–41.

Unlike Byrd's previous expeditions, this one was national and governmental. It was run by an interdepartmental committee in Washington. Nevertheless, Congress provided only a part of the funds needed; more than a hundred firms and individuals contributed money, supplies, and equipment. It was a new experience for Byrd to be taking orders in Antarctica, and one of his closest aides wrote later that they were often "disgusted with many half-thought-out orders dispatched to us from Washington."[60]

This expedition opened a new station, known as East Base, on Stonington Island, to reassert an American presence in the peninsula area. West Base was Little America III, six miles from its now unusable predecessors. Both were intended to be "more or less continuously occupied."[61] But as it turned out, there was little time except for sorties to plant the flag and set brass markers. The demands of approaching war that so altered the nature of this expedition also caused it to be ended prematurely.

Another Antarctic era had ended. With a few exceptions, expeditions thereafter would be government sponsored and directed. The days of private enterprise and private sponsorship were over, and although Antarctica continued to attract would-be heroes, they were more often seen as nuisances than as objects of admiration. Also, the continent and its surrounding seas were now viewed in a new light, as a large, uncertain piece in complex military strategies. It would be two decades before it was recognized that the Antarctic environment is so uncompromisingly hostile that there is little one can do there that cannot be done better elsewhere.

GEOGRAPHY OF A COLD CONTINENT

When Kerguélen wrote of South France that "the latitude in which it lies promises all the crops of the Mother country," he fell into a misconception that required many years and much suffering to eradicate. Iles Kerguélen, the barren, bitter-cold islands, are almost precisely the same distance from the South Pole as Paris is from the North Pole. What could be more natural, then, than to suppose that the climates were essentially the same? But the "Ant-Arctic" is opposite the Arctic in more than name and place.

The great geographer Isaiah Bowman once said that the Arctic is a hollow and the Antarctic is a hump.[62] The Arctic (from the Greek *Arktos,* the Bear—the constellation revolving around the North Star) is an ocean surrounded by continents where temperatures are frequently colder than they are at the North Pole. The Antarctic is an ice-encased continent surrounded by comparatively warm ocean. The difference is profound. The southern polar region is vastly colder. The ice covering Antarctica is permanent and reflects 80 to 90 percent of the sunlight it receives. In contrast, the layer of ice on the Arctic Ocean breaks up in summer, exposing the relatively warm water, never more than a few degrees below freezing and capable of absorbing 60 to 70 percent of the sun's heat.[63] Another substantial difference is the altitude of Antarctica, the highest continent in the world, although most of it is ice. At the South Pole, ninety-six hundred feet of ice cover rock that is about three hundred feet below sea level.[64] On this high plateau, which constitutes most of the continent, temperatures are comparable to those on Mars; the world's lowest reading has been recorded there—minus 126°F.[65]

Whereas in the north the maximum extent of sea ice is about 5 percent of the hemisphere, in the south it represents 8 percent of the hemisphere and the annual variation from summer to winter is far greater.[66] In each austral winter, the south polar icecap effectively doubles in size as sea ice forms hundreds of miles outward from the continent.[67] The pack ice in the South Atlantic may reach beyond 50°, a latitude that in the Northern Hemisphere falls to the south of the British Isles.[68] Each spring, the sea ice breaks away from most of the Antarctic continent as the result of tidal action and is blown northward by the prevailing winds. This expanding ring of ice often remains impenetrable until midsummer.

In the Southern Hemisphere, only rudimentary forms of terrestrial life exist south of 60° latitude. At that same latitude in the Northern Hemisphere are Oslo, Leningrad, and Helsinki. Indeed, all of Finland is north of 60°. Transposed to a comparable latitude in the south, the Soviet city of Murmansk, an ice-free port with a population of more than three hundred thousand, would either be permanently frozen in the continental ice sheet (if in the east) or have but a few months of open water each year (if in the west).[69]

Worse than the cold is the wind. Frank Debenham, who accompanied Scott on his second expedition, called it "the dominant, almost universal and even overwhelming feature of Antarctica." Its occasional cessation offers "something of the awed pleasure of a gnawing toothache that has miraculously stopped."[70] The gravity-fed or katabatic winds are the worst. They rip down from the high plateau, reaching speeds as high as 180 miles per hour by the time they reach the coast.[71] Although topography is clearly a factor, no one fully understands why these winds vary enormously from place to place along the coast, averaging 44 miles an hour year-round at one point (Cape Denison) and half that speed a few miles away.[72]

Snow falls in Antarctica not as flakes but as tiny pellets. Driven by the wind, snow stings like coarse sand.[73] Windblown snow also forms sastrugi, frozen waves that vary from a few inches to five feet in height.[74] Before the days of efficient tracked vehicles, sastrugi could make sledging agonizingly slow and exhausting. Wind also forms snow bridges over nearly bottomless crevasses that may be up to a hundred feet across.[75]

After his winter alone, Admiral Byrd wrote a particularly vivid description of an Antarctic storm in winter:

There is something extravagantly insensate about an Antarctic blizzard at night. Its vindictiveness cannot be measured on an anemoneter sheet. It is more than just wind: it is a solid wall of snow moving at gale force, sounding like surf. The whole malevolent rush is concentrated upon you as upon a personal enemy. In the senseless explosion of sound you are reduced to a crawling thing on the margin of a disintegrating world; you can't see, you can't hear, you can hardly move. The lungs gasp after the air is sucked out of them, and the brain is shaken. Nothing in the world will so quickly isolate a man.[76]

Most of this snow is simply being blown from one place to another, for in fact Antarctica is extraordinarily arid. In the central plateau, annual precipitation may be less than two inches (water equivalent), but it increases toward the coast. In some years, in some places, notably the peninsula, precipitation may amount to as much as thirty inches. Manmade structures anywhere in the Antarctic may be buried by snow in a relatively short time. The original South Pole station, built in the mid-1950s, has long since been buried and sealed off as hazardous. Little America, Admiral Byrd's base on the Ross Ice Shelf, had to be rebuilt for each successive expedition. The British Station at Halley Bay was buried in thirty feet of snow in less than a decade,[77] and the Russians built an additional floor every four years above their original permanent structure at Mirnyi.[78]

The marvel is that, despite so little precipitation, the greater part of the continent is blanketed in snow and ice to a depth of about two miles—in a few places, three. The weight is so enormous that it has depressed the continent by an average of nearly two thousand feet, pushing much of the land below sea level. Thus, if the snow and ice were removed from Antarctica, the western and geologically younger half would appear as an archipelago,[79] a fact that was suspected long before it could be proved.

About 80 percent of all the fresh water in the world is locked up at the poles as snow or ice—most of it in Antarctica. If anything should cause this ice to melt or to slide into the sea, the oceans would rise about two hundred feet, and more than half the population of the world would be drowned or driven from their homes.[80]

Strangely, about 2 percent of the continent is free of ice. One of the largest such areas is in Victoria Land, right across McMurdo Sound from U.S. and New Zealand bases. These so-called dry valleys are obviously of exceptional interest to scientists. What little flora exists is mostly on the peninsula, but lichens have been found on peaks three hundred miles from the pole. More than five hundred species of lichens have been identified as well as lesser varieties of mosses and algae.[81]

Rigidly as Antarctica appears to be locked in ice, there is constant movement outward from the center. By one estimate, a snow particle falling at the pole of inaccessibility (i.e., the point farthest from any sea) might take a hundred thousand years to reach the edge of the ice sheet, a distance of nearly twelve hundred miles. On the other hand, glaciers flowing onto the Ross Ice Shelf travel about eleven hundred feet a year.[82] The Ross Ice Shelf itself is moving seaward at a rate of half a mile a year.[83] Glaciers also form ice tongues that float as much as sixty miles into the ocean.[84] Ice shelves and tongues ultimately break off—or calve—to form spectacular tabular icebergs that may be larger than the State of Rhode Island.

The Antarctic continent, including its permanent ice shelves, has an area equal to the United States and Europe combined. In addition, within the area defined as the Antarctic regions are about a dozen islands and archipelagoes. The widely recognized although invisible boundary of the Antarctic regions is the Antarctic Convergence, where the Southern Ocean undergoes a rapid change in temperature, chemistry, and biology. The Antarctic Convergence is an undulating belt girdling the Southern Hemisphere where the very cold but fresher and therefore lighter water flowing northward from Antarctica plunges below the warmer, saltier water of the Atlantic, Pacific, and Indian oceans. This ribbon of mixing water, twenty to thirty miles wide, is not fixed but roughly follows the 50th parallel of latitude except in the Pacific sector, where it swings farther north. What is particularly striking about the Antarctic Convergence, apart from the rapid change in water temperature, is the barrier it forms to living species. With some exceptions, such as whales, the biological communities of the Antarctic regions are quite distinct from those in the so-called subantarctic regions to the north.[85]

The vast Southern Ocean, "probably the largest marine ecosystem on the globe,"[86] adds to the isolation of Antarctica. No other continent is without at least one close neighbor. The six-hundred-mile-wide Drake Passage, between the tips of South America and the Antarctic Peninsula, constitutes a significant constriction of the currents that otherwise swirl freely in a limitless sea. The distance from Antarctica to Africa is twenty-one hundred miles, to New Zealand, twelve hundred miles. The Southern Ocean is also unusually deep—twelve thousand to sixteen thousand feet over most of its extent.[87] The dominant movement of water is the Circumpolar Current or West Wind Drift, one of the major current systems of the world. The Russians have calculated that it is "equal in flow to six Gulf Streams."[88] This clockwise flow is reversed closer to the coast of Antarctica, where a weaker westward current is driven by the prevailing easterlies. In addition to these circumpolar currents, there are meridional water movements—northward at the surface and at the bottom, southward through much of the water column.[89] These movements have direct bearing on the climate of the Southern Hemisphere and the productivity of the Southern Ocean.

Nowhere south of the Antarctic Convergence is there any plant approaching even a shrub in size.[90] This terrestrial barrenness is as much due to salt-laden winds as to temperature. The biological poverty of the land, however, is made up for in the sea and the air. The nutrient-rich waters sustain twenty species of whales and eight species of seals that "comprise one of the greatest concentrations of mammals on earth."[91] Among the birds are seven species of penguins; the wandering albatross, with its unequaled wingspread of twelve feet; and Wilson's stormy petrel, believed to have the largest population of any bird species in the world except for the house sparrow and the common starling, both of which owe their abundance to human civilization.[92]

Some of this knowledge of Antarctica was acquired early in this century, but most is quite recent. What scientists have discovered about Antarctica is not only fascinating in itself; it is adding to man's understanding of the entire global environment (although not quite as much as is sometimes promised). Science is the principal activity in Antarctica and bears on every other aspect of the region—political, economic, and environmental. Hence to science we now turn.

CHAPTER

II

The Commonwealth of Science

For many, many years to come . . . the most important export of Antarctica is going to be its scientific data.

—*Laurence M. Gould*

Science has provided the rationale for everything undertaken in Antarctica. Scientific activity has been one of the principal ways that nations have substantiated their territorial claims in Antarctica, and one of the ways other nations cast doubt on those claims. Science sublimates historic rivalries and nourishes the remarkable cooperation achieved among nations there. Scientific study has revealed what little we know of the region's resources, and if environmental devastation is to be avoided, it will define the terms on which those resources may be exploited. Science laid the basis for the political regime under which Antarctica is now governed, and science informs all the coordinated actions taken by governments in respect to Antarctica. Therefore, some consideration of Antarctic science—activities, objectives, attitudes, organization, administration, and policy—is essential to a discussion of the future of what English historian H. G. R. King has called the Commonwealth of Science.

39

SCIENCE IN THE ERA OF EXPLORATION

Many who suffered or perished in Antarctica in the era of exploration would be startled to know how little significance has since been attached to their scientific efforts. A characteristic view is that of Phillip Law, an Australian scientist and Antarctic expedition leader. In the warm glow of achievement in the International Geophysical Year (IGY), 1957-58—a massive and highly successful enterprise that emphasized polar research—he wrote:

> For fifty years past, the main motive actuating Antarctic work has been territorial conquest. Expeditionary work was aimed primarily at discovering new territories, at establishing national sovereignty over such territories, at protecting and strengthening national claims. . . . Scientific work was, in general, of secondary importance. The IGY changed all this.[1]

At the opening of the Washington Conference of 1959 at which the Antarctic Treaty was negotiated, the Soviet delegate alluded to the IGY when he observed: "It may be said without exaggeration that, as a result of this international scientific cooperation, mankind has learned more about Antarctica in the last three or four years than in all the one hundred thirty years since the day of discovery."[2] Of course, Russia and her successor state had not been in Antarctica for those 130 years.

One of the principal architects of the U.S. Antarctic Research Program wrote in 1970 that "prior to the IGY, hoped-for resources, claims to territory, and national interests, including security, dominated the activities [in Antarctica]."[3]

Whether or not these statements are accurate, they appear to be a harsh judgment if only because the scientific work undertaken in earlier times was accomplished at such great effort and often under such appalling conditions. To be sure, from Captain Cook to Admiral Byrd, most explorers showed some ambivalence between desire for personal or national glory and the acceptance of the implicit demands of science. But often their commitment to science was intense—sufficient to endanger their lives.

A member of Scott's second expedition explained the failure of the South Polar party this way: "We were primarily a great scientific expedition, with the Pole as our bait for public support, though it was not more important than any other acre of the plateau. . . . We were discursive. We were full of intellectual interests and curiosities of all kinds. We took on the work of two or three expeditions."[4] There is much truth in this. On a sledge beside the tent where the bodies of Scott and his companions were found, there were thirty-seven pounds of rocks, their last remaining baggage, dragged to their very last stop. According to Sir Raymond Priestley, the samples included "priceless specimens."[5]

Most of the rocks were gathered from a moraine under the sandstone cliffs of Mount Buckley, where the five men took half a day off and "geologized."[6] There is nothing in their journals to indicate how the decision was made to look for rocks instead of getting on with the business of survival. Scott merely noted, "The moraine was obviously so interesting that . . . I decided to camp and spend the day geologizing."[7] They stopped again the next day to collect rock specimens, despite uncertainty about whether they would reach the next depot with its essential supply of food and fuel. And even in the last extremity, when other gear was being abandoned, the rocks were kept without question. Probably this was not entirely selfless devotion to science. Given the failure to reach the pole first, and then the probability of death, the pile of rocks became the men's last will and testament.

The most dedicated geologizer on the trip to the pole was Scott's chief scientist, Edward A. Wilson, who was suffering at the time from a damaged leg and snow blindness. Six months earlier, Wilson had led the famous Winter Journey, five weeks under the most desperate conditions imaginable. The purpose was to obtain eggs of the emperor penguin at the only rookery then known, at the only time of year they could be had. Penguins, wrote Wilson, "are the most primitive birds living now, and the Emperor is quite the most interesting of them all."[8] By obtaining early embryos for microscopic analysis, Wilson hoped to find a link between birds and reptiles from which birds evolved. Struggling in temperatures down to 77°F. below zero, against gale-force winds that blew away tents, in clothing and sleeping bags frozen stiff with the previous day's perspiration, Wilson and two companions obtained five eggs, of which three got back to base intact. Immediately pickled in alcohol, the embryos safely reached England, where they were little appreciated and added nothing to knowledge.[9] Wilson did not live to know this, but no doubt he would have consoled himself with the thought that man-hauling sledges on an extended journey in the Antarctic winter had never been done before.

"The British expedition," wrote Roald Amundsen, "was designed entirely for scientific research. The Pole was only a side-issue, whereas in my extended plan it was the main object."[10] Indeed it was. Of all Antarctic explorers, Amundsen was the most single-minded. Yet even he paid obeisance to science: His expedition kept accurate meteorological records, brought back about fifty rock specimens (none of much interest), and conducted some modest oceanography.[11]

Captain Cook was sponsored by the Royal Society, Britain's premier scientific body, and in his company were several astronomers and naturalists. Significantly, the Royal Society was even more impressed by Cook's techniques for maintaining the health of his crews than by his geographical exploits. Cook's men were kept virtually free of scurvy with a diet that included sweet wort, an unfermented malt.[12] In the autumn of 1839, Captain James Clark Ross sailed from England with 2,618 pints of vegetable soup, 2,398 pounds of pickled cabbage, and 10,782 pounds of carrots. Over four seasons in Antarctic waters his crew remained free of scurvy.[13] Yet scurvy was the scourge of later Antarctic explorers. It caused death on the *Belgica* and *Southern Cross* expeditions and, as late as 1915, in Shackleton's support party on the Ross Ice Shelf. It was the cause of Shackleton's being invalided home during the first Scott expedition. Scurvy was unquestionably a factor in the failure of Scott's party to get back from the South Pole.[14] Amundsen escaped only because he stockpiled seal along the route and ate his own dogs. It is surprising that early twentieth-century doctors and scientists advanced knowledge of nutrition hardly at all and appeared to have forgotten what their forebears had taught.

The effectiveness of citrus in avoiding and treating scurvy was first discovered in 1601 by an officer of the East India Company, James Lancaster. Yet the means to prevent this greatest of all killers of seafarers and explorers was disregarded for two centuries, despite further conclusive experiments by a physician, James Lind, in 1747.[15] It was not until 1795 that the British Navy began to use citrus juice regularly, and the results were so spectacular that the practice was made compulsory in 1803. Yet the merchant marine delayed until 1865 to provide its seamen with citrus juice; by then, the policy had fallen out of favor in the Royal Navy and had been abandoned. Apparently the reason was that the Navy, having changed its source of supply, had unwittingly adopted a variety lower in ascorbic acid and therefore less effective.[16] How remarkable that after this long history, the greatest threat to Antarctic exploration was again scurvy, and that scientists appeared to take so little interest in the problem. By then, differing opinions about scurvy were rampant. Even Edward Wilson, the able scientist and doctor in Scott's polar party, was ill informed, despite his interest in nutrition. On his remarkable Winter Journey of 1912, he and his companions conducted an experiment on themselves to find the best balance between fat and starch to maintain energy in subzero conditions. The most he or any of his contemporaries knew about avoiding scurvy was to eat fresh meat when possible.

Scott and his companions perished only months after evidence was found for the hypothesis that certain diseases are caused by a lack of specific vitamins in the diet. However, some years passed before it was proven that scurvy was caused by an insufficiency of Vitamin C, or ascorbic acid.

The lack of scientific curiosity about scurvy was an aberration; normally, the scientific spirit prevailed even against great odds. Bellingshausen expected to carry two naturalists, but they withdrew at the last minute, and he had to settle for an astronomer and an artist, while conducting his own scientific experiments. The flurry of expeditions in the 1840s was spurred primarily by the new interest in the earth's magnetism, which was of such importance to improved navigation. Among other travails suffered by Wilkes was the Navy's announcement that the findings of his scientists would have to receive security clearance before publication.[17] As a result, the best scientists could not be recruited; nevertheless, the expedition collected fifty thousand botanical items, three thousand insects, fifteen hundred bird skins, seven thousand mineral specimens, thirty to forty bushels of seashells, and two hundred glass jars, two barrels, and ten kegs filled with mollusks, fish, and reptiles.[18] Kenneth J. Bertrand, the leading historian of American Antarctic exploration, has written that the Wilkes expedition was "a milestone in American science . . . and to a great degree American science attained its majority in this effort."[19]

It was the Sixth International Geographical Congress that was instrumental in rekindling interest in Antarctica, after a hiatus of half a century, and in encouraging the first coordinated scientific expeditions. The purpose of the *Belgica* expedition was explicitly scientific observation. Borchgrevink, although financed by a newspaper publisher, took with him a highly qualified magnetic observer, a meteorologist, and a zoologist.[20] The Swedes, who suffered more terrifying tribulations than any expedition up to that time, were absolutely heroic in hanging onto their scientific samples. Shackleton, on man's first attempt to reach the South Pole, brought back the evidence on which so much subsequent science has been based—namely, that the continent once had a temperate climate. Ironically, the only scientist to head an Antarctic expedition until the second half of the twentieth century[21]—Australian Douglas Mawson—was more preoccupied with claimstaking than had been any of his peers.

The ambivalence of explorers toward science is reflected in a particularly revealing passage in Richard Byrd's *Alone,* the book in which he recounts the consequences of his reckless decision to winter alone in a prefabricated hut buried in the snow. Looking back on one of the low points of that five-month period of solitary confinement and illness, Byrd wrote:

> The one aspiration I still had was to be vindicated by the tiny heap of data collected on the shelf in the Escape Tunnel. But even as I seized upon this, I recognized its flimsiness; a romanticized rationalization, as are most of the things which men are anxious to be judged by. We men of action who serve science serve only a reflection in a mirror. The tasks are difficult, the objectives remote; but scholars sitting in bookish surroundings tell us where to go, what to look for, and even what we are apt to find. Likewise, they pass dispassionate judgement on whatever we bring back. We are nothing more than glamorous middlemen between theory and fact, materialists jobbing in the substance of universal truths.[22]

Sir Raymond Priestley, a scientist who as a young man served with both Shackleton and Scott, was critical of the Byrd expeditions as being more military than scientific. This seems a fair assessment only of the third and fourth expeditions, which bracketed World War II, although even the short-lived third expedition, in addition to exploring new territories, did original auroral work and the first studies of human adaptation to cold and perpetual night.[23] But Priestley would not have agreed with those who assert that science was always secondary. In his presidential address to the British

Association for the Advancement of Science in 1956, Priestley said that the Norwegian-Swedish-British expedition of 1949-52 had "purely scientific objectives" and that it did "first-class scientific work . . . of unsurpassed value."[24]

The reason for emphasizing the long tradition of science is to stress the legitimacy of science in Antarctica and the extent to which intellectual curiosity as well as pride and nationalism drove the early explorers. For more than a century, Antarctica has been a place of mystery, seeming to offer the opportunity for enhanced apprehension of earth and its place in the solar system. Yet always there has been tension between the expectations of scientists and the requirements of political reality. This was most pronounced in the period surrounding World War II. The third Byrd expedition, which took place just before the United States entered the war, was indeed different in character from those that went before. Among detailed orders from Roosevelt to Byrd, cabled after the ships had sailed, was one directing that at the end of the expedition Byrd must "require from every person under your command the surrender of all journals, diaries, memoranda, remarks, writings, charts, drawings, sketches, paintings, photographs, films, plates, as well as all specimens of every kind."[25] This was the more infuriating because most of the civilian scientists had signed on for ten dollars a month, expecting to be remunerated in other ways. "For a while, I expected a full-scale mutiny over this unfair and stupid ruling," one of the expedition leaders wrote later.[26] The civilian scientists decided unanimously to resign in a body and debark at the next port, but Byrd finally talked them out of it by promising to do his utmost to have the order rescinded. In the end, the issue became academic because World War II scattered the scientists to more urgent missions and prevented processing of the data.

The fourth Byrd expedition, in 1946–47, was patently military in purpose, and the commander of the operating task force, Admiral Richard Cruzen, considered the many scientists on the expedition "superfluous."[27] Operation Highjump, as it was called, constituted both a massive showing of the flag and an opportunity to conduct maneuvers in an environment not unlike the far north, where wartime allies glared at each other with growing hostility across the Arctic Ocean. Operation Highjump was run from Washington by an interagency committee. The expedition was composed of twelve Navy ships, including the aircraft carrier

Philippine Sea, nine planes, and forty-seven hundred men, of whom about two dozen were scientists. The planes, most of them military versions of the DC 3, flew thirty-seven thousand miles and photographed four hundred thousand square miles of Antarctica. As a gesture to internationalism, Admiral Byrd, overflying the South Pole once again, dropped the flags of all the members of the United Nations.[28]

For the British, too, strategic concerns became temporarily the highest priority. Between 1943 and 1945, Britain secretly established two bases in the Antarctic Peninsula area. (See Chapter IV.) Although the mission was military, the operation included a number of scientists, headed by James M. Wordie, who had been chief scientist on the Shackleton expedition of 1914-16. Quite a lot of solid science was accomplished and has continued without interruption to this day.[29]

Thus, in the early 1950s, when the International Geophysical Year was conceived, scientists had reason to feel that military strategy and territorial claims (Chapter IV) had come to dominate the thinking of national governments and that science was becoming more a rationale than a priority—conducted as long as it did not interfere with other objectives. Even with regard to the IGY as it was getting under way, the retiring director of Britain's Scott Polar Research Center could write: "It is the naive alone who will be persuaded that pure science is the sole stimulant."[30]

Few would disagree; yet the IGY was an event of broad importance. Apart from the enormous quantity of scientific data collected, it subdued in some measure the politicization of Antarctica. It established the preeminence of science in Antarctica for decades to come. In the judgment of Laurence Gould—the chairman of the Antarctic Committee of the U.S. National Committee for IGY, and the scientist quoted at the head of this chapter—the IGY was the "most comprehensive scientific program ever undertaken by man. It is the first attempt at a total study of his environment."[31]

THE INTERNATIONAL GEOPHYSICAL YEAR

The idea for the IGY was planted on an April evening in 1950 at a dinner party given by James Van Allen (of the Van Allen radiation belts in space) at his home outside Washington. Lloyd V. Berkner of the Carnegie Institution, who had been a radio engineer on the first Byrd Antarctic expedition, suggested that advances in trans-portation, communications, instrumentation, and other technolo-gies made it highly desirable to hold a Third International Polar Year without delay. The first had been held in 1882–83, when eleven nations sent expeditions to the Arctic. Fifty years later, the second polar year again gave scant attention to the Antarctic, primarily because at the depth of a world depression the costs seemed exorbitant. The scientists assembled at the dinner party agreed that to wait until 1982 for a third polar year was unacceptable. The time was ripe for a scientific assault on the poles.[32]

A major international effort in Antarctica might provide answers to questions on which little progress had been made since the turn of the century. How thick was the ice sheet? Was it waxing or waning? What was the topography beneath the ice? Were there two continents rather than one? Or was West Antarctica an archipelago? How did this immense mass of ice affect global weather? How did it influence the dynamics of the Southern Ocean? Multiple, simultaneous observations would also expand knowledge of *Aurora Australis*, cosmic rays, and the ionosphere.

The suggestion for a Third International Polar Year was received favorably by the International Council of Scientific Unions (ICSU), representing all the principal international scientific bodies. The initial idea was gradually expanded to embrace the entire globe— land, sea, and atmosphere—but emphasis remained on the poles, particularly Antarctica. An area given importance equal to that of Antarctica was outer space. The Soviet Union scored no small coup when it launched the first *Sputnik* just as the IGY was getting under way.

To organize and direct the IGY, ICSU created the Comité Spécial de l'Année Géophysique Internationale (CSAGI), headed by an eminent British geophysicist, Sydney Chapman, who had also been at the Van Allen dinner party. Ultimately, twelve thousand scientists from sixty-seven nations, serving at twenty-five hundred radio-linked stations around the world, participated in an eighteen-month IGY from July 1, 1957, to December 31, 1958. Not by chance, the timing coincided with a period of maximum solar activity.

During the IGY, twelve nations operated sixty stations in the Antarctic; of these, forty-eight were actually on the continent. Argentina, Britain, and Chile were already operating multiple bases on or near the Antarctic Peninsula, and Australia had recently opened a year-round station on the other side of the continent. Belgium, France, New Zealand, Norway, and the United States were prepared to reactivate old bases and to open new ones. Japan, which had had a brief encounter with the Antarctic in 1911–12, wanted to return, and South Africa, although it would not operate a station on the continent until the IGY was over, planned to expand operations on its subantarctic islands, Marion and Prince Edward, and to occupy the meteorological station constructed by the British on Gough Island.[33] Thus, eleven of the twelve countries—those that would later negotiate the Antarctic Treaty—had had some experience in Antarctica in this century. The twelfth nation, the Soviet Union, had shown no interest in the continent since Bellingshausen's circumnavigation in the early nineteenth century. As delegates of the eleven nations assembled in Paris in July 1955 to plan their cooperative effort, it was not known whether a Soviet representative would join them. When he arrived, it became clear that the Soviet Union planned a major program—at least three bases (soon to be six), including one at the South Pole. Since the United States had expressed a prior interest in this site, there was considerable relief when the Soviets deferred without argument and chose instead the Pole of Inaccessibility and the Geomagnetic Pole.

Considering the Cold War tensions of the 1950s and the fact that the Suez and the Hungary crises occurred while the IGY was being planned, the ease with which agreement was reached and the level of cooperation attained were extraordinary. The participating nations, with scientists, not governments, as negotiators, agreed on what they would undertake and where. They pledged to exchange all data and ultimately to make it available to all scientists of whatever country. Three data centers were established—one in the United States, one in the Soviet Union, and the third with elements scattered among Western Europe, Australia, and Japan. Scientists of each nation were posted to research stations of others. A Weather Central, to analyze all reports received from observers on land, sea, or air, was established at Little America, but other nationals, notably a Soviet meteorologist, were assigned there, while an American was regularly welcomed at Mirnyi, the principal Soviet base. Scientists from still other nations were invited to participate; U.S. stations, for example, included scientists from

Austria, the Republic of China, Denmark, West Germany, Lebanon, and the Netherlands.[34]

The success of the IGY was due in part to its well-ordered priorities. It did not try to do everything or to be all things to all scientists. It confined itself to those disciplines concerned with the earth and the forces that affect it—meteorology and upper-atmosphere physics, glaciology, and oceanography (actually, some fourteen disciplines in all). The highest priority was given to problems requiring simultaneous observation of the same phenomena at many points on the globe. Agreement was not always universal as to how stated priorities should be interpreted. After careful consideration, the CSAGI concluded that mapping in Antarctica was not an appropriate project. Mapping was controversial because it had political, even military, connotations. The Soviet Union did considerable mapping anyway; the United States apparently refrained primarily for budgetary reasons.[35] The Soviets also made no secret of their intention to study the mineral resources of Antarctica—a prospect frowned on by the scientific community.

Politics and national security intruded in other ways. The whole enterprise nearly floundered on the two-Chinas issue, although the Nationalists had shown no interest whatever in the IGY until Peking announced conditional participation. The matter never was resolved; the People's Republic simply withdrew without notice.[36] The large number of stations set up or expanded in the peninsula area of Antarctica had more to do with politics than with science (see Chapter IV). One reason the United States made such a large commitment to the IGY was that the National Security Council decided as early as 1954 that the United States would be second to none in Antarctica. The decision to establish so many U.S. stations (seven) was influenced by the Department of Defense.[37] And it was only under sharp protest by American scientists that the Department of Defense dropped from its list of objectives the reinforcement of U.S. rights in Antarctica. Indeed, all the participating nations were motivated in varying degree by a desire to establish or reinforce political beachheads.

The involvement of the military was inescapable because of the extraordinary logistical demands of the IGY in Antarctica. Operation Deepfreeze, as it was called, accomplished prodigies of transport and construction before the Year began. For the United

States to build seven stations required three thousand men, two hundred aircraft, three hundred vehicles, thousands of tons of cargo, and storage tanks for half a million gallons of fuel. The most ambitious undertaking was the construction of a base at the South Pole to be named for Amundsen and Scott. It was decided that, rather than haul matériel up the crevassed glaciers, it would be easier and safer to fly supplies from the depot at McMurdo and drop them from the air. Air Force Globemasters, then the largest of all cargo planes, flew more than sixty-five missions and dropped eight hundred tons of prefabricated buildings, radio equipment, supplies, and a fourteen-thousand-pound tractor.[38] Although much of the matériel was damaged on landing, a well-equipped base for eighteen men was nevertheless constructed where no man had visited since Scott. The chief scientist for the station was Paul Siple, who had been chosen in 1928 from among scores of thousands of Boy Scouts to accompany Byrd on his first Antarctic expedition. The original South Pole station is now buried under forty feet of snow; a new one has been built and covered with a huge geodesic dome.

At McMurdo, where solid, ice-free ground was available for an airfield, the Seabees erected thirty-five major buildings, some with bathrooms "each larger than the Scott hut"—as Debenham ruefully noted.[39] Little America V was again built on the Ross Ice Shelf, not because it was a good place to build but because (1) it was reasonably accessible to Marie Byrd Land, which was unapproachable from the sea, and (2) the continuity of meteorological and other records since 1929 was of some value.[40] Since the previous sites had all floated out to sea on calved icebergs, Little America V was constructed 30 miles to the east at Kainan Bay. Byrd Station, 650 miles from Little America in the interior of Marie Byrd Land, was established by a supply train consisting of seven forty-ton tractors towing twelve twenty-ton sledges, all following a crevasse detector mounted on a small tracked vehicle called the Weasel.[41] For part of the way, the crevasses were so bad that they had to be dynamited and filled in before the train could pass.[42] Other U.S. stations, all new, were Hallett, near the northern tip of Victoria Land (operated jointly with New Zealand); Wilkes, on the Budd Coast (taken over by the Australians in 1959); and Ellsworth, on the Filchner Ice Shelf, later operated by Argentina. Construction of Hallett involved the displacement of an Adélie penguin rookery covering two acres—a peculiar step to be taken in the name of science.[43] In subsequent years other U.S. stations have come and gone, but of these seven, only McMurdo and Amundsen-Scott are still in operation by the United States.

While the United States concentrated on West Antarctica, the Soviet Union placed all its stations in East Antarctica—two on the coast and four inland on the high plateau. Lacking airlift, the Soviets used giant caterpillar tractors instead. They encountered greater difficulties than anticipated and did not reach the Pole of Inaccessibility, 1,250 miles from their principal base at Mirnyi, until the IGY was formally ending. Although a small party reached the Geomagnetic Pole, a station was not built there until later.[44] Other nations were satisfied, with minor exceptions, to establish coastal stations involving less severe supply problems.

Important scientific work in Antarctica began before the IGY had formally started and continued without a break after it ended, although with some reduction in stations, staffs, and resources. One of the most astonishing discoveries of any period in Antarctica was made in early 1957 by a small team of scientists, all of whom were in their twenties and had never before been in the Antarctic.

For roughly fifty years, it had been assumed that the South Polar ice mantle was relatively thin—at most 2,000 feet thick—and that it generally followed the topography of the continent. In the course of a traverse from Little America into Marie Byrd Land, an American party discovered ice depths of more than a mile in several places and a maximum thickness of 8,500 feet. More remarkable, the scientists were at an elevation of only a few thousand feet when these measurements were taken, so clearly rock bottom was several thousand feet below sea level. Compared to the radio echo-sounding technique soon to be developed, their equipment was cumbersome and time consuming to operate, but nonetheless this represented one of the technical advances of which Berkner had spoken.[45] They detonated a half-pound of TNT in a hole ten inches deep and measured the time elapsed as the shock waves bounced off the rock below and returned. These seismic studies were supplemented by magnetic and gravity soundings, which were less time consuming but required careful calibration and a number of preliminary measurements (of latitude and elevation or the strength and inclination of the earth's magnetic field at that site). All in all, it is not surprising that their report was received with disbelief at the National Academy of Sciences and that the young scientists were asked to recalculate their findings. Not only were they correct, but much higher figures would soon be found in the same region: ice thickness of 13,940 feet and troughs as much as 6,500 feet below sea level.[46]

During the IGY, seismic traverses were also made by Soviet, Australian, and French scientists, and by the British Commonwealth Trans-Antarctic Expedition. Its leaders were the famous explorers Sir Vivian Fuchs and Sir Edmund Hillary, and their objective was to cross from the Weddell Sea to the Ross Sea by way of the South Pole. Although not part of the IGY, the expedition used some of its facilities and inadvertently stole much of its thunder. Fuchs very nearly became trapped in the Weddell Sea and encountered quite unforeseen difficulties in linking up with Hillary at the South Pole—where, by then, the Americans were comfortably ensconced and could offer their British guests hot showers and movies. One of the contributions of the expedition was to add significantly to the body of seismic measurements of the continent.[47]

As a result of all the seismic data collected over these few years in the late 1950s, what had long been suspected became certain: West Antarctica is indeed an achipelago. In fact, only about three-quarters of the South Polar Icecap is, strictly speaking, continental. If the estimated eight million cubic miles of ice were removed, however, the continent might rise as much as thirty-three hundred feet, lifting large submerged areas out of the sea.[48]

Conversely East Antarctica, sometimes called Greater Antarctica, was found to be a highly stable shield composed of a pre-Cambrian rock, the oldest type known (more than six hundred million years).[49] It would be many more years before something approaching a complete profile of Antarctic ice and topography would be achieved. This would come when, in the late 1960s, it became possible to measure ice thickness and ground level simultaneously by radar impulses from a low-flying plane.[50] Yet even today, more than 30 percent of the continent remains unsurveyed.[51]

Of the forty-eight volumes of the IGY *Annals,* ten are devoted to aurora and airglow, and nine are devoted to the ionosphere, compared to one each for such substantial fields as glaciology, oceanography, and meteorology.[52] The Antarctic is, of course, an unequaled place to pursue upper-atmosphere physics. Unlike the Arctic, it provides a stable, high-altitude platform from which to observe phenomena that are unique to the poles and to study the influence of the sun at the farthest reaches of the biosphere. The South Polar region is both an attic window with an exceptionally good view into space and a magnetic maelstrom, drawing into it a variety of extraterrestrial debris. The Earth's own magnetic field, bending in lines of force from pole to pole, ensures that the bombardment of particles from the sun and other stars will be heaviest at the poles. Some of the charged particles collide with air molecules in the upper atmosphere and are destroyed. Their energy is converted into heat (and light), which creates the auroras. The surviving particles are fated to bounce back and forth from pole to pole (in the magnetosphere) until they, too, crash into air molecules.[53]

Never, before 1957, were so many cameras, spectroscopes, neutron monitors, and other devices trained on the south polar sky to record and measure the auroras from many vantage points. Great effort was also made to understand airglow—that soft, faint, encompassing light that is by no means confined to the poles—but the cause eluded the scientists of the IGY. However, striking gains were made in the study of cosmic rays, which are not rays but particles of atomic debris and—as the IGY scientists discovered— are not primarily cosmic. Rather they mostly emanate from our own sun and are related in extremely complex ways to solar disturbances.

The ionosphere consists of multiple layers of electrified molecules that make short-wave radio communication possible. Unless the fifty-to-two-hundred-mile-high ionosphere is grossly disrupted by solar storms, it reflects radio waves of low frequency back to Earth, while waves of higher frequency, such as those of television and radar, pass through it. Disruption can also be caused by detonation of a nuclear bomb at high altitudes. During the IGY, the United States set off three small nuclear devices at a height of three hundred miles over the South Atlantic. Trillions of energetic electrons trapped in the Earth's magnetic field created a shell of intense radiation as far as four thousand miles from Earth. More than six months elapsed before any information about the experiment was released. Although it was then acknowledged that the effects of a nuclear explosion in space last for several weeks, the real significance of the tests was not mentioned—namely that nuclear explosions in space made radio communication virtually impossible for varying periods of time. Thus, the worst fears of the military were confirmed.[54]

The outer atmosphere is full of strange noises, and the strangest of these so-called sferics is the whistler. Whistlers had been heard by radio operators for decades, but it was just before the IGY that the phenomenon was explained. They are caused by lightning in the form of long-wave electromagnetic energy that has been caught up in the Earth's magnetic field, bounced to the opposite hemisphere, and quite possibly bounced back again in a fixed arc. These waves travel at approximately the speed of light, but the higher frequencies travel faster than the lower ones. Thus, what started as a click becomes elongated and sounds like a descending whistle. The matched pairs of landing sites for these streaking particles of energy—one in each hemisphere—are called conjugate points. During the IGY, Byrd Station and Great Whale River, Quebec, served as conjugate points for the study of electromagnetic phenomena.

Today, Byrd Station is closed, and studies of conjugate phenomena have been carried on at Siple Station at the base of the peninsula. After the first Siple Station was crushed under thirty feet of snow, a new one was recently built, with a radio antenna 14 miles long, sitting on ice thousands of feet above sea level. With this efficient instrument, Siple sent out radio signals of very low frequency (VLF) to its conjugate point at Roberval, about 150 miles north of Quebec City, in a region prone to heavy thunderstorms. These manmade signals originating in Antarctica and the natural whistlers originating in Quebec were used as diagnostic tools to probe the magnetosphere. In 1980–81, this work was supplemented by seven rocket probes and ten balloons packed with instruments. Scientists hope that these studies may have application in plasma physics theory, energy research, and communications.[55] Siple was closed in the winter of 1980, the victim of inflation and soaring fuel costs, but remained open throughout 1981. Its future is uncertain.

PLANNING FOR THE LONGER HAUL

Since it took seven years to create the IGY, it is not surprising that, even before the eighteen-month spectacular began, the question arose: Should it be continued after 1958? Having made a huge investment in plant, the United States was in favor of continuing; it argued that budgets could be reduced without a decline in scientific product. The majority on the Special Committee of the IGY were dubious. They anticipated difficulty in obtaining adequate funding and in recruiting personnel; they also contended that continuation would cause delays in processing the mass of data already collected.[56] But the last-minute announcement by the Soviet Union that it fully intended to carry on had a powerful effect in altering perceptions.

Within two weeks, in September 1957, ICSU had created the Scientific Committee on Antarctic Research (SCAR), which to this day plays an important part in maintaining the international character of science in Antarctica.[57] It is composed of one delegate from a designated scientific body in each of the countries involved in Antarctic research, plus representatives of eight scientific unions of which ICSU is composed, as well as delegates from a few other international organizations such as the World Meteorological Organization (WMO), an agency of the United Nations. SCAR was charged "with furthering the cooperation of scientific activity in Antarctica with a view to framing a scientific program of circumpolar scope and significance."[58] SCAR operates through ten Working Groups representing relevant disciplines as well as ad hoc groups of specialists. It conducts a biennial assembly, sponsors conferences and symposia, and publishes a *Bulletin,* which appears thrice yearly in the *Polar Record* (Cambridge). SCAR makes recommendations to its member bodies and is responsive to requests for special studies and directives from them, and indirectly from governments. SCAR is an unofficial body with virtually no funds of its own, so studies under its auspices must generally be financed by national governments. SCAR's very considerable influence stems from the distinction of its individual members and their authority within their national scientific communities.[59]

Nations organize their Antarctic research in various ways. The principal differences are whether responsibility is highly centralized, whether the scientists have their own logistics or depend on

SCIENTIFIC STATIONS
OPERATING IN WINTER 1981

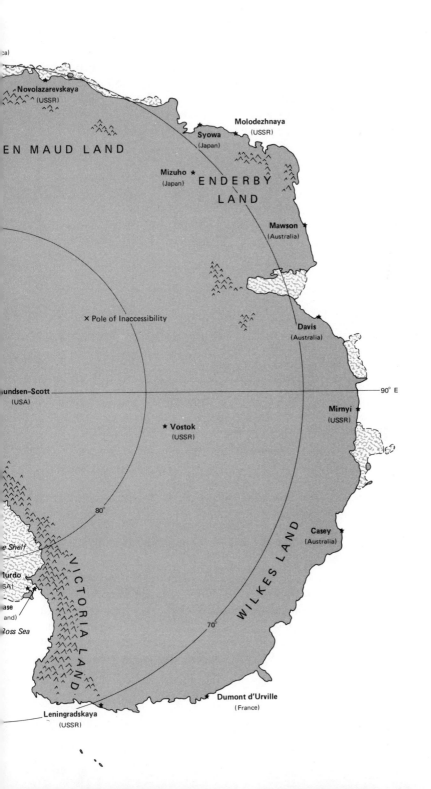

ca)

Novolazarevskaya
(USSR)

EN MAUD LAND

Molodezhnaya
(USSR)

Syowa
(Japan)

Mizuho ★
(Japan)

ENDERBY
LAND

Mawson ★
(Australia)

Davis
(Australia)

× Pole of Inaccessibility

90° E

undsen-Scott
(USA)

Mirnyi ★
(USSR)

★ Vostok
(USSR)

80°

Casey ★
(Australia)

e Shelf

lurdo
SA)

ase
and)

VICTORIA LAND

WILKES LAND

Ross Sea

70°

Dumont d'Urville
(France)

Leningradskaya
(USSR)

others, and whether those who set policy and administer programs also conduct research. The British Antarctic Survey, with a
staff of about 360, is an example of a highly unified, government-
supported body of scientists that has its own ships and planes and
conducts its own research at five stations.[60] The Australians are
similarly organized. France opted to continue giving government
support to an essentially private organization, Expeditions Polaires
Françaises, created in 1947 by the extraordinary Paul-Emile Victor.[61] In the United States, the Division of Polar Programs (DPP)
within the National Science Foundation (NSF) administers the U.S.
Antarctic Research Program (USARP). The division conducts no
research itself but administers grants to scientists—and teams of
scientists—most of whom are attached to universities. Since the
mid-1970s, after several years of transition, all funding for USARP
has gone directly to NSF. From a total budget of around $70
million, NSF pays the Navy for services rendered, including
operating McMurdo Station, flying planes and helicopters owned
by NSF, arranging air transport of supplies and personnel from the
United States to Antarctica, directing the work of supply ships and
Coast Guard icebreakers, and providing a variety of other functions such as communications. Some two thousand support personnel are involved. In addition, NSF pays a private contractor,
Antarctic Services, Inc., to operate South Pole, Siple, and Palmer
stations, as well as USARP's only research vessel, Hero, and to
perform other administrative functions.[62] After this enormous
overhead has been budgeted, the moneys available for research
grants are fairly modest—about $7.5 million.

Advice and counsel are offered to NSF by the Polar Research
Board of the National Academy of Sciences, which also represents
the United States in SCAR. Periodically, the sixteen-member board
conducts broad surveys to define major research objectives for the
years ahead.[63] But it is the Division of Polar Programs of the NSF
that finally determines the priorities, makes the decisions, and
pays all the bills for U.S. scientific research in Antarctica.

It was only with very strong backing from the White House that
NSF won its dominant position. As soon as the decision was made
in January 1958 to continue an extensive research program more or
less permanently, a power struggle arose over how the effort
would be organized and who would succeed to the authority of
those who had run the U.S. IGY program. The two key bodies had

been the Committee on Polar Research of the National Academy of Sciences and the Antarctic Working Group of the Operations Coordinating Board (OCB). Neither seemed well suited to adminis- ter a continuing program, and in fact the OCB, a creation of the Eisenhower White House, was soon to be abolished by President Kennedy.

The recommendation that the National Science Foundation take over was made by the Bureau of the Budget. The Department of Defense fought the proposal, determined to maintain the ascen- dancy it inherited from Admiral Byrd. During the summer of 1959, as he was about to retire, Admiral George Dufek, who had commanded all the support and construction forces for the IGY, wrote a long, secret report in which he said that direction of the U.S. Antarctic Program by NSF "would prove fatal to our national interests." He argued that preoccupation with science would lead to the neglect of our political, economic, and strategic interests.[64] Admiral Arleigh Burke, chief of naval operations, was reported to hold that "neither by law nor experience does the National Science Foundation seem equipped to manage a program with so many implications outside its usual field of endeavor."[65]

There was more opposition. The Committee on Polar Research (subsequently the Polar Research Board) was jealous of its preroga- tives. Its chairman, the redoubtable Laurence Gould, wrote angrily to NSF Director Alan T. Waterman when NSF approved two projects that Gould's committee had turned down. Gould wrote with all the prestige of the National Academy of Sciences behind him, whereas the NSF was less than ten years old, but Waterman replied as graciously as possible that NSF had ultimate authority.[66] When Waterman tried to relieve the political pressure by creating an Interdepartmental Committee on Antarctic Research, on which any federal agency could sit and communicate its views to NSF, Gould strongly objected, saying he feared "polar research becom- ing a completely governmental function."[67] But Waterman himself was much opposed to all funds being fed through NSF as they are today. The operating responsibilities of the Defense Department cannot be transferred, he contended, and NSF "should not be in a position of monitoring the logistic operation."[68]

Meanwhile, a number of congressional leaders were promoting the idea of either an independent or a quasi-governmental commis- sion to be named for Admiral Byrd. It would be a permanent body taking over responsibility for planning and conducting Antarctic research. The Department of Defense was ambivalent but inclined to lend support if it meant it could keep its dominant position as "Executive Agent" and be rid of the demeaning word "support," which was used to describe its function in relation to NSF.[69] The idea floated around until 1965, when it finally expired under the unbroken opposition of the Johnson administration.[70]

SCOPE OF THE CURRENT EFFORT

Ever since the IGY, there have been about thirty scientific stations operating year-round in Antarctica, of which four have been operated by the United States. In the 1980–81 season, USARP supported about 285 scientists working on eighty-six different projects in the fields of glaciology, biology and medicine, earth sciences, upper-atmosphere physics, meteorology, and ocean sciences. This includes all the sciences for which Antarctic research is particularly suited and represents a considerable expansion since the IGY—particularly in biology, geology, and marine sciences. For example, whereas oceanography was confined to charting major circumpolar currents during the IGY, in 1981 the United States spent about $3 million on marine ecosystem studies, excluding the cost of ships and shore facilities.[71] Another major area of research introduced since the IGY is the study of animal adaptation to extreme cold.

Because of inflation, especially in fuel costs and military pay increases, a declining proportion of the USARP budget goes directly for scientific research; the ratio is now about one dollar of science for nine dollars of support. The inflationary squeeze has been so severe that, at least temporarily, Siple Station is no longer operating as a year-round station; every gallon of heating oil burned at Siple requires six gallons of aviation fuel to get it there from McMurdo. The next cut may come in the number of Hercules C-130s (five of seven were active in 1980–81), which consume nearly a third of the logistic budget. The South Pole station could not be efficiently supported without them. No other country has more than small planes in Antarctica, and a reduction in C-130s would substantially alter the science program. Just getting to Antarctica is expensive—a flight of ten thousand miles from the U.S. West Coast to McMurdo via Christchurch, New Zealand.

(However, those assigned to Palmer Station in the peninsula area are serviced through Ushuaia in Argentina's Tierra del Fuego.)

Only the Soviet Union maintains an Antarctic research program comparable in size to that of the United States. In its first two decades in Antarctica, according to a Soviet source, nine thousand Soviet citizens served in Antarctica, and of these, thirty-four hundred wintered over (a figure far higher than that for the United States). The exact number of scientists is not given, but their work resulted in more than four thousand articles, a two-volume atlas, and more than sixty volumes of *Transactions of the Soviet Antarctic Expedition*.[72] In 1980, the Soviet Union increased its year-round stations from six to seven, compared to three for the United States. The newest base, Russkaya, is on the Ruppert Coast of Marie Byrd Land. The spectrum of disciplines covered by the Soviets is similar to that of the United States.

In terms of resources expended in Antarctica, Argentina, with seven year-round bases, is probably making an effort equal to that of the United States and the Soviet Union, but it is directed to settlement as well as to science. Britain and Chile have fairly comprehensive research programs, which, like Argentina's, are heavily concentrated on the peninsula and in the surrounding waters. Australia is the only other country to have a continuing program that encompasses the full spectrum of polar sciences. New Zealand works closely with the United States, which provides much of its logistic support in exchange for the use of facilities in Christchurch. France confines itself largely to its one station, named for Dumont D'Urville.

Since 1960, Norway has mounted only one expedition to Antarctica, in 1976–77, but it has generally had a few scientists there, frequently at one of the U.S. stations. However, in recent years, Norway has maintained an upper-atmosphere meteorological station on Bouvet Island, as a contribution to the U.N.'s Global Atmospheric Research Program.[73] Japan, too, has been an irregular participant in Antarctic research but is now extremely interested in the marine resources of the Southern Ocean and is conducting a three-year program of seismic surveys on the continental shelf.

Poland established its first permanent station in 1976 on King George Island (one of the South Shetlands) and named it Henryk Arctowski for the meteorologist on the *Belgica* expedition. Poland's scientific research is much influenced by its interest in krill but has been expanding into several disciplines. South Africa maintains one station, Sanae (close to 0° longitude), concentrating on the atmospheric sciences, while its supply ship conducts some ocean-ography. Belgium has not mounted an expedition of its own since the IGY.

The latest newcomer to the Antarctic in modern times is West Germany, which has for several years been doing krill research. For the first time since the *Schwabenland* expedition, Germany returned to the continent in 1979–80, primarily to find a suitable site for a year-round station on the Filchner Ice Shelf at the head of the Weddell Sea. In early 1980, the West Germans budgeted the equivalent of $150 million to plan more than seventy research projects, to build a base in Antarctica to accommodate about thirty scientists, to establish a polar research institute in Bremen, to construct a research vessel for work in ice, and to finance expedi-tions through 1983.[74] However, as it had often before, the Weddell Sea frustrated the German effort to build a base at 77°S. In January 1981, ice more than twelve feet thick halted the expedition a hundred miles from its goal. To the intense disappointment of the German scientists, an alternative site was selected nearly nine hundred miles to the northeast at Atka Bay, a well-studied area.[75] The next season, December 1981, the Germans had more ill luck when a supply ship was crushed by ice and sank in the Ross Sea, though without loss of life.

Although Antarctica is often referred to as the last unspoiled continent, it is not unsullied. True, the Antarctic is so vast that man's overall impact has been small, but pollution and ecological disruptions around research stations can be severe.[76] Even beyond the immediate environs of polar stations, there is some deteriora-tion. This is especially true in the dry valleys—the rare, snow-free areas that are of enormous interest to biologists. So many scientists have camped and conducted experiments there that the environ-ment has inevitably been altered.

At most stations, refuse and sewage are dumped into the sea. At inland stations waste must be burned or buried. The United States has by far the worst reputation for pollution around its stations.[77] The floor of McMurdo Sound, the most convenient site for marine biology experiments as well as for dumping, is littered with tons of old oil drums, tractors, aircraft parts, plastic, and thousands of beer cans. Perhaps more destructive is the organic material that is seriously upsetting the ecological balances in an environment where recovery may take decades, if it ever gets a chance.[78] These conditions are not confined to McMurdo, although at other U.S. stations refuse is more easily buried in the snow. Promised alternatives to these polluting practices have not been forthcoming. The NSF spent many years and many dollars to prepare an inch-thick environmental impact statement, which contained only the obvious, minimized every problem, evaded every issue, and announced that long-awaited "studies" were still in progress or yet to be undertaken.[79]

Although Antarctic architecture is not expected to win prizes, it seems significant that writers visiting McMurdo invariably comment on the ugliness of the station, particularly in contrast to the surrounding beauty.[80] The station is built on porous volcanic rock, and the exposed area has been greatly increased by consuming available snow as water. Vehicles pulverize the rock to a fine dust that in summer covers everything with a gray film. In addition, the buildings are unappealing to the eye, and outdoor storage of equipment gives the station the appearance of "a wartime supply dump."[81] Such visual pollution pales to insignificance, however, beside the sometime threat of atomic radiation.

NUKEY POO

Nowhere was nuclear power anticipated with greater optimism than in Antarctica, and nowhere was its failure more convincing. As early as 1957, Walter Sullivan, science writer for *The New York Times*, had written: "Atomic power packages are being developed which will largely eliminate the need for liquid fuels, constituting about 75 per cent of the resupply cargo which must be carried to Antarctic stations and airlifted to remote camps such as that at the Pole."[82] The cost of diesel fuel rose more than threefold by the time it reached McMurdo and fiftyfold by the time it reached the South Pole station. The Atomic Energy Commission (AEC) calculated that the cost of power generation at McMurdo could be almost halved by the use of nuclear energy and projected total annual savings of $1.67 million (in 1960 dollars).[83] Also, the fuel-oil storage capacity in Antarctica was limited and would have to be expanded unless an alternative could be found. Other advantages foreseen were a reduced danger of fire by eliminating oil stoves and electric heaters and the potential for creating large, temperature-controlled environments that would make Antarctica "a playground for rich tourists."[84] Paul Siple anticipated that Antarctica would become a center for nuclear research and industry.[85]

As the first of what was expected to be several reactors was starting up in Antarctica, Admiral Dufek, the former commander of Operation Deep Freeze, said that it "opens a dramatic new era in man's conquest of the remotest continent."[86] A leading Australian in Antarctic science observed that "the future development of Antarctica will, I am sure, depend upon the success of the American experience with nuclear power."[87]

The NSF was not so enthusiastic. Thomas O. Jones, who headed USARP, thought the design and planning of the reactor had been done too hastily and that the promised savings were exaggerated. He questioned whether Antarctica provided a suitable environment for an experimental reactor. Officially, his chief concern was the possible effect on the scientific program, especially on cosmic ray research.[88] Alan T. Waterman and Roswell Gilpatric, director and deputy director of the NSF respectively, shared these concerns but felt that the nuclear reactor was an AEC project with national implications, which was true.[89] Their reluctance to be obstructionist was encouraged by the fact that the project was strongly supported by the Department of Defense, with which NSF was then in a power struggle.

Congress swiftly appropriated funds, and by March 1962, Antarctica's one and only nuclear power plant came on line with eighteen hundred kilowatts of electricity.

Within its first year, the reactor broke down and was out of action for about eight weeks. Diesel generators were returned to duty, but fuel had to be flown in by helicopter from tankers that could get no closer than forty miles because of impenetrable ice. The helicopters provided little more energy than they consumed in the round-trip flights. Throughout the reactor's eleven-year history, such stoppages continued. Beyond question the plant was uneconomic. It rarely produced at its designed output; nearly thirty men were needed to operate it; and a large standby capacity for oil-powered generation was still required.[90]

But the so-called Nukey Poo came to an end, not because it was uneconomic, but because it was leaking. The reactor stopped generating in late 1972 and was never started up again, as it gradually became known that the gravel backfill used in place of the normal concrete shield (considered impossible to pour in Antarctic temperatures) was contaminated. So was the soil beneath.

The Antarctic Treaty permits nuclear power plants but not the burial of radioactive wastes. So, over three seasons, the Navy brought back to the United States nearly 800 tons of radioactive "junk," including the contaminated components of the dismantled reactor. In addition, 12,200 tons of earth and gravel were shipped to the United States for burial. It was the first time a used reactor had been disassembled and transported. Proving that it could be done without accident may be the only achievement connected with Nukey Poo.[91]

Thus ended the euphoric hopes of Admiral Dufek and others that nuclear power would permit enormous economies, reduce supply problems by nearly half, and in general serve as the key to unlock Antarctica. Despite the fact that five million gallons of petroleum products must be delivered to Antarctica each year, just for the U.S. program, and despite the tenfold increase in costs, no one is inclined to try nuclear energy again in Antarctica.[92] In fact, a new conventional power station has just been built at McMurdo.

ICE CORES, FOSSILS, AND METEORITES

The relative purity of the Antarctic environment is an important asset. Antarctica serves as a baseline for measuring pollutants in the biosphere. The discovery of strontium 90 in Antarctica after nuclear weapons testing in the atmosphere came as no surprise, but finding lead and DDT in recent layers of snow confirmed theories about how these substances are transported and added a new dimension to the hazard they represent. Airborne particles, nitrous oxide, and ozone levels are constantly monitored at the South Pole station.

In the exceptionally cold temperatures of Antarctica, snow traps and buries foreign material and preserves it, whether it is organic or inorganic, soluble or insoluble. Ever since the IGY, scientists have been drilling in Antarctica and extracting ice cores, which provide a remarkable record of the past.[93] For the first two hundred feet or so, each seasonal accumulation of snow is a visible layer, much like the rings of a tree. At greater depths, the snow is compacted into glacier ice. Increasingly sophisticated techniques are permitting the extraction of continuous cores to ever greater depths (more than three thousand feet) and the interpretation of more and more data from them. For past millennia, scientists can measure such things as solar activity, climate, and carbon dioxide.

Despite contradictory evidence as to whether the earth is warming or cooling, a growing school of thought is convinced that increasing carbon dioxide from burning fossil fuels and from the destruction of forests will cause a dangerous warming of the climate. The United Nations Environment Program (UNEP) believes that the issue "commands urgent and universal attention."[94] At present rates, carbon dioxide in the atmosphere is expected to double in about half a century, causing a significant increase in global temperatures. This is the so-called greenhouse effect by which increasing amounts of the sun's heat are trapped in the Earth's atmosphere, rather than being reflected out into space. A peculiar aspect of this phenomenon is that if the average global temperature rises 2°C as a result of carbon dioxide in the atmosphere, the average temperature at the poles will be up 5°C. This would be sufficient to cause severe melting at the poles and a gradual rise in sea levels. However, the reverse is also possible. If the ocean warms but the air above the ice sheets remains below freezing, the result could be increased snowfall, a growth in the ice sheets, and thus a lowering of the sea level.[95]

The reverse phenomenon seems more probable. A panel of experts concluded that "the disintegration of parts of the West Antarctic ice sheet . . . is a possibility and should be taken seriously."[96] This would raise sea levels as much as twenty-five feet, flooding the dwellings of eleven million Americans alone.[97] The consequences for agriculture, fishing, and forestry would be incalculable. Clearly, Antarctica is a critical place at which to monitor the growth and effects of carbon dioxide in the atmosphere. Also, a more accurate historic record of atmospheric carbon dioxide derived from ice cores may help to confirm or weaken predictions.[98]

An even more disquieting theory arises from the fact that for more than 90 percent of the time over the last million years the global climate has been colder, more glacial than today.[99] Although the present interglacial period seems reasonably stable, some believe that a large part of the ice sheets might slide or "surge" into the sea, forming a huge ice shelf that would not only raise the sea level disastrously, but also substantially increase the Earth's albedo (reflectivity). This would lead to global cooling, causing glaciation in the Northern Hemisphere—or perhaps merely offsetting the warming (greenhouse) effect of carbon dioxide. What makes the improbable possible is that much of the Antarctic ice sheet is believed to rest on slush or pools of water melted by heat from the Earth's core and probably friction (between rock and moving ice) as well. Some evidence exists that a surge occurred about ninety-five thousand years ago and may have initiated the last glaciation.[100]

One of the most exciting scientific events in Antarctica since the IGY was the discovery in December 1967 of skeletal remains of a land vertebrate—the first ever found there. It was a four-footed amphibian, of the genus *Lystrosaurus,* and virtually identical to fossils found in South Africa and India. Two years later, the same Ohio State team found hundreds more amphibian and reptilian remains, again in the area of the Beardmore Glacier in rocks of the Triassic Period of two hundred million years ago. These fossil vertebrates could be linked positively to those found in South America and Australia, as well as in India and Africa. These discoveries provided the missing link in the theory of continental drift and place the remaining skeptics in an untenable position.[101] New finds of fossil vertebrates continue to be made. In 1977–78, a team of Americans and Australians found a cache of almost complete skeletons that included not only species found on other continents but also species never seen before.[102]

In 1982, a team from Ohio State's Institute of Polar Studies again found what paleontologists had been sure were there all along— the fossil remains of a land mammal. The bones were those of a small marsupial. They strongly support a long-held theory that these pouched creatures migrated from South America to Australia by way of Antarctica before these continents broke apart about sixty million years ago.

Another noteworthy discovery was algae growing in profusion in almost total darkness on the bottom of permanently frozen lakes. Even in the brief summer season, the light filtering through eighteen feet of ice is less than one-tenth of one percent of that on the surface—far less than was believed to be the minimum for any photosynthesis to take place. A great deal of work has been done on the ecology of Antarctic freshwater lakes, some of which are free of ice in summer and teeming with life. Another feat of adaptation is the growth of lichens beneath the surface of porous rock found in the dry valleys of Antarctica. Unlike the surface, the tiny crannies below provide a relatively constant temperature and enough retained moisture to sustain a rich microbial colony.[103] This discovery has raised hopes that a similar form of life may yet be found on Mars, which the dry valleys closely resemble in appearance and chemistry.

The vast expansion of gravity studies over a large part of Antarctica have been useful to NASA. Biological studies of the dry valleys, which bear striking similarities to the moon, had an impact on the Apollo program. Biology was one of the sciences entirely neglected by the IGY; therefore, since that time, it has been an especially productive area for research. A continuing study that has attracted particular attention focuses on the process by which fish avoid freezing to death. Arthur De Vries of the Scripps Institution of Oceanography at La Jolla, California, has isolated an antifreeze protein that lowers the freezing point of blood to $-2.1°C$.[104]

One of the richest finds in Antarctica has been meteorites—some three thousand of them discovered just since 1969.[105] What makes them especially valuable is that, whereas meteorites found elsewhere are few (about ten a year) and are often weathered and eroded, those discovered in Antarctica have been preserved in the pristine condition in which they reached the Earth. Although the oldest residency in the icecap so far dated is 700,000 years, it is possible that meteorites yet to be discovered may have been there as long as the icecap, perhaps 20 million years. This would be a mere instant in their lifetime, for meteorites are believed to have a common origin with the Earth about 4.6 billion years ago. Nearly 800 million years older than any known rocks from Earth, most meteorites have plunged from the asteroid belt that revolves around the sun between the inner, rock-ribbed planets and the outer gaseous planets.[106] A relatively rare type and the oldest of the meteorites, called carbonaceous chondrites, contains complex organic molecules and water bound structurally to their minerals.[107] While these organic molecules do not prove that life exists elsewhere, they show that the conditions necessary for the creation of life occur outside our biosphere.[108] The carbonaceous chondrite has been called the "Rosetta stone of the solar system"[109] because it can tell us about processes that took place before the planets were formed and about their evolution since. When they are found in Antarctica, having moved with the glacial flow of the icecap until terrain conditions push them upward and expose them by ablation, they are accorded the care and respect of moon rocks: They are transported in cold, sterile containers to the Johnson Space Center in Houston, Texas, for classification and study.[110] An interesting bonus is that when more is known about the movement of meteorites in Antarctica, more will be known about the flow of the icecap itself.

The growth of remote sensing and automated devices for recording data might have been expected to reduce manpower needs in Antarctic research. In fact, the reverse seems to be true: Remote sensing and electronic recorders have been used to extend man's scientific reach rather than relieving him of tasks. For example, Landsat-3, Nimbus-7, Tiros-N, and the very similar NOAA-6 satellites are all in near-polar orbit and all have multiple scanners producing quantities of information from six different sensors. McMurdo has a ground station—a so-called high resolution picture transmission system—that can pick up much of this data either as visual images or in digital form on tape. Among other things, remote sensing monitors the waxing and waning of the ice pack and tracks the movement of icebergs, some for up to twelve years. All this tends to make for additional work because there are more data requiring analysis and interpretation.[111]

ARE WE GETTING THE SCIENCE WE DESERVE?

Although the National Science Foundation completely dominates U.S. research in Antarctica, other departments and agencies have interests and responsibilities: The National Oceanic and Atmospheric Administration (NOAA) is involved in climate research and marine resources; the Department of the Interior—especially the Geological Survey—has responsibilities for resource assessment and for endangered species; the missions of the Council on Environmental Quality (CEQ) and the Marine Mammal Commission (MMC)[112] unquestionably embrace Antarctica. The National Aeronautics and Space Administration (NASA), which provides some of the rockets used in research, is concerned with the magnetosphere and is custodian of Antarctic meteorites; and the Department of Energy[113] is interested in the region's potential resources.

However, none of these agencies has funds specifically for Antarctic research, and each can make a contribution only as a spinoff of its respective mission. The NSF may seek counsel of these agencies or provide funding for special projects. But if these agencies are too aggressive in advancing their points of view or their perceptions of scientific requirements in Antarctica, they may be accused of wishing to assume NSF's responsibilities.

As a practical matter, no American can conduct research in the Antarctic or even visit Antarctica (except as a largely shipbound tourist) without the approval and support of the NSF. It alone has the money and the legislative authority. Monopoly is no more desirable in science than in other fields, although there may be no practical alternative. Logistics represents such a high fraction of the total costs of Antarctic research that not even the wealthiest private foundation could compete. Nor would it have any motive; no relevant field of science is being seriously neglected. But the very fact that there are no alternatives available places a particularly heavy responsibility on the NSF.

For the quarter-century that Big Science has burgeoned in Antarctica, science administrators have not resisted the temptation to overstate the relevance, the applicability, and the immediacy of research in the south polar region. The former chairman of the National Academy of Science's Polar Research Board and now U.S. representative to SCAR has said that the IGY was sold largely on the promise of improved weather forecasting. He readily admitted it was a promise unfulfilled.[114] In 1974, the National Research Council (NRC) was issued a series of reports calling for "emphasis on understanding the physical role of Antarctic and Arctic phenomena in world weather and climate change." A summary report issued by the NRC acknowledged that, after nearly two decades of intense study, the impact of the poles on global circulation of oceans and atmosphere "is understood crudely at best."[115] Thus, after nearly thirty years of intensive research in Antarctica—much longer in the Arctic—little progress has been made. Meanwhile, oceanographers, glaciologists, and upper-atmosphere physicists continue to claim that their studies will improve weather forecasting.

The tendency to oversell the capabilities of science and the immediate relevance of research is not peculiar to the Antarctic. But that cold continent does possess an aura of mystery that promises much in some very "hot" fields, such as weather, climate, and resources. The present director of the NSF, John B. Slaughter, testifying before Congress in 1978 on the exploitation of Antarctic resources, said: "The aspects we are most interested in are the marine resources and the mineral resources. Our scientific programs are to a large extent addressed to these specific issues."[116] If members of the committee had had time to study the U.S. Antarctic Research Program in detail, it is unlikely they would have accepted this as a statement of fact. The USARP environmental impact statement, mentioned earlier, seeks to give a similar impression without supporting evidence.[117] Some critics within the scientific community believe that the Dry Valleys Drilling Project and the Minerals Assessment Project conducted by airborne radiometer are enormously wasteful boondoggles that have no purpose other than to give an impression that USARP is doing important research related to resources.

There is something approaching a conspiracy between scientists and the NSF's Division of Polar Programs to give the impression to Congress and the small public that may be listening that Antarctic research is resource-oriented and of almost instant applicability. It is not, nor should it be necessarily. But the conviction runs strong in NSF that, if Congress is not constantly reassured that the taxpayer is getting his tangible money's worth, funding will dry up.

There is no reason to doubt that a great deal of very good basic research is being done in Antarctica. Funding is not likely to dry up, although whether it will or should keep up with inflation is debatable. The Reagan administration has shown no inclination to cut the USARP budget and seems likely to remain responsive to the argument of a ranking naval officer associated with the support of USARP: "Our first job in Antarctica is to be there, to exert a presence. Science is secondary—a benefit of being there."[118] The Director of the Division of Polar Programs, Edward P. Todd, has said the same thing on more than one occasion, and the point is well understood by science administrators in Washington and other capitals.

Although breakthroughs continue to be made occasionally, it

might be said of polar science that it is moving from a period of
discovery to one of quantification. Inevitably, there is somewhat
less excitement as the once virgin icescape becomes more familiar. The biggest change since the IGY, according to one old Antarctic hand, is that scientists in Antarctica today are no longer
philosophers; they are too preoccupied with their own immediate
specialty.

Another change observed by some is an atmosphere at U.S.
Antarctic stations less conducive to creative work. Voluntary duty
by support personnel is no longer the norm. The large naval
contingent in Antarctica is not there out of choice but under orders,
and the civilians employed by the major contractor are there not
out of intellectual curiosity but because the pay is good. Although
the Navy maintains that the Antarctic provides a valuable experience, those who serve there consider it a poor road to advancement, if not a career dead end. None of this contributes to good
morale. American scientists who have served at the stations of
other countries often note the far pleasanter environment, where
everyone from chief scientist to cook's helper is enthusiastic about
being where he is. By making the U.S. armed services functionar-
ies of the NSF in Antarctica, the executive branch has ensured a
total lack of interest by the Department of Defense and widespread
dissatisfaction among those assigned to what they consider undesirable and even dangerous duty.

A remarkably skeptical view of Antarctic science was offered
more than ten years ago by a highly qualified observer. A. P. Crary
was chief scientist of USARP and, with Thomas O. Jones, was the
principal architect of the continuing U.S. research program after
the IGY. In an article first published in 1970, Crary chided
scientists in several disciplines (notably glaciology and meteorology) for pretentiousness, faulted the program for inflexibility, and
criticized U.S. scientists for failing to make a genuine commitment
to international cooperation.[119] Since scientific research in Antarctica has often been presented as something almost unworldly in its
detachment or, conversely, of marvelous relevance, it is worth
quoting Crary at some length, especially as the points he makes
seem even more valid today.

Looking back at the progress and the mistakes we have made in
Antarctica in the past dozen years, perhaps we should ask ourslves:

Have we done too much? What was the big hurry? Must we continue to entice hundreds of scientists to the continent each year? How will future generations of scientists view our work, with those from only a few decades getting the real opportunities? What have been the criteria for justifying the budget figures? Could we have done all that was really needed at half the cost?

I would say that our decisions on Antarctica have the same basis as that of many other national budget decisions over the years. Starting at any level, the trend continues up and up. Like all facets of American life, there is no hint of retreat. Every added project, each additional scientist, represents something to build on. . . . For science, there is another subtle difficulty. The real breakthroughs in science generally come from the young scientists, but it is extremely difficult for a young scientist to get a start in the system. The old ones do not fade away fast enough. Neither, of course, do the civil servants who have nurtured these same scientists through the years. Obviously, the system has many inequities.

I have sometimes thought that the proper way to handle the Antarctic effort would be to have one three-year expedition every decade, with no repeat performers permitted from one decade to the next. This would allow each scientific team time to collect adequate data and to work it up thoroughly so that the next group could absorb the information and adequately plan its expedition.[120]

This last suggestion is not to be taken entirely seriously. Continuity in data gathering has great advantages and the economies would not be nearly so substantial as the numbers suggest, because a station abandoned for seven years would be expensive to rehabilitate. More important, if the United States withdrew from the South Pole station, most observers believe, the Soviets would occupy the site instantly—even though they might have to develop a whole new supply system to support it. Scientifically, the Amundsen-Scott station may not be worth its very high operating costs, but—as we shall see presently—it is of inestimable value politically.

Most of Crary's queries deserve reconsideration today. The strength of the Division of Polar Programs is also its weakness. The law creating the NSF prohibits the staff from conducting research; its task is to choose among deserving proposals submitted to it. This has had the advantage of encouraging hospitality to new ideas and avoiding some bureaucratic rigidities. But by interpreting this procedure inflexibly, the division denies itself any leadership role, fails to shape a coherent program, and rejects responsibilities not foreseen when USARP was created. Eighty-six separate research projects in Antarctica in one season seems too many. They have no defined relationship to one another. They reflect no clear priorities, but rather a balancing of political and academic pressures. They represent no systematic effort to close some of the most important gaps in knowledge. And they are unresponsive to the requests of other agencies of government that need hard answers to hard questions. These points will be developed further in later chapters.

CHAPTER

⫟⫟⫟

Guessing at Resources

The idea that Antarctica can be held forever as a scientific
laboratory is losing ground.

—*J. H. Zumberge*

  The resources of Antarctica are largely speculative. They consist
of the Southern Ocean fishery, notably krill; the probable presence
of oil, whether or not it is feasible to extract it; hard minerals that,
even if they exist in useful quantities, are mostly buried under
thousands of feet of ice; icebergs as a source of fresh water, if they
can be transported to where they are needed; tourism, which
might someday be a source of revenue or simply a continuing
headache; and various uses of the continent once considered
promising—as a deep freeze for emergency food storage, for
airfield sites on Great Circle routes between the southern continents, and as a burial ground for radioactive wastes. Each of these
will be discussed.

MARINE LIVING RESOURCES

  The Southern Ocean represents the world's last great undeveloped fishery. Despite the reckless harvesting of marine mammals
in Antarctic waters over a period of two centuries, the idea of the
Southern Ocean as a rich source of food is comparatively recent.[1]
Two circumstances have given greater urgency to the possibility.

75

First is the apparent fact that exploitation of conventional fisheries may have reached or exceeded their limit.[2] The total harvest from the seas grew very slowly in the 1970s and only with increased effort, while the decline in stocks of herring, mackerel, and Peruvian anchoveta has been alarming.

Second, the major fishing nations have been shut out of waters they customarily exploited because of the nearly universal adoption by coastal nations of the two-hundred-mile exclusive economic zone (EEZ), which has now been formalized in the Convention on the Law of the Sea. Alternative fishing grounds have become a matter of urgency. These developments have occurred in parallel with the growing perception that food supplies generally may become increasingly critical and that command of food resources is an important element of power.

South of the Antarctic Convergence are to be found squid and octopus (cephalopods), crabs and lobsters, and fin fish, but little is known of their quantities. Of the twenty thousand kinds of fish in the world's oceans, only about a hundred have been found in the southern seas.[3] Of these, perhaps twenty species hold potential for commercial fishing, especially various kinds of Antarctic cod and icefish, which are already being harvested. A large proportion of Antarctic fin fish swim at depths that make recovery difficult; yet in some areas, overfishing may have already begun. In addition, the coasts of Antarctica are rich in seaweeds, including many already in use in other parts of the world, as food or for the production of algal products. Since the use of seaweeds—and new products processed from them—is constantly increasing, the benthic marine algae of Antarctica represent a potential resource.

But it is not cod or squid or seaweed that has attracted so much recent attention, but krill, a small, shrimplike crustacean of exceptional nutritional value. Of the six species of krill found in the Southern Ocean, *Euphausia superba* is the largest, most abundant, and alone in being of commercial interest. It almost surely constitutes the world's largest unexploited source of animal protein. Krill—the word is a Norwegian whaling term for tiny fish or whale food—has a protein content of 50–60 percent (dry weight); it is high in all essential amino acids and is rich in minerals (calcium, copper, iron, magnesium, and phosphorous) and vitamins (notably A and the B group complex). Nutritionally, krill compares favorably with soybean and is the equivalent of fish protein concentrate. In early experiments, Soviet investigators have found krill superior to beef paste as a feed supplement for animals.[4] It yields a nutritious oil and a high-quality chitin (the principal component of the shell) used in the pharmaceutical, cosmetic, photographic, and other industries.

The krill's habit of swimming (or drifting) in large swarms makes it possible for baleen whales to sift vast quantities from the sea; it also makes krill convenient for trawlers to catch. The previous high estimates of the size of these swarms were dwarfed in 1981 by the discovery of a shoal containing some ten million metric tons of krill. Theoretically, that would be enough to provide five hundred million of the world's most undernourished people with forty-four pounds of krill per person. Measured by acoustical and netting techniques, the swarm covered several square miles and ranged in depth from about sixty to six hundred feet.[5] Previously, densities had been estimated from six to sixty kilograms of krill per cubic meter of water and from five hundred to forty-nine thousand individuals per cubic meter.[6] The West Germans once caught thirty-five tons in eight minutes and believe that daily catches of two hundred or three hundred tons are practicable.[7]

As the dominant zooplankton of the Southern Ocean, krill is also the principal consumer of phytoplankton, primarily diatoms, which prosper in the coastal waters of Antarctica. The Southern Ocean is enriched both by warmer currents from the north that well upward and from the meltwater of glaciers and ice shelves that appear to have absorbed nitrogen from the atmosphere.[8] Distribution of krill is by no means uniform; although they are found all around the continent, the largest concentration seems to be in the southwest Atlantic in the region of the Scotia Sea.

All higher species in the ecosystem of the Southern Ocean depend on krill directly or indirectly, in whole or in part. Whales, seals, penguins, squid, fish, and winged birds are all consumers. Moreover, the Antarctic food chain is uniquely short: No group is more than three steps away from phytoplankton; and krill, a crustacean five centimeters in length and weighing about one gram, is the principal food of the great whales—the world's largest mammals. Normally, species at the upper levels of the food chain are harvested, rather than one species that forms the foundation of the entire food web. There is no precedent for the commercial exploitation of a species so far down on the food chain—

and so central to a vast and virtually enclosed ecosystem.[9]

This is what troubles scientists, conservationists, and all those who hope that mankind will not repeat its past performance in virtually exterminating several species of seals and whales. And despite the fact that krill and the marine ecosystem of which it is the most important component have been studied for half a century, areas of ignorance are vast and potentially dangerous. For example, we do not know:

- how many krill there are—estimates of standing stocks or biomass range from 300 million to 6 billion metric tons;
- annual krill production—estimates range from 200 million metric tons to 6.6 billion metric tons per year, a thirty-three-fold difference;
- how much krill is consumed by its natural predators;
- to what extent the production of krill is limited by the availability of food and to what extent by predation;
- how and why the krill swarms and with whom—its own age group or indiscriminately;[10]
- how long the krill lives, when it becomes sexually mature, whether it spawns more than once, what it does in winter when it cannot be easily observed, and whether it consists of a single genetic stock or of several discrete populations.

The usual explanation for the paucity of data is that, until very recently, krill could not be maintained in the laboratory for long-term study; now at Palmer Station, in aquaria with flow-through seawater, krill are being reared with some success, although they have so far succumbed to invasion of bacteria before reaching maturity.[11] Also, in estimating krill abundance, figures must be extrapolated from relatively small samples of a species that is not only unevenly distributed around the ocean but whose swarming density varies enormously. The costs of research in this field are particularly high and a coordinated, international effort has heretofore been lacking. Finally, much of the data and analyses still used today were gathered decades ago, notably by the British *Discovery* expeditions of the 1920s and 1930s, whose scientific chronicler was James W. S. Marr.[12] Nevertheless, considering that a recently published krill bibliography contains sixteen hundred titles,[13] the extent of our ignorance is astonishing.

Until better data on the size of standing stocks, annual production, and predator consumption become available, it is obviously impossible to determine how much krill can be harvested without throwing the Antarctic ecosystem out of kilter and endangering the creatures that depend on krill for their survival. In setting harvest levels, productivity is far more important than the total size of the stock.[14] Many scientists seriously question the assumption that there is now a substantial surplus of krill because there has been a sharp decline in their once principal predators, the great whales. It seems more likely that other species have benefited from the lower consumption to build up their own populations. For example, there is strong evidence that chinstrap and Adélie penguins and crabeater seals have doubled or tripled in recent decades.[15] At Signy Island (one of the South Orkneys), chinstraps increased 35 percent over ten years, and Adélies increased 55 percent over twenty years.[16] Fur seals, which were virtually extinct sixty years ago, are now conservatively estimated to number about four hundred thousand and are increasing by 17 percent a year.[17] Even when comparative figures for population growth are not available, they can be inferred from evidence of earlier sexual maturity, a phenomenon that occurs when food is more easily available. These generally substantial increases in the populations of most penguins and seals may have absorbed a large proportion of the theoretical excess of krill, estimated at between 100 and 150 million metric tons (mmt), made available by the decline in baleen whales.

The table on the next page provides very rough estimates of the present stocks of krill predators and their consumption of krill.[18]

Not all krill predators would suffer equally if krill were harvested too heavily. The first to be threatened would be the baleen whales, which depend on dense swarms and swim in the same latitudes in which trawlers hunt for krill. This point is critical. If harvesting krill reduced the density of swarms below some unknown level, the consequences for baleen whales might be catastrophic, no matter how many krill were left in the sea. Crabeater seals and Adélie penguins inhabit the ice farther south, and it is possible that harvesting krill would affect them minimally. Species that do not show up on the table at all, because they are not direct consumers of krill, would be no less seriously affected by overfishing. The sperm whale, for example, depends heavily on squid, which, as one of the largest consumers of krill, would certainly decline if its primary source of food were significantly reduced.

ESTIMATED ANNUAL CONSUMPTION OF KRILL

	Present Stocks (individuals)	Consumption of Krill (in metric tons)
BALEEN WHALES		
fin	84,000	16,400,000
blue	10,000	3,400,000
sei	50,000[a]	2,900,000
humpback	3,000	300,000
minke	200,000	19,800,000[b]
		42,800,000
SEALS		
crabeater	25,000,000	106,000,000
other	4,000,000	3,100,000
		109,100,000
PENGUINS		
Adélie	50,000,000	9,000,000
chinstrap	4,000,000	1,500,000
other	16,000,000	3,400,000
		13,900,000
WINGED BIRDS	100,000,000	500,000
SQUID		100,000,000[c]
FISH		64,000,000[c]
	Total Consumption	330,300,000

Sources: Estimated consumption figures are adapted from Green, "Role of Krill in the Antarctic Marine Ecosystem," pp. 17 and 21. Stock estimates are drawn from Everson, The Living Resources of the Southern Ocean; Bengtson, Review of Information; and McWhinnie NSF Report.

Notes

a. This assumes that only half the population feeds south of the Antarctic Convergence.
b. Only the minke whale is believed to remain south of the Convergence year-round. Hence, its consumption is larger in relation to its total biomass. Prior to the last decade, the minke was considered hardly worth catching and as a result is the only baleen whose population has not been depleted and may have grown.
c. These are hardly more than guesses, but they have been raised substantially on the basis of recent research.

Although rarely noted, it seems significant that at least two of the largest consumers of krill—squid and crabeater seals—have potential commercial value. If krill are to be harvested, it would seem desirable to exploit their chief predators (other than whales) at the same time, in order to maintain balance within the food web.[19] With present knowledge, this is not, of course, easily accomplished.

At present, there is no commercial sealing in Antarctica, and any that may take place will be regulated by the International Sealing Convention, which came into force in 1978. The species traditionally taken by sealers—fur and elephant seals—are still recovering from near extermination. But the misnamed crabeater seal, which weighs up to nine hundred pounds and whose diet is 95 percent krill, may be the most abundant seal in the world, certainly in the Antarctic. Among the early explorers, who depended on seals for food, the flesh of the crabeater was preferred; it was said to be about the same color as beef and to taste equally good.[20] Despite the fact that there may be thirty million crabeaters (some say seventy million), they have not proved economical to catch because they do not congregate in the manner of other species.[21] Crabeaters are quite probably one of the major beneficiaries of the decline in whale stocks, yet they may not in fact be competing directly with the baleens, which generally feed farther north. Thus we do not know whether culling crabeaters would be helpful. It might be more useful to raise the quota on minke so as to reduce their numbers, which may have increased enormously while they were immune from the hunting that decimated the stocks of blue and humpback.[22] But, as biologists remind us, once an ecological balance has been upset by man, it is nearly impossible to restore.

Among those worried about the consequences of unrestrained fishing for krill, concern for the great whales is uppermost. Although totally protected, the blue, the fin, and the humpback show no sign of increasing.[23] Scientists are not agreed on what constitutes a safe harvest of krill. At a meeting of experts in 1974, "There was a consensus that . . . the potential yield appeared to be at least 100 million tons."[24] This estimate was picked up and accepted as revealed truth in the press and in organs of the United Nations, but it made many scientists increasingly uneasy. Today, the consensus is that we do not know enough to make such estimates, and that a large safety factor should be built in to compensate for our ignorance. Most scientists are reluctant to hazard a guess, although Katherine Green has speculated that between 30 and 60 mmt might be feasible.[25] One is more likely to see estimates of annual productivity, on which all else depends. Not surprisingly, fishing nations give credence to much higher figures than do such nations as the United States and Britain that are not engaged in krill fishing. Although there is as yet no formal policy, scientists are urging Washington to assume annual productivity no higher than 250 mmt and a safe harvest as no more than 5 mmt. This is not to say that they believe the latter figure to be the ultimate limit, but rather a total that should be adhered to until far more data are available.

Virtually all students of the marine environment of Antarctica make the point that the Southern Ocean must be managed as a single ecosystem in which all the trophic interrelationships—not simply one species—are considered. To fish for krill on the basis of maximum sustainable yield (msy)—the traditional way of managing fisheries—could well be disastrous for other species in the food web.[26] Another area of agreement, at least among scientists, is that all exploitation of marine resources should be prohibited in certain specified areas of the Southern Ocean so that these can serve as baselines for comparative study.[27] The very highest priority is given to acquiring and exchanging information on which sound decisions can be based.

STUDYING KRILL AND THE MARINE ECOSYSTEM

The major international effort to learn more about the Southern Ocean and its fauna is known by the somewhat labored acronym BIOMASS—Biological Investigations of Marine Antarctic Systems and Stocks. It was born at a conference at Woods Hole, Massachusetts, in August 1976—the product of initiatives and studies by the Scientific Committee on Antarctic Research (SCAR) and the Scientific Committee on Oceanic Research (SCOR), and also involving the International Association for Biological Oceanography (IABO) and the Advisory Committee on Marine Resources Research (ACMRR) of the Food and Agricultural Organization (FAO). All of these became the sponsors of BIOMASS. In the words of the convener of the conference, Sayed Z. El-Sayed of Texas A & M University, "The principal objective of BIOMASS is to gain a deeper understanding of the structure and dynamic functioning of the Antarctic marine ecosystems as a basis for the future management of potential living resources."[28]

The ambitious program of research initially contemplated was too large and too unfocused, and there was virtually no money except what participating governments would provide for their own researchers. BIOMASS has thus increasingly become a program for assessing the abundance and distribution of krill—a project on which all interested nations could agree. In February 1981, ships of ten nations participated in an acoustic survey concentrated primarily in the southwest Atlantic, where krill are especially abundant, but also in the southwest Indian Ocean. FIBEX—First International BIOMASS Experiment—had other aspects, but the principal objective was to achieve a better estimate of the total population of krill and to assess the feasibility of acoustic surveys for measuring krill stocks.[29] The masses of information gathered will take a long time to analyze, but a preliminary estimate of the standing stock of krill based on FIBEX data is 650 million metric tons.

In July 1977, the NSF asked El-Sayed what the U.S. contribution to BIOMASS should be. El-Sayed assembled an ad hoc Group for U.S. BIOMASS the following month and by November had produced a seventy-six-page report outlining research projects in a dozen subject areas. He also prepared budget estimates for a ten-year program that totaled a minimum of $38 million and an optimum of $107 million.[30] For a nation without commercial interests in the Southern Ocean, this was a sizable sum. Moreover, the program was so diffuse, so lacking in priorities, that it seemed (perhaps unfairly) to have been conceived to appeal to the largest number of scientists by offering something for everyone. Despite the fact that American scientists have played the leading role in planning and conceptualizing BIOMASS, nothing came of the report; it has been largely neglected by the U.S. government and the scientific establishment (although the United States did have one ship in FIBEX). Five years after the Woods Hole meeting, the United States still has no official policy toward BIOMASS, although in the summer of 1981 a joint committee of the Polar Research Board and the Ocean Sciences Board of the National Academy of Sciences recommended that "the United States should support the general aims of BIOMASS and contribute to its goals." Adding to the impression of tepid support, the committee went on to say that "general approval of the aims of BIOMASS is not inconsistent with special directions for United States studies."[31] This unofficial but long-awaited guidance could be interpreted any way one pleased.

Although the NSF is highly skeptical of the value of BIOMASS, it nevertheless increased its research awards for the study of krill from a hundred thousand dollars in 1977 to half a million dollars in fiscal 1980. In that same year, total U.S. funding for research on the Antarctic marine ecosystem amounted to six million dollars, including support costs.

A quarter of a century ago, two knowledgeable students of the Southern Ocean wrote: "It is not beyond the bounds of possibility to conceive of a floating plant, anchored in deep water, powered by the ever-blowing westerly winds, uninhabited and automatic, and visited at intervals of months for the removal of the crustacean sludge extracted by mechanical separation. Such development would seem more promising than direct fishery in antarctic waters."[32]

It was not until five years later that experimental fishing for krill was begun by the Soviets, followed by the Japanese, Chileans, Poles, West Germans, Bulgarians, and half a dozen others on a smaller scale (Norwegians, Taiwanese, East Germans, Spaniards, Koreans, and Argentines). According to FAO figures, which may be low, the total harvest of krill in the 1978–79 season was 386,000 metric tons, of which 326,000 tons were caught by the Soviets.[33] The latter figure represents an increase of nearly 400 percent over the previous year, but it may reflect not so much an actual quadrupling as more honest reporting. The Soviets' data have been suspect in the past, and a possible reason for greater candor now is that the Soviets are anticipating the assignment of quotas based on past catches. In 1981, thirty-five Soviet trawlers were counted in the vicinity of the ten-million-metric-ton swarm mentioned above, suggesting that annual increases may continue to be large. This runs counter to the trend for other countries fishing in the Southern Ocean. For two principal reasons having nothing to do with the cautionary counsel of ecologists, the harvest is expected to grow slowly: Krill is difficult to process and no substantial market for krill yet exists.

Although krill swarms are not easily seen from shipboard, they can be found with relative ease by directional echo sounder— essentially the same sonar device that submarines use to "see."[34]

Experiments have also been conducted on the remote sensing of krill—with limited success.[35] But even if modern sensors fail to identify krill, the Coastal Zone Color Scanner carried in Nimbus-7 shows concentrations of phytoplankton.[36] With further refinement, it may be possible to locate krill patches (groups of swarms) by spotting their sources of nourishment.

Thus, finding krill should not be a problem, but variations in the daily supply—the tendency toward feast or famine—may be troublesome. The physical act of catching krill will be relatively easy, although advances are needed in the way trawlers haul their catch aboard so as to minimize damage to the crop. The rate at which krill is taken may be seriously constrained by the danger of crushing the animal and thereby preventing its use for anything but meal. The next step is more difficult. Krill is highly perishable and within a few minutes or hours (depending upon temperature), disintegration (autolysis) begins and discoloration may occur. Therefore preliminary processing (buffer holding) is necessary almost immediately. The krill may be shelled, gutted, beheaded, boiled, steamed, dried, or quick frozen—or some combination of these. The procedures will depend on the ultimate product desired —whether for human or animal consumption—the condition of the krill, and the technology available. Most of the technology is still experimental and details are sometimes withheld as privileged information. The points to emphasize are that even preliminary processing is complex and involves sophisticated technologies; krill fishing is capital intensive and, if it is to be economical, must be undertaken on a substantial scale; and for some time, the catch is likely to be limited by the capacity of the factory ship to process it.

Another serious limitation is the absence of consumer demand for krill. Although a wide range of products has been tried, marketing has not flourished. There appears to be a difference of opinion about the taste appeal of krill, perhaps because quality control is a problem. Y. I. Tolstikov, head of the Soviet delegation at the Tenth Consultative Meeting of the Antarctic Treaty Powers, told this writer that the Soviets are finding it difficult to develop demand for krill. People do not much like it, he said, and it is not cheap to produce. If used as fodder, he added, people complain that the meat tastes of fish. Similar reports have come from the Japanese.[37] Nevertheless, none of the starters are abandoning their efforts to develop a profitable krill industry.

So far, the largest proportion of krill taken has been made into meal to be used as an animal feed supplement. But since krill is not ever expected to be cheap, a considerable effort has gone into developing appetizing products for human consumption. Among them are:

- whole tail meats, frozen, canned, or dried. (As with shrimp, the tail is the edible part.) These may compete with small shrimp tails or be converted into other products, such as the breaded krill sticks being marketed in Chile. In Japan, dried krill are eaten rather like peanuts.
- krill mince, which has potential for a variety of other uses, such as in pie fillings, soups, and salads, or as a component of fishcakes and fishballs.
- coagulated paste, which has been used primarily as a flavor and nutritional enhancer in butter, processed cheese, snacks, sauces, sausages and the like, or as a spread. Paste products have been developed in the Soviet Union, Japan, West Germany, Poland, and Chile.
- krill protein concentrate and soup powders, which might have high potential as food supplements in developing countries.

In the United States, krill is consumed primarily as pet food imported from Japan and West Germany. However, at least one food product for human consumption (whole frozen unpeeled krill) is imported from Japan, but it appears to be marketed only in Hawaii and California.[38] Despite the fact that the United States does no krill fishing, research and development on krill products have been conducted in this country, and krill processing machinery manufactured here has played an important role in the emergent krill industry.[39]

As yet there is no commercial fishing for krill; hence, the economics are not clear. Expeditions so far are experimental and government-sponsored or -subsidized, and the pricing of krill products is arbitrary. The enormous distances between the Southern Ocean and the principal fishing nations and the soaring cost of fuel are deterrents. So are the shortness of the season and the absence of navigational aids. At least one environmental organization that had long been concerned about the consequences of krill fishing announced in 1980 that there was nothing to worry about because the market for krill would remain so small as to pose no threat to the Antarctic ecosystem.[40]

In addition to all the known difficulties of harvesting, processing, and marketing krill has come one puzzling surprise. After years of chemical analysis of krill, after it was deemed free of toxic effects and indeed—in the opinion of Soviet scientists—therapeutic in the treatment of stomach ulcers and artereosclerosis,[41] krill is now said to have high concentrations of fluoride, making it unfit for human consumption.[42] This report has not caused any apparent lessening of interest in krill. Some believe the situation is analogous to the mercury-in-tuna scare of a few years ago. Others see the problem as real but surmountable.

As late as 1977, FAO considered it "probable that a commercial fishery for krill in the Southern Ocean will prove economically viable."[43] Although developments have been slower than expected, few seriously doubt that a substantial krill fishery will be developed. Many would argue the slower the better to allow for the acquisition and exchange of knowledge; to reduce the risk of irreversible changes in the ecosystem; to develop management strategies acceptable to all nations; and to find means of ensuring that poor countries are among the direct or indirect beneficiaries of this potentially vast source of protein.

MINERAL RESOURCES

The expectation of finding significant deposits of minerals in the Antarctic is based in part on the simple fact that all other continents contain mineral deposits—some of them, as we know, very rich. There is no reason to believe Antarctica is an exception, but with 98 percent of the continent covered by ice, the problem of finding minerals is formidable; the further problem of exploiting them economically, given the environmental conditions and the distances from supplies and markets, is one that may never be solved.[44]

That Antarctica contains minerals is more than an assumption, however. There are known to be large deposits of iron in East Antarctica, especially in the Prince Charles Mountains. Ample coalfields are scattered throughout the Transantarctic Mountains and elsewhere, but the quality is poor, and despite the high cost of transporting heating oil to Antarctica, mining of coal for local use holds no attraction. The world does not lack for iron or coal, and it is difficult to foresee a time when they could be extracted competitively in Antarctica—unless they were used locally in some emergent industry. Sand and gravel are available in many areas and might become important in future construction, although their utility is reduced by a climate that has so far precluded the pouring of concrete.

Evidence of copper has been seen in many places, but most deposits have been found on the peninsula. None is especially large or rich. Such other minerals as have been identified have been found in what geologists call "occurrences"—small amounts that may or may not be of any significance, their quantity as yet undetermined. Thus, in the Dufek Massif in the Pensacola Mountains—an area of particular promise—trace amounts of chromium, nickel, cobalt, and platinum have been found. Copper, lead, zinc, tin, gold, and silver have been seen in the Transantarctic Mountains, generally in concentrations so low as to discourage future prospecting. Manganese and molybdenum occur on Stonington Island and elsewhere. Although most authorities believe East Antarctica is less well endowed with minerals, it is said to contain (in addition to coal and iron) beryllium, copper, niobium, titanium, zirconium, graphite, mica, phosphate, and quartz of optical quality. On the sea floor beyond the continental shelf, there are manganese nodules, but so poor in metal content compared with those found nearer the equator that it is unlikely they will be mined.

It is perhaps not surprising that, in the case of metals, only occurrences have been found so far, since ostensibly exploration has not begun and discoveries have been incidental to scientific research. Nevertheless, distinguishing between what is done when seeking knowledge for its own sake and what is done as a result of an interest in minerals may be very difficult. Although a gentleman's agreement suspending mineral exploration until ground rules can be agreed upon by all the interested nations is in effect, it is intended primarily to postpone exploratory drilling for oil. There is every reason to believe that the nations conducting research in Antarctica have been interested in its resources from the beginning.

A U.S. presidential directive of October 13, 1970, stated that cooperative scientific research should include "prediction and assessment of resources." It has not been superseded, despite the voluntary restraints on exploration agreed to by the treaty powers. What concerns most governments at this stage is that (a) whatever exploration is done should not disrupt the environment, and (b) whatever is learned should be freely and fully communicated.

The Soviets have made no secret of their desire to learn everything possible about Antarctica's mineral resources. As early as 1960, after only three years in Antarctica, the Soviets had searched for minerals at sixty bare-ground points and shown their findings on a map. Although the results were not announced, they were not secret.[45] Ever since the IGY, there has been a debate within the Western scientific community as to whether the Soviet Union is communicating its research findings fully (as it is obligated to do under the Antarctic Treaty) or whether the Soviets simply have difficulty in processing raw data into usable form rapidly—not an unusual problem in science.

An interesting example of ambiguity in Antarctic research is the work of Edward J. Zeller of the University of Kansas. Since 1976, he has been conducting "a uranium resource evaluation" with an airborne gamma-ray spectrometer. Although Zeller insists he is not prospecting, his research has raised some eyebrows. Using mostly helicopters, he has taken radiation measurements in the Darwin Glacier area of the Transantarctic Mountains, Marie Byrd Land, the Ellsworth Mountains, and Victoria Land without finding any uranium—only some thorium, of which the world has an ample supply. His work, which is supported by the NSF and the West Germans, is limited by the fact that his radiometric equipment cannot see through ice. Nevertheless, Zeller has plenty of ice-free topography at which to aim his spectrometer; so far, he has covered only 0.2 percent of the exposed land area of Antarctica.[46]

THE RELEVANCE OF PLATE TECTONICS

Suppositions about the mineral resources of Antarctica do not depend entirely on the discovery of occurrences in exposed outcrops. The elaboration of the theory of continental drift into the science of plate tectonics has provided an important tool for locating the most promising areas for investigation, as we shall see. From the sighting of coal by the earliest inland explorer to the relatively recent discovery of the three-hundred-million-year-old jawbone of a freshwater amphibian, it was evident that the

Antarctic had not always had a polar climate. Thus, either the poles had moved or Antarctica had moved; no other explanation was possible.[47]

The theory of continental drift, first expounded in 1912, is generally attributed to a German, Alfred Wegener, although he owed much to others.[48] He was especially indebted to Austrian geologist Eduard Suess, who conceived the supercontinent Gondwanaland and named it for the region of India where he first began accumulating evidence that the Indian peninsula, southern Africa (including Malagasy, *i.e.*, Madagascar), South America, and Australia had similar geological and climatic histories. Alexander Du Toit further developed the Gondwanaland thesis in the 1930s, correctly making Antarctica the centerpiece, but because the most fundamental questions as to how and whither such vast land masses moved remained unanswered, the theory of continental drift was generally in disrepute for half a century.

"Answers of startling cohesion"[49] began to emerge coincident with the IGY, and by the end of a decade, plate tectonics provided something like a unified field theory for geophysics—one that satisfied various concerns of the earth sciences. The timing seemed appropriate because the Antarctic played so central a role both in the IGY and in the continent of Gondwanaland—geographically, historically, and scientifically.

Plate tectonic theory is now almost universally accepted.[50] It postulates that the Earth's crust is made up of approximately two dozen rigid plates moving over the interior mantle. Where these plates are drifting apart, as in the case of Gondwanaland, there is a spreading at the ocean ridges, an upwelling of lava from deep in the earth, and the formation of new crust. Where plates are moving into one another, the crust is pushed up and mountains are born. Thus, the Indian subcontinent, after breaking away from Gondwanaland, smashed into Eurasia and created the Himalayas, which are still rising. Fragments of Gondwanaland exist in central Iran and Afghanistan.[51]

The compelling evidence for Gondwanaland and its breakup is found in rocks and fossils, but the Earth provides another clue of particular importance in establishing time and place. The Earth's magnetic field periodically reverses its polarity, from north to south and south to north. By knowing when these reversals occurred, it is possible to date quite accurately when rock was formed. More than this, just as a compass needle dips as it approaches a magnetic pole, so lines of force solidified in rock tell the scientist the latitude at which a geological structure was formed. It is this kind of sophisticated knowledge that has permitted scientists to speculate that the rupture of Gondwanaland began with the breakaway of South America and Africa about 180 million years ago, followed by India some 100 million years ago, and finally Australia a mere 50 million years ago.

The map on the next page shows how Gondwanaland presumably appeared 200 million years ago.[52] The broken lines mark orogens—mountain systems uplifted in the same geological period. It is the presumed similarities within orogens that lead scientists to believe mineral deposits found in Chile, for instance, are likely to be found in the Antarctic Peninsula and part of Marie Byrd Land. Equally, there is a presumption that minerals found in southern Africa, which has some of the world's richest deposits of chromium, gold, and diamonds, also exist in the Ellsworth Orogen and the Transantarctic Mountains (the Ross Orogen). But the southern part of the Andean chain in Chile, for example, is "practically barren" mineralogically,[53] and there has been a "paucity of reported mineral occurrences in the Antarctic Peninula."[54] Thus there are no assurances, and commercial exploration, if it ever begins, will be playing for long odds, even before the problems of extraction arise.

It was noted earlier that a region of high mineral promise was the Dufek Massif, often called the Dufek Intrusion because layers of molten rock have intruded into older rock. Geologists call the formation "a stratiform igneous complex." This one is comparable in thickness (eight kilometers) and area (fifty thousand square kilometers) to South Africa's Bushveld Complex, with which the Dufek Massif lay in a common bed, so to speak, in Gondwanaland. The Bushveld Complex is the largest and richest mineral complex in the world;[55] by its own account, South Africa has 86 percent of the world's known platinum reserves, 83 percent of the chromium ore, 64 percent of the vanadium (for high-strength steels), 49 percent of the gold, and 48 percent of the manganese.[56] The United States categorized three of these—the platinum-group metals, chromium, and manganese—as among the five most critical strategic metals (cobalt and titanium being the others).[57] If hard minerals are ever to be mined in Antarctica, it is likely to be a large deposit of

GONDWANALAND

a high-grade ore of a high-value metal such as one might expect to find in the Dufek Massif.

David H. Elliot, director of the Institute of Polar Studies at Ohio State University, has imagined the operation of a mine in the Dufek Massif, exploiting a deposit of platinum-group metals.[58] He hypothesizes a mine where 510,000 tons of ore and 40,000 tons of waste rock per year are extracted with the expectation of ultimately producing 100,000 ounces of refined metals. Because the mine must be operated year-round in ferocious weather, the entire operation is underground. Five caverns are required to house the mine, the crushing and grinding room, the flotation mill, the smelter, and the power plant. This calls for the removal of about 200,000 tons of rock, exclusive of underground living facilities for some 450 people. The generating plant has a five-megawatt capacity, for electricity powers all the heavy machinery and furnaces, and provides much else, including meltwater used in the mining operation. Since the site is three hundred miles from the nearest open water (in the best of times and seasons), an oil-fired plant is out of the question; nuclear power must be used. The 486,000 tons of tailings do not include 28,400 tons of furnace slag and 3,750 tons of sulfur dioxide. Clearly the environmental impact locally would be devastating; a number of such mining operations would almost certainly degrade the nearly pristine atmosphere of Antarctica, thereby jeopardizing science and possibly affecting the global climate.[59]

This hazard is not imminent. Elliot calculated that, at mid-1976 prices, the product of this hypothetical mine would be worth just over fourteen million dollars. But the cost of operating the mine would be more than forty million dollars annually. For a hypothetical chromite mine, the ratio of costs to revenues is even worse.[60] Economists have since pointed out factors Elliot failed to consider and have concluded that the situation is even more unfavorable than his estimates indicate.[61]

Indeed there seems to be almost total agreement that hard minerals will not be mined in Antarctica for at least a generation. The single greatest obstacle is the energy required to convert ice to water, needed in all forms of mining operations. No combination of circumstances—supply, demand, discovery, technology—can be foreseen well into the twenty-first century that would make extraction of hard minerals economically attractive. This is not to say that the presumed hard minerals of Antarctica are unimportant —indeed, the expectation of future wealth makes them important now (see Chapter VI).

THE PROSPECT FOR OIL AND GAS

The heightened interest in the nonrenewable resources of the Antarctic focuses not on hard minerals but on the possibility of finding oil and gas. Attention is directed to the continental shelves, where unmetamorphosed sedimentary beds are of sufficient thickness to offer the prospect of oil and gas deposits. Much was made in 1973 of the finding of ethane, ethylene, and methane in three of four holes drilled by the scientific research ship *Glomar Challenger* in the Ross Sea; the first two of these hydrocarbons are often found in association with petroleum. Further expectations were raised the next year when part of a National Security Council study was leaked, indicating that the U.S. Geological Survey estimated deposits of 45 billion barrels of oil and 115 trillion cubic feet of natural gas on the continental shelves of West Antarctica.[62] Although the USGS insisted this was a misinterpretation, since only a third of the deposits were recoverable, the figures were given further credence when they appeared in *Science* without qualification.[63] They have appeared again and again since.[64] It has gradually become apparent, however, that minimal seismic surveys are not a basis for estimating petroleum reserves; until exploratory drilling begins, there is no way to assess this resource with even a pretense of reliability.

Before that day comes, far more multichannel seismic and other geophysical surveys will be needed. In this effort, the United States has been inactive despite a National Security Council directive that the mineral resources of Antarctica should be assessed.[65] The Soviet Union, with far less expertise in seismic work, has been active, as has Norway. Japan is conducting a three-year study centering on the Bellingshausen and Amundsen seas. The German Federal Institute for Geosciences and Resources has conducted surveys in the Weddell Sea and more recently in the Ross Sea. Ice conditions in the Ross Sea are far more favorable than the others, and a reconstruction of Gondwanaland suggests close affinities with the rich Gippsland Basin off the southeastern tip of Australia. Thus, it was in the Ross Sea that Gulf Oil proposed to

conduct a joint seismic venture with a consortium of oil companies
and the U.S. government. Nothing came of the proposal, but it is
being resurrected. Under the terms of the Antarctic Treaty, whatever is learned from these studies must be made known to all—a
matter of great importance at this time.

Despite the paucity of data, some oilmen believe that exploratory drilling will begin within a decade.[66] This will present awesome
problems, which will become greatly magnified if production wells
are bored. The continental shelves of Antarctica are roughly half as
wide and twice as deep as the global norm, presumably because
the land mass has sunk under the enormous weight of ice. The
weather makes all other drill sites, including the Arctic's Beaufort
Sea, appear benign by comparison, and weather forecasting is
entirely inadequate. The season for drilling is uniquely brief: From
the time the sea ice breaks up to allow a drillship to get on station
to the time it must depart or risk getting locked in for the winter
may be less than ninety days.[67] Icebergs will endanger drillships
and scour the sea bottom to depths of three hundred to four
hundred meters. Thus experience in the Arctic has little relevance.
There, artificial islands have been built in the shallow water to
serve as protected drilling platforms; threatening icebergs, incomparably smaller than those in the Antarctic, have been towed away;
and weather forecasting is comprehensive. Nevertheless, the Ca-
nadians spent three years and twelve million dollars assessing the
risk of drilling in the Beaufort Sea and now appear to have more
unanswered questions than they started with.[68]

The technology for exploratory drilling in Antarctic waters does
seem to be available. Drillships can now operate in more than a
thousand meters of water and, if threatened by storms or icebergs,
have the capacity to disengage from a wellhead quickly after
sealing it. Wellheads can be sunk below (or in valleys of) the sea
bottom to escape iceberg scouring. Blowout preventers are now
more reliable, and in case of failure, a second drillship can be
required to stand by to drill a relief hole.

All of these capabilities would be doubly important if exploration
advanced to exploitation, but they would not be enough. For
year-round operations (which alone would be economical), drilling
installations would have to be placed on the seabed, either buried
or beyond the reach of iceberg scour. Here the steepness of the
Antarctic shelf might actually be an advantage. To avoid enormous

shore installations for which space is inadequate, oil would probably be stored in submerged tanks floating at great depths. Since storage for nine or ten months of the year would be immensely costly, it would probably be necessary to construct large, ice-strengthened tankers that could operate year-round—if not everywhere, at least in the Ross Sea area where the pack ice is lighter than in, say, the Weddell, Bellingshausen, or Amundsen seas.[69] Clearly, the technology for oil production in Antarctic conditions does not yet exist.

The consequences of a major spill have been the subject of much speculation. The blowout of Extoc 1 in the Bay of Mexico in June 1979 shook a lot of experts who were wont to emphasize how statistically rare blowouts were and how little oil had been spilled in this manner. In the case of Extoc 1, 3.5 million barrels escaped over a period of nine months before it was brought under control, making it incomparably the largest oil spill in history. If this could happen in the relatively gentle waters of the Caribbean, what might happen in the brutal environment of Antarctica?

Opinions obviously differ. The optimistic theory—but one given considerable credence—is that the effects of a spill on wildlife would be local, even if severe. Dispersal through northward drift into the immense Southern Ocean would minimize the environmental impact. Others believe that the effects of the northward drifting oil on the phytoplankton and zooplankton—the very pulse of the ecosystem—might be devastating to higher species. Fortunately, both sides are prepared to admit that their knowledge is inadequate. At least for the present, there is a disposition to proceed with caution.

The fear that a large spill or series of spills might actually have severe climatic effects seems now to be generally discounted. The notion was that a large oil slick might lower the albedo of the sea ice sufficiently to cause its melting, thereby exposing more water, upsetting the heat balance further, and bringing on a rise in sea level. It has now been fairly convincingly demonstrated that the annual variation in sea ice through natural causes is so much greater than any possible melting caused by a hypothetical oil spill that concern on this point is unwarranted.[70] Others hold that such things are unknowable and that any tampering with heat balances in a polar context is extremely hazardous.

The costs of oil production in Antarctica are expected to be so

high that only a very large oil field will seem worth developing—
one capable of yielding more than a quarter of a million barrels a
day. Any gas associated with the oil can be put to use locally but
cannot be economically transported to markets. Every aspect of the
Antarctic environment will tend to increase costs over norms
elsewhere. For example, costs of drilling increase exponentially
with water depth,[71] and the cost of obtaining one additional daily
barrel of oil in a thousand meters of water will be nearly twice that
in five hundred meters.[72]

A 1969 study of resources for the future found that freight costs to
and from McMurdo Station were between two and ten times those
of transporting similar goods over similar distances in other parts
of the world. Exceptional costs include docking facilities in severe
ice conditions, the need for reinforced hulls and icebreakers, and
the short shipping season of ten to twelve weeks. Costs of shipping
to inland stations are two to three times as high as those for
McMurdo.[73] At shore points, unit costs would decline with volume, however, since one icebreaker can serve an almost unlimited
number of ships using the same approach channel.

Until recently, conventional wisdom held that the likelihood of
finding petroleum on the continent itself was virtually nil. This
remains true for East Antarctica, but as more is known about the
construction of West Antarctica, geologists have come to believe
that oil may be found there in the interstices between Gondwanaland fragments. West Antarctica, including a zone extending all the
way up to New Zealand, is perhaps the only remaining area of the
world where even the number of tectonic plates is unknown.
Nevertheless, geologists can discern four discrete areas of a
continental character. They are the peninsula, the Ellsworth Mountains extending eastward almost to the Transantarctic Mountains,
Marie Byrd Land (geologically a somewhat smaller area than maps
suggest), and Thurston Island off the Eights Coast between the
Amundsen and Bellingshausen seas. Between these continental
chunks are areas of very deep ice lying over sedimentary basins
formed when Gondwanaland was breaking up. These zones of
stretched continental crust are believed to be analogous to the
North Sea, which was formed by the incomplete departure of the
British Isles from continental Europe. Thus, there is high expectation that these basins of West Antarctica contain oil.

It is difficult to assess the significance of this hypothesis. If oil is found, it will be in deposits buried beneath thousands of feet of slowly moving ice in an area virtually inaccessible to the sea. Whether the advantages of a stable platform will more than compensate for these obstacles, only the further development of technology and the relative size of deposits will tell.

Interested scientists are now proposing a concerted, international effort to answer the remaining questions about the structure of West Antarctica and how it relates to East Antarctica. Specifically, they propose a series of what are called geotraverses, beginning with a line from the Transantarctic Mountains to the base of the peninsula. The idea is that, instead of random, uncoordinated site studies, much more can be learned from a geological survey along a defined line with several countries cooperating to share the costs and speed completion.

Assuming there is oil in Antarctica, opinion differs widely on when and whether it will be exploited. Some contend that production in Antarctic conditions will involve a net energy loss—that is, more energy will have to go into the operation than is taken out. Some believe that the technological problems will remain insuperable or that the costs will be prohibitive, at least until such time as other petroleum sources are exhausted. By that time, oil and gas would no longer be used as fuels, but might still be essential for the chemical industry. Even skeptics believe that exploratory drilling will begin soon, although production wells might not follow for decades.

Others point out that as the oil prices have risen, so have the estimated costs of exploiting alternative energy sources. Calculations made only a few years ago are already wildly out of date. As things are going, if one or more large oil deposits can be found in the Antarctic, exploitation before the end of the century is quite probable, especially if the cost/benefit analysis includes political considerations.

TOURISM

Some anticipated that Antarctica would become "a playground for rich tourists."[74] A group of Australians sought to raise money to build an Antarctic ski resort.[75] Others saw Antarctica as an unequaled site for sanatoriums where people with pulmonary diseases would recover in the purest, germ-free air.[76] Not long ago, it was rumored that Argentina would build a hotel on the peninsula. Although these plans did not come to fruition, Antarctic tourism is a reality. The extremely high costs have kept the industry of modest size, which is just as well because tourism in Antarctica creates large problems.[77]

The first cruise to Antarctica was conducted in 1958 by the Argentines, who continued the practice regularly until 1976, when fuel costs became a serious deterrent. The ships used could generally accommodate 400 or 800 passengers, and one cruise is believed to have carried 1,250 persons. From time to time over the past decade, cruises have also been conducted by firms in West Germany, Italy, Spain, Chile, the United Kingdom, Australia, and New Zealand. But since 1966, by far the largest number of cruises have been under the auspices of Lindblad Travel, followed closely in later years by Society Expeditions. Both are U.S. firms and appear to be alone in going beyond the peninsula and into the Ross Sea. In a fairly typical season, 1980–81, the *Lindblad Explorer* with 92 passengers made three departures from Ushuaia, the southernmost port in Argentina. Two cruises of three weeks each visited the Falkland Islands and points along the west coast of the Antarctic Peninsula to about 65°S. Stops were made at Soviet, Chilean, Polish, Argentine, and U.S. stations (one each). The third, a so-called Antarctic Circumnavigation Cruise of five weeks, sailed down the peninsula to the Ross Sea and included visits to stations and historic sites in the area of McMurdo Sound, where Scott and Shackleton had their bases. The ship then headed northwest to New Zealand, where passengers disembarked at Lyttelton.

A somewhat similar schedule is followed by Society Expeditions, based in Seattle. In 1980–81, its *World Discoverer*, with accommodations for 120 passengers, made four cruises, sailing from Punta Arenas in southern Chile or, in one instance, from Rio de Janeiro. One of the four cruises went into the Ross Sea and on to New Zealand. On one of the three peninsula cruises, passengers were exclusively associates of the Smithsonian Institution. The costs of these cruises vary greatly with accommodations, from a low of about four thousand dollars for a three-week cruise to a high of fifteen thousand dollars for a five-week cruise, with Lindblad generally the higher. These figures are exclusive of air fares to and/or from Rio, Buenos Aires, Santiago, and Auckland. One of the better things that the tourist gets for his money is excellent briefings by competent, on-board scientists, including such luminaries as Sir Peter Scott (son of Robert) and Roger Tory Peterson (Lindblad) and George Llano (Society Expeditions), formerly biology program director of the NSF's Division of Polar Programs. As many as a dozen landings may be made on each cruise, and the techniques developed for getting people in dubious physical condition from ship to shore and back are said to be remarkable.

The first tourist flight over Antarctica was conducted by the Chilean National Airlines in December 1956. Early the following season, a chartered Pan Am Boeing Stratocruiser flew from Christchurch, landing at McMurdo with 160 passengers, mostly journalists and U.S. Navy personnel. But the United States turned down all requests for commercial flights to land at Williams Field, McMurdo, for both technical facilities and accommodations were inadequate. Except for occasional flights by small planes, there were no tourist day trips until 1977, when both Qantas and Air New Zealand began regular flights, using mostly 747s and DC10s, both of which are too large to make an emergency landing at McMurdo. In each of the next two seasons Qantas conducted a dozen flights and Air New Zealand, four. The flights take ten or eleven hours, of which perhaps ninety minutes are spent over the continent. At least one 747 Qantas flight in early 1978 retraced the steps of Douglas Mawson on his harrowing trek in 1912 on which both of his companions perished (see Chapter I). On board as occasional commentator was an eighty-three-year-old survivor of that expedition.[78]

The crash of an Air New Zealand DC10 on Mt. Erebus in late November 1979, killing all 257 people aboard, dramatized in a particularly terrible way what most worries those with responsibilities in Antarctica. For the tourists in their light summer garb, it was probably a mercy that all were killed, apparently instantly. The plane carried no cold-weather survival gear.[79] For pilots and other support personnel working in Antarctica, the thought of scores or hundreds of survivors on the slopes of Mt. Erebus is terrifying. The rescue attempt would have cost many lives. (For two days after the crash, there were snowstorms with gale-force winds.) Scientific work everywhere on the continent would, for all practical purposes, have come to a halt. As it was, twenty hours of C-130 flying time and uncounted hours of helicopter time were diverted from the tightly scheduled scientific program. With VIPs already gathered in Christchurch, the commemorative flight to the South Pole, marking the fiftieth anniversary of Byrd's achievement, had to be canceled. But four days later, a Qantas 747 with more than 300 passengers departed from Sydney as scheduled for a daylong flight over Antarctica.[80]

Tourist flights over Antarctica depend on McMurdo Station for weather reports, but whether or not planes fly, on what route, and at what altitude are entirely at the discretion of their captains.[81] The New Zealand plane, whose captain and co-pilot had never flown in Antarctica, struck 12,400-foot Mt. Erebus at less than 1,500 feet. The flight recorder and cockpit tape were both recovered; after investigation, the crash was officially ascribed to pilot error in bad visibility, but apparently, Air New Zealand planes routinely flew in the vicinity of Ross Island at 1,000 to 4,000 feet.[82] Nevertheless, the families of the seventeen crew members are attempting to sue the United States Navy for one million dollars each on the grounds that radar operators were negligent in failing to warn the pilot that he was headed into the mountain. This bit of gall overlooks the facts that the plane crashed in territory claimed by New Zealand, that the overflights were not approved by the Antarctic Treaty powers, and that the United States Navy never assumed any responsibility for the safety of the tourist planes.

In the verbiage of an intergovernmental statement prior to the crash, "The present level of tourist overflight activity exceeds existing capabilities for air traffic control, communications and search and rescue in the Antarctic."[83] It is also unfair to those who work in Antarctica and to those who support their labors.

Ships are not immune from accident either. The *Lindblad Explorer* has twice run aground, with considerable damage to the ship but no injury or loss of life. Unlike the flying visitors, waterborne tourists go ashore and, at least to some extent, disrupt the work of scientific stations. The United States has asked tour operators to schedule visits to Palmer and McMurdo stations on weekends, but stations on the peninsula are too close together to permit such courtesy to all nations. Palmer Station has had as many as 90 tourists at one time, and Argentina's Esperanza base has accepted up to 900.

A relatively few sites bear a disproportionate burden of tourists. The area of richest biota—the peninsula—is of prime interest to tourists and also the most accessible. The historic sites on Ross Island are also vulnerable, although the number of tourists there is far less. A further cause for concern is that tourists may introduce nonindigenous species or diseases that might have serious consequences for Antarctic fauna. Seamen are incorrigible dumpers overboard, and even Jacques Cousteau's *Calypso* and the U.S. research ship *Hero* have been seen dumping garbage over the side or pumping bilges in Arthur Harbor, the site of Palmer Station.[84] Inevitably, tourism causes some marine pollution. If the numbers of shipborne tourists remain as low as they are now (under 1,000), and if the tourists continue to be well briefed in protecting the environment, the problems are manageable. But it is widely believed that tourism will grow, if slowly.

There has been one major mountaineering expedition, in the 1966–67 season. With authorization of the National Science Foundation and support from the American Alpine Club, the expedition climbed in the Sentinel Range at the head of the Ronne Ice Shelf.[85] Not all tourists arrive in organized parties or with official sanction. There have been private mountaineering expeditions, solo airplane flights, and sailboats in Antarctic waters.[86] All the challenging mountains in Antarctica have now been climbed, and the last private mountaineering expedition was in 1976.[87] Perhaps fortunately, Antarctic snow is not ideal for skiing. The most ambitious nongovernmental expedition in many years is the British party that crossed the Antarctic continent in 1980–81 on its way around the world on a polar axis. The Transglobe Expedition, consisting of three men and a woman, landed at Sanae in Antarctica on January 4, 1980, and airlifted two hundred tons of stores to its winter camp two hundred miles into the mountains. Despite airdropped supplies at four-hundred-mile intervals, the three men had a harrowing journey to McMurdo by way of the pole. (After serving as radio operator and aircraft dispatcher, the woman flew across.) Except for a hot meal and a shower at Amundsen-Scott Station, the party received no outside assistance, but the question arises what would have been expected of others if the expedition had gotten into real trouble.[88]

U.S. policy on tourism in Antarctica was formulated in 1967 and has not been altered significantly since:

> The United States does not control access to Antarctica by either U.S. citizens or foreign nationals. However, the United States does reserve the right to judge whether or not tourists can be admitted to any of its Antarctic stations, and under what conditions.

The United States expects tourist expeditions to be self-sufficient. . . .

Except in emergency United States Government resources will not be used for support of tourist enterprises.[89]

These ground rules—essentially similar to those of other concerned nations—have made it possible to refuse, for example, the request of ABC Sports to broadcast live by satellite a mountain-climbing feat in Antarctica. The application of an automobile battery manufacturer to tape a television commercial was similarly turned down.

Some scientists believe that tourism in Antarctica should be banned as hazardous, distracting to them, and burdensome to the environment.[90] Others believe that those who have seen the beauties and wonders of the Antarctic become ambassadors of goodwill and contribute to the small body of informed support for scientific research in Antarctica. For the decision-makers in those countries that have assumed responsibility for Antarctica, the alternatives are neither so simple nor so stark. As the following chapters will show more clearly, claims of sovereignty and treaty obligations affect the issue of tourism as so many others. There is a strong and proper disinclination on the part of concerned governments to give the impression that anyone is being excluded from Antarctica. Indeed, the Antarctic Treaty ensures the openness of the continent but provides no means to enforce rules of behavior that private individuals or groups may choose to ignore.

Ironically, the rising cost of energy may afford Antarctica its best defense (from tourism) or its greatest vulnerability (to oil companies). For the present, the frequent assertion—found even in official documents—that tourism in Antarctica is increasing appears to be unsupported by evidence. If the industry should ever reach the proportions once cheerfully anticipated by some, it might be necessary to impose new restraints to reduce the burden on the Antarctic environment and on the scientists who work in it, thereby raising a whole new set of political problems. Meanwhile, if tourist overflights are to continue, Australia and New Zealand must impose far higher standards on their own national airlines.

ICEBERGS AS A WATER RESOURCE

For four days in October 1977, 110 scientists and engineers from eighteen countries met in Ames, Iowa, to discuss the feasibility of

towing tabular icebergs from Antarctica to arid areas of the world
and converting them to desperately needed water. It was not a
new idea, and it was not the first international conference on the
subject.[91] What made the meeting especially noteworthy was that
(1) the principal sponsor was a Saudi prince presumed to have
access to millions of dollars for research and development; (2) the
NSF provided part of the funds for the meeting, thereby giving the
topic a measure of credibility;[92] and (3) attending the conference
were such eminent administrators of science as Thomas Malone,
Guy Stever, and Roger Revelle,[93] whose presence endowed the
ideas discussed with a new respectability. In short, the notion that
icebergs might be a source of drinking water and irrigation for
fields seven thousand miles away was no longer preposterous and
unworthy of examination. The proceedings of the First International Conference on Icebergs ran to 760 pages and contained about
seventy articles in which the skeptics were at least as well represented as the enthusiasts.[94]

The Saudi prince was Mohammed al-Faisal, who had recently
formed Iceberg Transport International (ITI), retaining France's
leading polar explorer, Paul-Emile Victor, as consultant.[95] Faisal
promised to start delivering icebergs to the Northern Hemisphere
by 1980 at half the cost of desalinization (on which Saudi Arabia
has already spent fifteen billion dollars).[96] This schedule slipped
considerably in the face of so basic a problem as how to keep a
chunk of ice perhaps a mile long by fifteen hundred feet wide and a
thousand feet deep from melting as it crosses the equator at one
mile per hour.

The idea of using the flat-topped icebergs that break away from
Antarctic ice shelves was first suggested only for the Southern
Hemisphere—the arid areas of western Australia or northern Chile
or Namibia (South West Africa). This was the concept first elaborated in 1973 by Wilford F. Weeks of the U.S. Army Cold Regions
Research Engineering Laboratory and W. J. Campbell of the U.S.
Geological Survey's Ice Dynamics Project.[97] The concept was
relatively simple. Antarctic icebergs are found naturally as far
north as 45° south latitude (occasionally even 30°S), and at the end
of the last century, small icebergs were towed up the coast of Chile,
even as far as Peru.[98] To pull larger ones on a systematic basis
seemed feasible. But almost immediately there were those (notably
Hult and Ostrander) who declared it was possible to transport

Antarctic icebergs to southern California and Arabia, although it seemed obvious, in Weeks's words, that if you tried to haul an unprotected iceberg to the north temperate zone, "you would end up with nothing but a towline."[99] In order to cross the equator, icebergs will have to be sheathed above, below, and at the waterline to prevent excessive melting and erosion in passage. The ITI plan, drawn up in 1977, recognized this but was inadequate. For the present, the idea seems impractical or uneconomic or both.

Some questions, however, have received tentative answers. How will suitable icebergs be located? By satellite imagery. How can one minimize the danger of the iceberg's breaking apart along some flaw such as a closed crevasse? By inspecting the iceberg with echo sounders mounted on helicopters. What method of propulsion will be used? After eliminating all manner of exotic alternatives, fleets of tugboats towing the bergs seem most probable.

More attention has been given to transporting icebergs than to processing them after delivery. If the berg survives the heat of the equator, the danger of fracturing, the power of crosswinds on an expanse of perhaps 1.5 million square feet of ice, and other perils of the high seas, the next problem is that the iceberg, drawing hundreds of feet of water, goes aground far from where it is needed. If the destination is Saudi Arabia, the iceberg hits bottom before it can enter the Red Sea. At enormous expense, the berg will have to be cut up and hauled in pieces from the Gulf of Aden to a mooring off Jeddah. It must then be melted in a way that will ensure a large, constant, and unpolluted flow of water to shore. One plan is to use parabolic reflectors to speed melting in shallow basins, from which the water would be pumped ashore.[100] Another idea is to use a process similar to ocean thermal energy conversion (OTEC), which exploits the difference in temperature between deep water and surface water to capture usable energy. ITI has entered a patent application for a system by which it hopes the temperature gradient between the iceberg and the tropical seawater will produce energy not only to help melt the ice but also to propel it.[101] Another possible use for this energy will be to pump the water to where it is most needed—a potentially high cost in some instances. (For example, Santiago, Chile, in an area of water shortage, is eighteen hundred feet above sea level.) An Antarctic iceberg melting off a tropical desert coast "should yield thousands of megawatt-years of energy" through such a process.[102]

Many questions remain. Who owns the icebergs? Are they free
for the taking? What impact may they have on weather? (They are
likely to cause fog, for example, but may have a moderating effect
on hurricanes.) What are the implications of taking water *from* a
desert *to* a desert?[103] What will be the effect of melting ice on the
marine ecology where a beached berg radically alters water temperature and salinity?[104]

Answers to these and to fundamental technological questions
are likely to be a long time in coming. ITI failed to attract reputable
scientists, the original plan was found to be faulty, and Prince
Faisal cut off ITI's line of credit. This deprivation is not necessarily
permanent, but until ITI is refunded, there is no institution with
the resources and motivation to conduct applied research. In April
1980, ITI did underwrite a conference in Cambridge, England,
where the focus was almost entirely on the physical characteristics
of icebergs, including the way they break and roll over.[105] The next
step is said to be an experiment in which an iceberg of modest size
is towed to western Australia with a minimum of surface shielding.

The bright prospect for cheap and unlimited water from Antarctic icebergs is dead for the foreseeable future, but the concept of
iceberg utilization is not. A world in which water will become an
increasingly critical resource cannot forever ignore the estimated
five thousand icebergs calved from Antarctic glaciers and ice
shelves every year—each containing about a billion tons of fresh
water.[106] The idea of capturing this water is worth pursuing, but
with more realism and careful study than before. If Saudi Arabia
were in the Southern Hemisphere, more substantial progress
might now be under way.

DISPOSAL OF RADIOACTIVE WASTES

Although the treaty that came into force in 1961 prohibits the
disposal of nuclear wastes in Antarctica, and although the treaty
powers reaffirmed this principle in 1975, the idea will not quite die.
The obvious reason is that year by year the wastes mount, the
technology for disposal remains questionable, and the issue becomes increasingly politicized. Disposal sites that are suitable both
geologically and geographically are hard to find—in some cases,
impossible, as, for instance, in Japan, a small country entirely in an
earthquake zone. If each country using nuclear fuel must solve the

problems individually, the costs will be extremely high and an inadequacy by one may endanger all. The National Academy of Sciences has said that "the inviolate storage/disposal of such materials poses the most serious environmental problem that is currently facing mankind."[107]

It has been generally assumed that, since the Antarctic ice cap moves constantly outward toward the sea, high-level radioactive wastes buried in the ice would by no means be isolated for the required 250,000 years. Moreover, if, as has been proposed, canisters of nuclear waste are simply allowed to sink through the ice, melting their own way down, they would ultimately reach hard rock, where the heat would cause melting, which in turn might enhance the danger of a surge. That is, nuclear wastes would aggravate a hazard already believed to exist—namely, that the ice cap may periodically slide into the sea because the interface between ice and rock is liquid, heated by the Earth's interior or friction or both.

There are those who believe otherwise.[108] They contend that computer model studies show the rate of ice flow from the heart of East Antarctica to be so slow that a buried object would not reach the sea for 500,000 years. They argue that the theory of periodic surges is unproven and that if the ice-rock interface is *not* substantially below zero, the canisters could be tethered in such a way that they would sink to a predetermined depth, well above the rock surface. Most geologists and glaciologists are skeptical.

A safer alternative would be to bury radioactive material in tunnels dug into Antarctic mountains. The cost of construction would, of course, be very high; even the feasibility studies would be extremely expensive. But if the costs were shared on a pro rata basis by all nations now seeking means of nuclear waste disposal, they might be manageable. Maintenance would be negligible and the danger of sabotage would be minimal, although there would, of course, be hazards involved in shipping the material such long distances into a hostile environment.

For the present, these solutions are academic. A change in the Antarctic Treaty to permit nuclear waste disposal would be strongly fought by many groups. But as time goes by, it is possible that waste burial in the frozen continent will seem the least unattractive alternative.

GEOTHERMAL AND WIND ENERGY

There are more than a dozen active volcanoes in Antarctica, and theoretically, they could be tapped as an energy source to meet local needs. The proposition might seem particularly attractive since the largest U.S. station and the principal New Zealand base are both on Ross Island, which consists of four coalesced volcanoes —Mt. Terra Nova, Mt. Terror, Mt. Bird, and Mt. Erebus.[109] In fact, the idea has not seemed practical enough even to conduct a feasibility study, presumably because it would be an enormous engineering feat rarely tried anywhere and because geothermal energy may create serious environmental problems.

Since Antarctica has some of the strongest, most constant winds in the world, they have been mentioned as a source of power. Whether or not he was the first to suggest it, Frank Debenham long ago proposed that Antarctic winds be harnessed not only for electricity for lighting and heating but also for conversion to hydrogen as a fuel for transportation.[110] This forward-looking concept was advanced when oil was cheap and research on the technology to capture wind energy was nil. In the intervening years we have learned how difficult it is to design a wind turbine that is reasonably efficient over a range of wind speeds. Nevertheless, in 1981 the National Science Foundation made a grant to the University of Arizona to study the feasibility of using wind power to generate "a significant part" of the electricity needed at McMurdo Station. The study is designed to answer such questions as whether a suitable wind turbine is commercially available, what the best site would be, and whether wind power would be cost effective.[111]

TRANSPORTATION AND COMMUNICATION

During the early decades of air travel and long-distance radio communication, Antarctica seemed a natural site for a major airfield and one or more radio relay stations to serve the Southern Hemisphere. A whole generation of Antarctic enthusiasts seems to have believed the continent would play an important role in international transportation. As late as the end of 1959, Admiral George Dufek, the commander of Operation Deep Freeze, just then retired, was excited by the prospect of heading a civilian consortium to build a modern, commercial airfield at Marble Point or Cape Bernacchi, forty miles across McMurdo Sound from the principal U.S. station.[112] Further study showed, of course, that there simply was not enough intercontinental air traffic in the Southern Hemisphere.[113] Within another decade, planes could fly nonstop between Australia and South Africa.

Technology also overtook the notion that Antarctica would play a major role in radio transmission. Before the need for ground relay stations became urgent, communications satellites were serving the purpose more effectively.

COLD STORAGE

Long-term storage of meat and grains in the natural deep freeze of Antarctica is an idea almost as old as this century. The continent seemed an ideal place to store food against a rainy day, without costs of maintenance or electricity. But on examination, the economics have never proved attractive. Possibly, if the perspective had been global instead of national, the analysis might have been different, but in a world which cannot even implement the decision to create an adequate grain reserve, the possibility of using Antarctica for storage is remote. The questionable notion survives that food shortages are local and that improved transportation has removed the danger of starvation.[114] It cannot be gainsaid, however, that the Antarctic is very far away both from the principal sources of any surplus and from the likeliest points of urgent need; that the technology for freezing has improved; and that the costs of carving storage lockers out of the ice would be heavy. While still mentioned, food storage in Antarctica has never been a going proposition.

Some of the hoped-for resources of Antarctica are unlikely ever to materialize; others lie in an uncertain future. But even though the harvest of krill is insignificant as yet and the existence of oil is only hypothesized, anticipation of these resources makes them international political issues now. If these resources prove substantial, who will benefit? Under what arrangements will they be exploited? Will access be open to all nations? Is there a basis for adjudging Antarctica "the common heritage of mankind"? Before addressing these questions, it is first necessary to look in some detail at (1) the claims to sovereignty that affect every Antarctic issue, and (2) the negotiation and evolution of the Antarctic Treaty, which is central to any resolution of the resources issue.

CHAPTER

IV

Territorial Claims

The law is whatever is boldly asserted and plausibly maintained.

—*Aaron Burr*

By letters patent of July 21, 1908, Great Britain made the first claim to territorial sovereignty in Antarctica. The governor of the Falkland Islands was directed to administer, on behalf of the Crown, undefined lands lying to the south. The lands were not those made vivid to Englishmen by Ross and Scott and Shackleton. As finally delimited in 1917, the territory claimed as the Falkland Island Dependencies consisted of the South Orkney, South Sandwich, and South Shetland islands; South Georgia; and the Antarctic Peninsula.[1] A principal objective was to gain control of some of the best whaling grounds in the Southern Ocean. The motive was not entirely selfish: Britain was rightly concerned with the overexploitation of whales and the destruction of a highly profitable industry.[2] But in closing the commons, Britain began a process that had troublesome consequences.

There were no official protests. In 1923, by Order-in-Council, Britain formally claimed the Ross Ice Shelf and its surrounding coasts as a "British settlement" and placed it under the administration of the governor-general of New Zealand. Just ten years later, Britain carved out a third and largest slice of the continent, placing

TERRITORIAL CLAIMS

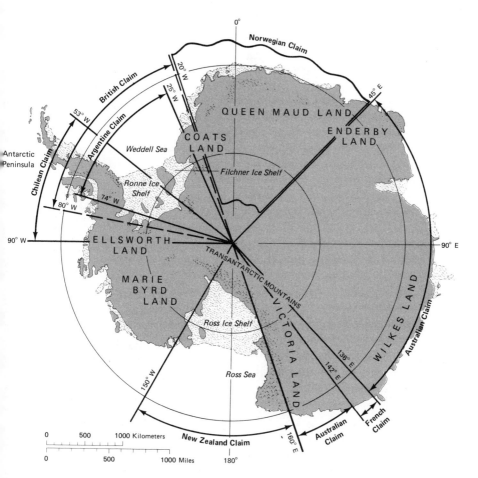

it under the authority of Australia. Together, the three territorial claims, each extending to the geographic pole, embrace more than two-thirds of Antarctica.

In anticipation of the claim in Australia's behalf, France, in 1924, formally annexed Adélie Land, although no Frenchman had ever set foot on it.[3] It consists of a relatively small wedge sandwiched between slices of the Australian Antarctic Territory. Australia was unhappy but raised no sustained objection. The French claim included the islands of St. Paul, New Amsterdam, Kerguélen (previously annexed), and Crozet. Adélie Land was not extended to the pole until a presidential decree of 1938, when agreement was reached with Australia on the precise boundaries between their territories.

Norway had two reasons for staking a claim in addition to its primacy as explorer of Queen Maud Land. As a preeminent whaling nation, Norway was growing weary of being pushed out of Antarctic coastal waters by the territorial claims of other nations. Even as it annexed the remaining sector between the Australian and British claims, Norway promised not to exclude any other nation from its territorial waters.[4] But a more immediate motive was the fact that in January 1939, with tensions high in Europe, a German expedition was pushing through the pack ice to Queen Maud Land. A preemptive declaration of sovereignty by Norway was therefore welcomed by the Allies. Norway was alone in claiming only the "mainland coast," and to this day the southern boundary of Norway's claim is undefined. Because the practice of making pieshaped claims is disadvantageous to Norway in the Arctic, where it was originally applied, Norway has taken care to avoid it in the Antarctic.

The war, when it came, awakened an interest in Antarctica on the part of Chile and Argentina. Despite later protestations to the contrary, neither country had been much involved in the Antarctic during the first four decades of the century. Argentina had continued to man the weather station bequeathed it in 1904, and by executive decree in that same year, it took possession of the South Orkney Islands, where the station was situated. Chileans established a whaling station on Deception Island in 1906. Otherwise Argentina and Chile showed no disposition toward exploration, claimstaking, or research in Antarctica until World War II, when other nations with Antarctic interests were otherwise engaged and the continent appeared to have some strategic importance. Argentina sent expeditions to the peninsula and the South Shetlands in 1942 and 1943. Chile, in November 1940, delimited a broad sector that it claimed had been national territory all along. Argentina took the same position and much of the same territory. Hence, Chile and Argentina became, depending on one's viewpoint, either the first claimants or the last. In any event, their claims overlapped each other as well as the 1908 claim of Great Britain.

There are now fourteen nations that have consultative status with respect to the Antarctic Treaty—that is, they are members of the inner circle making decisions affecting Antarctica. They are evenly divided between those that claim parts of the continent as sovereign territory—Britain, Australia, New Zealand, France, Norway, Chile, and Argentina—and those that make no claims and recognize none. These are Belgium, the Federal Republic of Germany, Japan, Poland, South Africa, the Soviet Union, and the United States.[5] The claimant states recognize one another's sovereignty on the continent except where claims overlap in the peninsula quadrant. About 17 percent of the continent remains unclaimed.

The hope that the claims issue would simply go away has not been fulfilled anywhere in Antarctica. Argentina and Chile, where a succession of harried governments have found Antarctica a popular, unifying issue, defend their claims with an almost religious zeal. Their people have been led to believe that the national patrimony is at stake and that untold riches lie at hand in their sovereign territories to the south.

THE LEGAL BASES OF CLAIMS[6]

Historic Right. In the fifteenth century, the kingdom of Portugal and the kings of Castille and Aragon were in growing dispute over the territories discovered by their navigators. Acting as arbiter, Pope Alexander VI issued four Bulls in 1493, in effect awarding Africa to Portugal and the New World to Spain. By the Treaty of Tordesillas the following year, the two powers agreed to move the pope's proposed longitudinal boundary 270 leagues farther west (as measured from the Cape Verde Islands). The treaty stated that the line should be drawn "from the Arctic to the Antarctic Poles."[7] The boundary falls between 46° and 49° west longitude.[8]

Since maps of that day showed *Terra Australis* as a huge continent almost touching South America, it was perhaps natural to infer that whatever lay to the south belonged to Spain or its heirs—certainly not to Britain (in the Latin view), for by the Treaty of Madrid of 1670 Spain and England agreed not to poach on each other's preserves in the New World.[9] The extent of Spain's preserve and whether it can be said to encompass an unknown, unseen continent are legitimate questions.

Chile departs from Argentina to assert a superior claim when it declares itself the only legitimate Spanish heir to those territories "stretching from the southern shore of the Strait of Magellan as far as the South Pole."[10] By exclusive concessions, it is maintained, these territories were granted by Charles V to one Pedro Sanchez de Hoz and in due course to the captaincy general of Chile. A royal decree of 1558 is cited in which the governor of Chile is requested to "send a report on all the territories situated on the other side of the Strait and to take possession of them."[11]

Finally, when Chile and Argentina began their struggle for independence from Spain in 1810, both countries buttressed their claim to the unknown lands to the south by invoking the doctrine of *uti possidetis juris* (retain possession by right), applying it to mean that no territory in the New World could be considered *res nullius* (belonging to no one). Today, Chile, especially, insists that this principle takes precedence over occupation.[12] Further, Chile asserts that, when Britain was demonstrating a proprietary interest in the South Shetlands in the early nineteenth century, Bernardo O'Higgins, hero of Chilean independence, sent a reminder in 1831 that Chile had exclusive rights to that part of the Antarctic.

Anglo-Saxon writers, in particular, are wont to ridicule all of this and even to consider the argument beneath rebuttal. Certainly, it is at best questionable whether Spain could bequeath to its former colonies lands that it did not possess, had never seen, and could not place on a map. Referring specifically to these arguments for centuries-old rights, a writer in *The Yale Law Journal* held that such theories of international law "are arcane and cannot be taken seriously."[13] However, they are taken very seriously indeed by Chile and Argentina, and a number of non-Spanish scholars of international law with roots in the Roman tradition support their view.[14] But neither Chile nor Argentina rests its case on these arguments alone.

Contiguity/Proximity. Of the two terms, contiguity has more status in international law. It was used principally in the nineteenth century as a basis for claiming sovereignty over offshore islands. But whether contiguity theory can support Antarctic claims is dubious. When hundreds or thousands of miles of ocean separate land masses, it stretches common sense to assert that they are contiguous. Therefore, proximity or propinquity has increasingly been used as an argument for asserting a superior claim. By a small margin, the argument favors Chile over Argentina, although it is used primarily to discredit the British claim.

Geological Affinity. It has been argued that, since structurally the Antarctic Peninsula and Ellsworth Land are a continuation of the Andes, these regions are natural extensions of Chile and Argentina. If this argument were to be accepted as controlling, then the Chilean and Argentine claims could not be extended to the pole, since geologically the Transantarctic Mountains and the polar plateau bear no relation to the Andes.

The Sector Principle. All the claimant states except Norway apply some version of the sector principle, which was proposed in 1907 by a Canadian senator, Pascal Poirier, as a means of drawing territorial boundaries in the Arctic. The idea was that a meridian line should be drawn to the pole from the eastern and western extremities of each country surrounding the Arctic Ocean. The concept was embraced by Russia and Canada, the countries with the longest base to their triangular sector. Other affected countries either opposed the idea or merely tolerated it.

Applying the sector principle to the Antarctic is more difficult. Large parts of the Antarctic, especially in the Pacific, are opposite no country from which meridians could be drawn. Africa and South America are themselves triangular, with their apex toward the south. Thus, if every country could assert an Antarctic claim merely by drawing lines of meridian to the pole, there might be dozens of claimants—among them Uruguay, Brazil, and Peru, which continue to take this "theory of projections" seriously.[15] And how could Northern Hemisphere countries make claims at the opposite pole on the basis of a sector principle?

Given the shortcomings of the sector principle as applied to Antarctica, adaptations were required. The triangular sectors reaching the pole had their bases measured not by the boundaries of a country but by a stretch of Antarctic coast explored by the claimant country. This was an effort to validate the sector principle by that of continuity or "hinterland" used by the colonial powers in Africa and the thirteen colonies in America to claim inland areas over which effective control had not been established. This helped to rationalize such anachronisms as France's Adélie Land's being opposite Tasmania or Australia's claim's being far larger than it would be if meridian lines were dropped from Brisbane and Perth. Although the Ross Dependency is opposite New Zealand, its boundaries were not drawn in strict conformity to the sector principle, and Britain's claim, of course, bears only remote relation to its Falkland Islands possession.

Conflicting positions on the acceptability of the sector principle are rampant among scholars of international law. For example, a writer in the *American Journal of International Law* could say in 1939 that "the sector principle as applied at least to Antarctica is now a part of the accepted international legal order."[16] Two decades later, Philip Jessup, who would later serve on the International Court of Justice, testified before Congress that "the so-called sector theory . . . has never become established in international law."[17] As for Chile and Argentina, they support the sector theory as it has evolved in Antarctica, but in conjunction with strong emphasis on proximity. "When two countries occupy the same sector, the occupation of the adjacent country should prevail over that of the other and non-adjacent country."[18]

Symbolic Acts. These are methods of asserting sovereignty without the bother of settlement or of reinforcing claims made by other means. Raising flags, burying claim documents, and setting up brass plaques are symbolic acts widely practiced by Antarctic explorers. A common practice among claimant (and some nonclaimant) nations is to establish a post office at one or more Antarctic stations and to issue special stamps. Expedition leaders or members of their staffs may be given civil appointments, whether or not real duties are involved. To these symbolic acts Chile and Argentina have added some of greater substance. The presidents of both countries have visited Antarctica to reaffirm their conflicting sovereignties. The first to do so was Chilean President Gabriel Gonzaliz Videla in 1948. When President Arturo Frondizi of Argentina visited Deception Island in 1961, there were riots in Santiago.[19] President Augusto Pinochet Ugarte of Chile toured Antarctica as recently as January 1977, to the dismay of Argentiniens.[20] The foreign ministers of both countries have traveled to Antarctica often.

In the middle 1950s, Argentina and Chile altered government administration so as to incorporate their Antarctic territories into their southernmost provinces, placing them under the authority of provincial governors. Although administration is an important factor in establishing sovereignty, these were in fact symbolic acts because real control remained where it had been—at the center. In the case of Argentina, real control lay with the Argentine Antarctic Institute within the Ministry of the Army.

An event that Argentina hopes will prove much more than a symbolic act was the birth of a boy in Antarctica in January 1978.[21] Since Argentine military personnel are now allowed to bring their families with them to Antarctica, the event has frequently been repeated, giving some substance to the claim that Antarctica is now truly settled and effectively occupied by Argentina.[22]

Pan-American Primacy.   In asserting the superiority of their claims over that of Britain, Chile and Argentina have used an argument long employed in the dispute over the Falkland Islands —namely, that the peninsula quadrant of Antarctica is geographically and geologically American territory. At various times, the Monroe Doctrine has been invoked, without much support from the United States. But in 1941, following the failure of talks on their own territorial dispute in Antarctica, Chile and Argentina found it possible to agree that "a South American Antarctic exists and the only countries with exclusive rights of sovereignty over it are Chile and Argentina."[23] After the war, the two countries would invoke the Inter-American Treaty of Reciprocal Assistance (Rio, 1947), which defined the area covered by the pact as extending from pole to pole between 24° and 90° W.

Although this sector amply covered the disputed Antarctic territory, the treaty carried a U.S. reservation designed especially to avoid taking sides on Antarctic (and Falkland Islands) claims.[24] The following year at Bogotá, the Organization of American States came into being, reinforcing the unilateral Monroe Doctrine and strengthening the basis of claims to an "American" Antarctic.

Effective Occupation.   This is the principal method of perfecting a territorial claim and the only one applicable to Antarctica that is universally recognized in international law. Unfortunately, there is no agreement as to what it means. Legal scholars differ as to how strictly standards should apply in a region without permanent population and with a climate that precludes normal habitation over most of its extent. When the interior of the continent was first being explored at the start of this century, it was generally assumed that acquisition of territory was impossible precisely because occupation was impossible.

Gradually in this century some legal scholars have been inclined to make exceptions for uninhabitable areas, and international tribunals have established precedents affording more flexible interpretation of effective occupation. In ruling on the Legal Status of Eastern Greenland in 1933, the Permanent Court of International Justice wrote that "a claim to sovereignty must be based on two elements: the intention and will to act as a sovereign, and some actual continued display of such authority."[25] Furthermore, the conditions for fulfilling these requirements were not unduly rigorous. In the same decision, the justices wrote:

> It is impossible to read the records of the decisions in cases of territorial sovereignty without observing that in many cases the tribunal has been satisfied with very little in the way of the actual exercise of sovereign rights, provided that the other State could not make out a superior claim. This is particularly true in the case of claims to sovereignty over areas in thinly populated or unsettled countries.[26]

What country has a superior claim in the American quadrant is, of course, a matter of long dispute, the bitterness of which is only superficially disguised at present. For Chile, even a gesture toward effective occupation was late in coming. The first permanent Chilean base was not established until 1947, although others followed quickly. On the other hand, Argentina can claim continuous occupancy and uninterrupted activity at the weather station on Laurie Island in the South Orkneys since 1904.[27] At Hope Bay on the tip of the peninsula, Argentina maintains the nearest thing to a normal human settlement to be found anywhere in Antarctica; its purpose is clearly more political than scientific.[28]

CONFLICT WITH BRITAIN

With so many arguments in support of the claims of Chile and Argentina, what case does Britain have? First, discovery and exploration. South Georgia was probably discovered by English merchant Anthony de la Roche. Captain Cook was the first to land there and to discover the South Sandwich Islands, both of which he named and claimed for the English Crown. William Smith was the first to sight the South Shetland Islands—or at least the first to report it.[29] All of these are, of course, in the disputed sector. Britishers discovered and named more of the offshore islands than any other nationality, with the possible exception of the Americans. Whoever was first to see the continent, it was not a Spaniard nor an heir of Spain. And while Englishmen (as well as Americans and Scandinavians) explored the peninsula, South Americans showed little interest or concern for nearly four decades.

Discovery does not itself grant title. Hugo Grotius's dictum, although qualified today, still is considered to have bearing on all territorial claims in Antarctica:

> No one is a sovereign of a thing which he himself has never possessed and which no one else has held in his name. . . . To discover a thing is not only to seize it with the eyes but to take real possession thereof. . . . The act of discovery is sufficient to give a clear title of sovereignty only when it is accompanied by actual possession.[30]

As seen in the discussion of effective occupation, above, this rule has been bent but not broken.

In international law, the term "inchoate title" means that for an indeterminate period the discoverer has first rights—an opportunity to perfect its title before another nation can establish a counterclaim. The difficulty is that no one agrees on what length of time an inchoate title is valid. It was first interpreted to mean a few years, but in the Antarctic, it has often been stretched to decades or to more than a century. If any nation could claim inchoate title to the Antarctic Peninsula, it would be Britain, but the interval between discovery and formal claim, occupation, and administration was certainly extended, as it was for all claimants to Antarctic territory.

It is of some importance in international law that Britain holds precedence in declaring its sovereignty over the islands and lands to the south of the Falkland Islands. Further, neither Chile nor Argentina protested or submitted a counterclaim until many years later.[31] Still more important, when whaling began early in this century, Chilean and Argentine whaling companies, among others, made annual payments to the British government for the right to use harbors and shore stations in South Georgia and the South Shetland Islands.[32]

And finally, Britain asserts that settlements on South Georgia and Deception Island, established prior to the declaration of sovereignty in 1908, clearly constitute effective occupation. This was further perfected in 1910, when a resident magistrate, a post office, and administrative offices were operating at Port Foster on Deception Island.

The friction between Britain and Argentina over Antarctica has sometimes led to violence, although what might have been the most serious confrontation was avoided because one party did not show up. Between 1943 and 1945, as the war in Europe was coming to a climax, Britain dispatched one small ship to Antarctica "to deny the use of certain sheltered points to enemy submarines or raiders"[33] and to ensure that Argentina (friendly to Nazi Germany) would not seize control of the south side of the Drake Passage. Earlier, in January 1941, off Queen Maud Land, German raiders captured three Norwegian whaling factory ships and eleven catchers totaling forty thousand tons, plus a precious supply of fuel oil. By the time Britain's Operation Tabarin had established a base on Deception Island, which affords the most secluded harbor in the area, and another on the Antarctic Peninsula itself, the German raiders were using the more northern Kerguélen Islands, from which they went forth to sink or capture several hundred thousand tons of Allied shipping.[34]

The evidence suggests that Operation Tabarin was more concerned with the Argentines, with whom it could cope, than with German raiders, who would have made life very difficult had they shown up. But they did not, and the Argentines had already departed, leaving behind several bronze plaques representing their recently defined claim. Early in 1943, the British ambassador to Buenos Aires ceremoniously returned one of the plaques to the Argentine government.

In 1947–48, with diplomatic notes between London and Buenos

Aires reaching new heights of acrimony, warships were for the first time introduced into the Antarctic. With a naval force of two cruisers and six destroyers escorting troopships, the Argentines entered the harbor at Deception Island and proceeded to build a base across the bay from a long-established British station. By the time a cruiser and a frigate of the Royal Navy arrived, the Argentine warships had departed, leaving a party of ten at the new station. The British did not attempt to remove them, and the station has been manned ever since. Soon thereafter the three competing nations reached a temporary agreement (renewed annually thereafter) not to send warships south of 60° latitude.

It was in this period that Britain made the first of many offers to submit all or part of the territorial disputes in Antarctica to the International Court of Justice. Argentina and Chile declined the proposal, as they did again specifically in 1955, when Britain applied unilaterally to The Hague for arbitration.[35]

Violence continued. In 1952, Argentine soldiers in Hope Bay fired a machine gun over the heads of a British party as it was landing to rebuild one of its own stations that four years earlier had tragically burned with the loss of two lives. Just a year later, British forces on Deception Island tore down Argentine and Chilean huts that had been built only a few hundred yards from the British station. Two Argentines were arrested and deported. By 1955, Argentina had almost as many bases on the peninsula as Britain, and more personnel. Chile was not far behind.[36]

The Falkland Islands, although they lie north of what is regarded as the Antarctic regions and outside the area covered by the Antarctic Treaty, have been associated with the southern continent historically and politically. For the Argentines, the disputes over both areas "are frequently viewed as one and the same."[37] The 1982 war in the south Atlantic will have a continuing impact on the Antarctic and will magnify the problem of conflicting claims there. Since generations of Argentines have been taught that not only the Malvinas, as they call the Falklands, but all the other islands to the south and east, plus the Antarctic Peninsula, are their sacred patrimony, failure to hold the Falklands may serve to redirect Argentine jingoism to Antarctica.[38]

Another reason for the close relationship between the Falklands and Antarctica is the application of the sector principle as a means to strengthen territorial claims to the south. Whether in fact the

Argentine junta believed that the capture of South Georgia and the Falklands would reinforce Argentina's claims cannot be known, but it may have added a further motive for the invasion. Another motive may have been the expectation of finding offshore oil and gas in the islands, although this consideration was probably less important than the American press suggested. Unquestionably, seizure of the Falklands was designed primarily to divert the Argentines' attention from horrendous domestic problems. In this the junta certainly succeeded for a time. But the Argentines erred in underestimating the British response, misreading the reaction of the United States, and assuming that the false issue of colonialism could be made to obscure the more central issue of self-determination. The British erred, during the protracted negotiations with the Argentines, in allowing eighteen hundred islanders to dictate Britain's position. And they erred in underestimating the depth of the Argentine feeling about a patch of ground for which they would gladly fight, though on no account would they wish to live there.[39] So a tragic war was fought where no serious national interest was at stake.

Argentina's overt act of agression and Britain's strong response seemed for the moment to make history irrelevant. But the war, of course, has settled nothing, and sooner or later the antagonists must get back to reality, of which history is a part. Strangely, even British sources disagree on some fairly important particulars.[40] All that can be said with some certainty is, briefly, that the Falkland Islands have at various times been occupied and claimed by the French and Spanish, as well as the English and Argentines; that several attempts to create settlements there in the eighteenth and early nineteenth centuries failed and the islands were abandoned by authority; that the Argentines were able to sustain a settlement there for only five years; that the British did not retake the Falklands by force in 1833–34, because there was at the time no established authority and no resistance except by convicts and murderers who held the islands in thrall; that the British established order and, reluctantly, in 1841, made the archipelago a Crown Colony, which it has remained ever since.

Yet the Argentines believe the islands belong to them by historic right, first occupation, and proximity, of which the last is the strongest argument. Their case for claiming the South Sandwich Islands and South Georgia, where the war began, is far weaker and less insistent. Soon after the British occupation of the Falklands in 1834, the Argentines sought to invoke the Monroe Doctrine, but Secretary of State Daniel Webster, considering friendship with Britain more important, committed the United States not to interfere in the Falklands dispute.[41]

Now the parties must find their way back to the negotiating table. The islands mean infinitely more to the Argentines than to the British, and prolonged occupation will not weaken Argentina's determination to regain them. When Britain's heroic defense of principle begins to lose its luster, the cost of ensuring the defense of the archipelago will seem intolerable. Further, the United States will find an extended British stay in the Falklands unacceptable; the burr under the Pan-American saddle is now a sore that must be healed.

Britain and Argentina must also try to minimize the consequences of the war, particularly for the Antarctic, where both countries have mutual, as well as conflicting, interests. It seems likely that for a time, at least, the two antagonists will assert their claims in Antarctica with heightened vigor and that negotiations on outstanding issues, such as the exploitation of mineral resources in Antarctica, will be in suspension.

Argentina also has sharp conflicts with Chile, although in Antarctica, each acknowledges that the other has some rights (in contrast to Britain), and each firmly believes its claim to be superior. Repeated efforts to delineate a boundary have come to naught. After renewed negotiations failed in early 1948, they issued a joint declaration saying:

> Until such time as the [boundary] line of common neighborliness is covenanted . . . in the antarctic territories of Chile and of the Republic of Argentina, . . . both Governments will act in common accord in the protection and juridical defense of their rights in the South American Antarctic, included between the meridians of 25° and 90°, Longitude West of Greenwich, in which territories it is conceded that Chile and the Argentine Republic have indisputable rights of sovereignty.[42]

Yet before the end of the year they had nearly come to blows; without a common enemy in Britain, they almost surely would have on more than one occasion.

Conflicts over their common boundary at the tip of South

America have flared between Chile and Argentina periodically since 1843. The current phase of the controversy—the Beagle Channel dispute—must be mentioned because it bears on their Antarctic claims and because it affects the capacity of the two countries to act in concert on some Antarctic issues. When a boundaries treaty of 1881 came into dispute, Chile and Argentina entered into a 1902 treaty providing for compulsory arbitration by the British Crown. The initial award of that year designated the eastern reaches of the Beagle Channel as the boundary— Argentina on the north, Chile on the South.

More than half a century later, Argentina argued that the award was not specific with respect to a group of islands—principally, Picton, Nueva, and Lennox—at the eastern extremity of the Beagle Channel. Although the islands are barren and uninhabited except for a handful of fishing families, national pride, the possibility of offshore oil, and Antarctic claims based on the sector principle all became involved. Also at stake, at least in the minds of Argentines, was the historic definition of Chile as a Pacific power and Argentina as an Atlantic power, and the perception that the disputed islands were in the Atlantic.[43] When bilateral negotiation failed, the two countries were legally bound to return to Her Britannic Majesty for a further arbitration decision. After pondering the matter for six years, the Court, on February 18, 1977, decided unanimously that the islands belonged to Chile.[44] Ignoring the compulsory nature of the arbitration, Argentina declared the award "insuperably null and void."[45] After a sharp exchange of notes, Chile and Argentina agreed by the Act of Puerto Montt, February 20, 1978, to resume bilateral negotiation in defined stages. The first stage, which was largely technical, was successfully negotiated, but the second stage, which got to matters of real substance, collapsed after the fifth meeting in mid-August. Through the rest of the year, tensions between the two countries rose to the very verge of war.[46]

At the eleventh hour, the United States persuaded the Holy See to intercede, and Argentina and Chile accepted the pope's mediation. When this failed, the Vatican in late 1980 proposed a solution acceptable to Chile but not, as yet, to Argentina. Although never made public, the proposal is reported to agree that the disputed islands belong to Chile, but qualifies the offshore rights that would normally accrue. It creates what the pope calls "a sea of peace" in which resources would be shared. Although the Argentines allow that this is an improvement on the arbitration decision, the government lacks the political courage to accept it. "My plight," a leading Argentine military figure is quoted as saying, "is that I cannot set aside national honor for the sake of peace."[47]

The implications of this or any other solution of the Beagle Channel dispute in respect to Antarctic claims are by no means clear—to anyone. All that is apparent is that in the minds of the principals, the national patrimony, oil, and Antarctica are all involved. And because the Chilean and Argentine governments have both elevated Antarctica to a domestic political issue of great moment, both have severely limited their options.

Does any country have a perfected claim to sovereignty in Antarctica? Before the IGY began, in 1957, the answer was almost certainly no. Most legal experts are unimpressed by arguments other than those of effective occupation, possession, and administration, which are generally found to be wanting. Writing in an international law journal in 1934, the year following Britain's claim in behalf of Australia, an American scholar was caustic. He ridiculed the sector principle, which "attempts to set up claims in advance of discovery." He wrote that the French and Australian claims involved absurdities hardly less than those of Spain and Portugal negotiating the Treaty of Tordesillas in 1494.[48]

Legal scholars seem extraordinarily responsive to the policies and viewpoints of their own governments. This appears to be as true of Anglo-Saxon experts as of others. It is of course inconceivable that a legal scholar in Chile or Argentina could publicly question the validity of his country's claim. To the contrary, after forty years they remain inexhaustible in marshaling, explicating, and analyzing arguments supporting their country's territorial sovereignty in Antarctica. It was not especially unusual to find in one issue of *Current Antarctic Literature* that, under the heading "Political Geography," eleven of twelve articles were by Argentine writers on Argentine claims (to the Falklands, however, as well as to Antarctica).[49]

Whatever the invalidity of original claims, the situation has been altered by much continuous occupation since the beginning of the IGY. Today, it is regarded as possible that, were an international tribunal asked to rule—absent the Antarctic Treaty—it might award some portions of the continent and immediate islands to some of the claimants. For several reasons, however, the possibility is hypothetical—not least because the nonclaimants would reject the decision and the political problems would merely be exacerbated.

Some countries clearly feel more confident of their claims than others. New Zealanders seem especially uneasy. The Ross Dependency is not part of New Zealand, and the British government has never formally authorized the transfer of the British claim in that area to New Zealand. All that exists is the 1923 Order in Council by which the British Parliament placed the Ross Dependency under New Zealand's governor-general, who represents the English Crown. As recently as 1967, the New Zealand government year-book referred to "the Ross Dependency, the administration of which is exercized by New Zealand, on behalf of the United Kingdom Government."[50] In 1980, the Public Issues Committee of the Auckland District Law Society published a statement lamenting that "New Zealand has done virtually nothing to confirm any rights in the area" and urging that New Zealand "acquire by legal process the British rights to the Dependency."[51]

Also, New Zealand is particularly affected by legal questions arising out of conditions peculiar to Antarctica. These have complicated the claims issue and have spawned a vast literature, largely sterile and academic.[52] The related questions are whether ice is land or water; whether there are legal differences between fixed ice and floating ice, permanent ice and impermanent ice; and whether it is legally significant that much of the "continent" is below sea level (although if the ice were removed, much submerged land would rise out of the sea). Then, too, all ice moves—very slowly in the deep interior of the continent, more rapidly on the margins. Thus, territorial boundaries cannot be drawn on the ice surface, but only as connected points of latitude and longitude. The discussion can appear extremely esoteric until the prospect of drilling for oil or the utilization of icebergs is considered. Nevertheless, as we shall see in later chapters, the legal niceties so amply explored by experts are largely irrelevant. Political decisions made by the treaty powers and to a lesser extent by the Law of the Sea Conference will be controlling.

THE UNITED STATES AND THE CLAIMS ISSUE

Among the nonclaimant nations, the United States is distinctive in (1) having been most active in Antarctica, particularly in that sector that remains unclaimed; (2) having bases for a claim as strong as any nation's; (3) having at various times been under considerable pressure, external as well as internal, to assert a claim; and (4) keeping its options open and under periodic review, while giving the appearance of consistency.

Today, as for decades past, the United States recognizes no claims in Antarctica but reserves its right to make a claim of its own. The issue first arose in 1924, when, in response to an official inquiry by Norway, Secretary of State Charles Evans Hughes wrote: "It is the considered opinion of this department that the discovery of lands unknown to civilization, even when coupled with the formal taking of possession, does not support a valid claim of sovereignty unless the discovery is followed by actual settlement of the discovered country."[53] Hughes's statement, which assumed that "actual settlement would be impossible," was a sharp departure from an earlier position taken in an altogether different context. In 1896, offering the American interpretation of "effective occupation," Secretary of State Richard Olney had said: "The only possession required is such as is reasonable under all the circumstances in view of the extent of the territory claimed, its nature, and uses to which it is adapted and is put. . . ."[54]

Hughes's dictum was as close to a policy as the United States was to have for many years. A study by the Navy in the same year (1924) was largely ignored. It expressed a lively interest in Antarctic sovereignty, "particularly in view of the possibility of the discovery of fuel and other mineral resources."[55] At that time, it must be remembered, the United States had not made an appearance in Antarctica for more than eighty years.

Richard Byrd set about changing the United States from the least active to the most active nation in Antarctica. One thing he neglected to ask before his departure was whether he should claim heretofore undiscovered lands for the United States; Washington had offered no instructions on this point. When Byrd inquired by cable, the Department of State dawdled and finally avoided any direct answer.[56] As noted earlier, Byrd and his lieutenants, acting on their own, did indeed stake claims, notably in what is now Marie Byrd Land.

The expedition established Little America I on the Ross Ice Shelf—territory claimed by New Zealand. There followed an amicable cat-and-mouse game in which Britain and New Zealand

(which was not yet independent) sought to obtain U.S. acknowl-
edgment, however indirect, of New Zealand's sovereignty, while
the United States went to absurd lengths to avoid doing anything
that could be so interpreted. A note from the British ambassador in
Washington offering to "send instructions to the appropriate
authorities in the Falkland and Ross Dependencies to give every
possible assistance to Commander Byrd while he was in their
territories" went unanswered for a year and then was merely
acknowledged.[57] The British even offered nonexistent facilities.
While the Department of State was being evasive, Byrd sent a cable
from his staging area in Dunedin to Secretary Kellogg, saying that
the New Zealand government was withholding its assistance
because it had not been officially notified that the expedition was
"accredited" by the U.S. government. Wellington was then informed through the American consul that the Byrd expedition
was entirely of a scientific nature and that New Zealand's assistance in fulfilling the expedition's objectives would be appreciated.[58] Since Byrd was then in New Zealand, this need not be
interpreted as a request for assistance in Antarctica.[59]

During the second Byrd expedition, the diplomatic exchanges
were a bit less gracious. In behalf of New Zealand, Britain strongly
protested what it considered high-handed disregard for Commonwealth rights. In particular, Britain quarreled with the establishment of a post office at Little America and the issuance of special
stamps. It also criticized the failure to ask permission to operate
radio and aircraft. The Department of State did no more than
acknowledge the communication.

In 1930, while the first Byrd expedition was still in progress,
Senator Millard Tydings of Maryland introduced a resolution
authorizing and directing the President "to lay claim to all areas in
the Antarctic which have been discovered or explored by American
citizens."[60] No action was taken, but it was the first of many efforts
by members of Congress to induce the U.S. government to claim
"our rights" in Antarctica. Since the Australian claim had not then
been asserted, more than half the continent was still up for grabs,
including the vast territory whose coast had been cruised by
Lieutenant Wilkes. Some elements in the United States were
indignant when, in February 1933, what is still known as Wilkes
Land was claimed for Australia by the British Crown, along with
immense territories farther west.

Meanwhile, Senator Tydings's initiative had had one interesting result. A memorandum prepared by the Department of State's geographer, Samuel W. Boggs, discussed the elements of a U.S. Antarctic policy and proposed that the United States either assert a claim or seek an international solution.[61] With a world depression preoccupying political leaders, it is not surprising that neither alternative was pursued. As Boggs voluntarily continued his study of the issues, he was admonished by the Department of State's Legal Adviser in a handwritten note not to say "the U.S. has made no claim of a formal nature . . . say only what we *have done.*"[62]

Although by the late 1930s the United States was still adhering to the Hughes doctrine, the unclaimed sector of Antarctica centering on Marie Byrd Land had been liberally sprinkled with American flags and cairns and brass cylinders containing declarations claiming the territory for the United States. But these claims by American citizens were never formalized. As the war loomed in Europe, it appeared that Washington might indeed be reconsidering. In 1938, President Roosevelt ordered a complete reexamination of U.S. Antarctic policy, and Lincoln Ellsworth, who was leaving on another expedition, was secretly given some quite remarkable instructions.

They reached him in the form of a cable, signed by Secretary Cordell Hull, to the U.S. consul in Capetown, Ellsworth's jumping-off point. With italics added, the communication read in part as follows:

Upon the arrival of Mr. Ellsworth in Capetown you are requested to inform him, in strict confidence, that it seems appropriate for him to assert claims in the name of the United States as an American citizen, to all territory he may explore, photograph, or map which has hitherto been undiscovered and unexplored, *regardless of whether or not it lies within a sector or sphere of influence already claimed by any other country.* It is, of course, preferable that such claims shall relate to territories not already claimed by any other country. Reassertion of American claims to territory visited by American explorers several decades ago would seem to be appropriate if he should desire to explore such areas. You may suggest the possibility of dropping notes or personal proclamations, attached to parachutes, containing assertions of claims, and subsequently making public the text of such claims, together with approximate latitude and longitude of all the points concerned. It should be made clear to Ellsworth that he

should not indicate or imply advance knowledge or approval of the
Government of the United States but that he should leave it for this
Government to adopt its own course of action.[63]

Ellsworth, who was an old hand at claimstaking in the Antarctic,
was even given detailed instructions on how the British do it. But
he was not given a copy of the cable "because of the highly
confidential nature of that instruction and the department's desire
to avoid any possibility of its contents coming to the knowledge of
any person not an American citizen."[64] The consul was ordered to
paraphrase the key paragraph (quoted above) and type it on plain
paper. Ellsworth acted on these instructions with enthusiasm and
claimed a three-hundred-mile swath now known as the American
Highland in the interior of Australia's claim.[65]

Meanwhile, the Department of State study was delivered to the
President in early January 1939.[66] It proposed to modify the
Hughes doctrine and recommended that the United States seriously consider making a claim. But it failed to make a very persuasive
case. What particularly bothered the department was that "effective occupation" was no longer an "impossibility" as Hughes had
assumed. However, the study was unable to resolve the dilemma
that to keep the Hughes doctrine would make it difficult for the
United States to make a valid claim, while to drop it would make
nonrecognition of existing claims more difficult. Nevertheless, a
letter from Hull to Roosevelt, dated February 13, 1939, indicates
that the department was thinking about a claim that would include
not only Marie Byrd Land but also the so-called American Highland in the Australian zone and part or all of the Antarctic
Peninsula.[67]

Aspects of the claims issue have had a comic-opera character—
illustrated by an exchange of notes between the United States and
France in January 1939, as the world stood on the edge of
cataclysm. The United States made clear to its allies that it intended
to overfly Antarctica wherever and whenever it pleased in order to
keep track of the Germans and any other unfriendly outsiders.
French Foreign Minister Georges Bonnet replied with a quite
irrelevant restatement of France's Antarctic claim, concluding:
"Under these circumstances, I take pleasure in thinking that the
reserves formulated by the United States Government do not

concern Adélie Land, over which the rights of the French Government have, for nearly a century, been regularly established and have never given rise to contestation." Although the Department of State took nearly three months to answer, it could not hide its irritation. "So far as my Government is aware," wrote Walton Moore for the Secretary of State, "Admiral Dumont d'Urville did not even land on the coast claimed for France by him, nor has any French citizen visited the area . . . since then. . . . The United States Government cannot admit that sovereignty accrues from mere discovery."[68]

By mid-1939, Roosevelt had pushed through Congress an appropriation of $340,000 with which to create the United States Antarctic Service and to launch the first official Antarctic expedition in a century. This was the third Byrd expedition, and its aim—in the words of Roosevelt to Hull—was "to make an investigation and survey of the natural resources of the land and sea areas of the Antarctic Regions."[69] At the same time, U.S. ambassadors in Latin America were instructed to deliver a "confidential memorandum," which included the statement that part of the expedition's mission was "to determine and make recommendations regarding the practicality of making permanent or semi-permanent establishments in Antarctica."[70] But according to the congressional testimony of a member of the interdepartmental committee responsible for administering the Antarctic Service, the main purpose of the expedition was to strengthen the bases for U.S. claims in the Antarctic.[71] On this expedition, for the first time, the United States established a base in the peninsula area, which would soon be overcrowded with stations.

Roosevelt presented Byrd with pages of formal instructions, including the following under Item 6:

(f) The United States has never recognized any claims to sovereignty over territory in the Antarctic regions asserted by any foreign state. No member of the United States Antarctic Service shall take any action or make any statements tending to compromise this position.

Members of the Service may take any appropriate steps such as dropping written claims from airplanes, depositing such writings in cairns, et cetera, which might assist in supporting a sovereignty claim by the United States Government.[72]

Earlier Roosevelt had sent Byrd a personal letter, dated July 12, 1939, which read in part:

> The most important thing is to prove (a) that human beings can permanently occupy a portion of the Continent winter and summer (b) that it is well worth a small annual appropriation to maintain such permanent bases because of their growing value for four purposes—national defense of the Western Hemisphere, radio, meteorology and minerals. Each of these four is of approximately equal importance as far as we now know.[73]

Less than a month later, the President wrote another personal letter, this time to Under Secretary Sumner Welles, in which he put forward an idea that appears to have been his alone:

> I am inclined to think in regard to the Antarctic Expedition that we should give some study to a new form of sovereignty, i.e., a claim to sovereignty of the whole sector lying south of the Americas in behalf of, and in trust for, the American Republics as a whole. Under this the United States, being the only Republic which has taken the initiative in exploring and possibly settling the area, would act not only in behalf of its own exclusive sovereignty but would include all the other Republics—and in the future if the American sector proved valuable in any shape, manner, or form, its sovereignty could be managed by an inter-American Republic governing body.
>   That is a new one. Think it over.[74]

In making this suggestion, Roosevelt was no doubt influenced by the approaching war in Europe, which was only weeks away. Soon, too, Chile and Argentina would be preoccupied by fruitless negotiations after Chile announced its Antarctic claim or—as Chile insisted—delimited its long-existing sovereign territory. In any event, the suggestion came to naught.[75]

Again in 1939, the British ambassador to Washington informed the secretary of state "that His Majesty's Government in New Zealand will be pleased to afford Admiral Byrd's expedition facilities to establish a base in the Ross Dependency." Sumner Welles replied stiffly that "it is not anticipated that Admiral Byrd will have need to call upon the New Zealand authorities for any special facilities. . . ."[76] Congress, which had not appropriated nearly enough money for even one season in Antarctica (the difference having been made up by private donors, the War

Department, and the Navy), declined entirely to support the expedition for another year. Its abrupt end involved waste of resources and data, but for a nation rearming for the very real possibility of involvement in the war, expeditions to Antarctica seemed unessential. Most of the information gathered was not even processed, much less published, as scientists were called to other duties.

The mammoth Operation Highjump, launched in 1947, and Operation Windmill immediately following have already been discussed in terms of their military as opposed to their scientific emphasis. But they also had the unstated objective "of consolidating and extending United States sovereignty over the largest practicable area of the Antarctic continent."[77] This was not revealed until 1955, when the Operation Plan of Deepfreeze was announced. Although ostensibly designed to prepare for the International Geophysical Year, the plan acknowledged that one purpose was to establish "permanent stations in the Antarctic . . . in support of United States 'rights' in the area."[78] Even as the ships of Operation Highjump were arriving in Antarctic waters, it appeared that the United States was about to assert a claim, and *The New York Times* of January 6, 1947, so reported. But the Department of State hesitated. Relations between Britain, Argentina, and Chile had become so explosive that Washington feared a U.S. claim might worsen the situation. As a result, the United States began to reexamine its goals and policies in Antarctica once again.

THE FIRST ATTEMPT TO INTERNATIONALIZE

A year later, the Department of State had a plan. It would propose international administration of Antarctica by the seven claimant nations plus the United States, which would declare its sovereignty over the unclaimed sector "to forestall any Soviet attempt to become a territorial claimant," as well as over any and all other parts of Antarctica "to which we have the best right by virtue of discovery and exploration." This not only would put the United States "on an equal juridical footing" with the claimant states but would also apply pressure to accept internationalization.[79]

The arrangement preferred by the United States was an eight-power trusteeship under the United Nations. "It is important to our international position that we maintain our full support of the United Nations and that any onus of weakening and disrupting the United Nations remain exclusively upon the USSR."[80] Of course, the trusteeship system was conceived primarily as a temporary bridge—a means to protect and guide non–self-governing territories to independence. In the words of Article 76b of the U.N. Charter, a basic objective of the trusteeship system was "to promote the political, economic, social and educational advancement of the inhabitants of the trust territories." Without an indigenous people in Antarctica, the concept of trusteeship seemed to many irrelevant.

When the idea was tried out privately on the British, they made clear they did not want the United Nations involved in any way in Antarctica, especially as it would give the Soviet Union an opportunity to interfere.[81] Therefore, the United States moved toward the concept of condominium, in which authority and control would be retained by the directly interested nations acting in concert. The Department of State prepared a draft agreement wherein the eight nations would "merge and join their claims . . . and interests in the special regime here established."[82] Secretary James Forrestal wrote that the Department of Defense would approve only if the Soviet Union were kept out and the idea of demilitarizing Antarctica was dropped.[83] The British were equally adamant regarding the Soviets, and Under Secretary Robert Lovett replied: "The Department shares your view that no occasion should be given to the Soviet Union to participate in an Antarctic settlement or administration, and would not propose or accept any arrangement to the contrary."[84] Only a few years later, the occasion would be given and an arrangement accepted, when the IGY was launched.

"I should like as soon as possible to be prepared to announce the American claim," Lovett wrote to Forrestal in August 1948, enclosing the first broad definition of the proposed claim. "It would therefore be appreciated if this matter could be given urgent attention."[85] The United States was preparing to claim territory in every sector except between the meridians 35°W and 13°E, a relatively small slice of the Norwegian and British/Argentine/Chilean claims. In all other sectors, Washington was to claim "all Antarctic territory which has been explored and mapped by United States expeditions" with certain specified exceptions.[86]

On August 9, 1948, formal invitations were issued to Argentina, Australia, Chile, France, New Zealand, Norway, and the United Kingdom (with all of whom Washington had already been consulting) to open discussions on the territorial problem. The note suggested that "the solution should be such as to promote scientific investigation and research" and foresaw "some form of internationalization." In conclusion, the note made clear that Washington was not in favor of a conference until there had been extended study and exchange of views.[87]

The American invitation was addressed only to the claimant states, disregarding others that at one time or another had shown an interest in Antarctica. Belgium and South Africa privately objected,[88] but to invite a nonclaimant state might open the door to the Soviet Union, which was particularly anathematized at this time because the Berlin Blockade was two months old and the airlift was heavily taxing the British and Americans. Furthermore, the Russians had shown no interest in the Antarctic for nearly 130 years—other than whaling in the Southern Ocean. The only hint of the reaction to come had been provided in 1939, when Norway's claim included Peter I Island, which was first sighted by the Russian, Bellingshausen. The Soviet government sent a note saying that it "would reserve its opinion as to the national status of territories discovered by Russian citizens."[89] Ten years later, this seemed to Western diplomats a mere aberration, explained by Stalin's approaching pact with Hitler, who had forces standing off Queen Maud Land at that very time. Previously, no Soviet had ever claimed that Bellingshausen "discovered Antarctica" or had even seen the continent.[90] In any case, a Soviet decree of April 15, 1926, had ruled out the doctrine of discovery because in the context of the Arctic it was convenient to do so.[91]

Nevertheless, at a meeting of the Geographical Society of the U.S.S.R. in February 1949, the president of the society spoke on "Russian Discoveries in the Antarctic and Present-Day Interest in That Area." The members then adopted a three-part resolution, which asserted Russian priority in the discovery of Antarctica and spoke of "the indisputable right of the Soviet Union to participate in the solution of problems of the Antarctic." The resolution continued: "No attempt to solve the problem of a regime for the Antarctic without participation of the Soviet Union can find any justification." And finally: "No solution of the problem of a regime

for the Antarctic without the participation of the Soviet Union can
have legal force, and the U.S.S.R. has every reason not to
recognize any such solution."[92]

In due course, the Soviet government made it official. In a
memorandum dated June 7, 1950, delivered to the claimant nations[93] plus the United States, the Soviet Union stated its position
in very similar language:

> The Government of the U.S.S.R. cannot agree to such a question as
> that of the Antarctic regime being settled without its participation.
> In this connection the Soviet Government deems it necessary to call
> to mind the outstanding services rendered by Russian navigators in
> discovering the Antarctic. It is a universally recognized fact that at
> the beginning of the nineteenth century the Russian voyagers
> Bellingshausen and Lazarev were the first to reach the shores of the
> Antarctic and circumnavigate this continent, thereby proving that
> the widespread view existing at that time to the effect that there was
> allegedly no land beyond the South Polar Circle was erroneous. This
> service rendered by the Russian navigators is no less important than
> the explorations conducted later on the continent itself and around
> its shores by expeditions of certain countries whose representatives
> now declare their interest in defining the regime in the
> Antarctic. . . .
>
> In view of the preceding statements, the Soviet Government
> cannot recognize as lawful any decision on the Antarctic regime
> taken without its participation.[94]

By the time the Soviet memorandum was received, the U.S.
initiative was for all practical purposes already dead, and it was
almost literally buried when the North Koreans invaded the South
on June 25, 1950. Chile and Argentina were adamantly opposed,
Norway saw no need for international administration, Australia
was dubious, France stalled, and New Zealand favored U.N.
trusteeship; only Great Britain favored the plan as a way of getting
out of its territorial disputes with Argentina and Chile. The latter
did present a counterproposal—the so-called Escudero declaration. It totally rejected internationalization but welcomed scientific
cooperation and suggested a five-year moratorium on territorial
claims. The concerned nations fiddled with the idea for months,
but it ultimately came to nothing.

A U.S. CLAIM RECONSIDERED

With the rejection of internationalization, the United States came under increased pressure to assert a formal claim in Antarctica. There followed a period of almost a decade when U.S. Antarctic policy appears so inconsistent and contradictory that it is difficult to make any sense of it—in part, no doubt, because many relevant documents are still classified—but more probably because under the mounting tensions of the Cold War, policy analysts and decision-makers were simply unable to define U.S. interests in Antarctica. The region did not seem to fit into any coherent political strategy. Yet the pulling and hauling were strenuous between those who favored a U.S. claim and those who opposed, between those who believed a large U.S. presence was essential and those who considered Antarctica of only scientific importance.

Examples of inconsistencies abound. Exclusion of the Soviet Union from any political involvement in Antarctica was a cornerstone of U.S. and Allied policy. National Security Council memoranda of 1954 and 1955 set forth as U.S. objectives in Antarctica:

1. Orderly progress toward a solution of the territorial problem of Antartica, which would assure control by the U.S. and friendly parties.

2. Freedom of exploration and scientific research for the United States and friendly parties.

3. Access by the United States and friendly parties to natural resources discovered in Antarctica.[95]

The reiterated reference to "friendly parties" clearly did not include the Soviet Union. Yet Washington virtually ensured Soviet active participation by converting the International Geophysical Year in Antarctica from a moderate-sized scientific program to a large national program. Not surprisingly, the Soviet Union joined on an equivalent scale. Six months after the IGY had started, Washington was forced to face reality and abandon its opposition to Soviet participation in a political settlement of Antarctic problems.

In 1954 President Eisenhower had rejected the recommendation of an interdepartmental study group that the United States
formally claim a large part of West Antarctica; but during 1956 and
1957 alone, the United States deposited thirty-one claims in various
parts of Antarctica, including the South Pole.[96] And in March 1956,
"in answer to public inquiries," the Department of State issued a
memorandum restating U.S. policy in familiar terms (reserving the
right to make a claim but recognizing none), but adding a new
paragraph no doubt designed to appease the territorial hawks:

> As yet knowledge of the Antarctic Continent is insufficient to
> permit an informal decision as to what value United States sover-
> eignty over parts of the continent would have. Traditionally the
> United States does not take lightly the obligation to protect areas
> under its sovereignty. Until more is known it may be questioned
> whether it is advisable to advance claims which would conflict with
> those of other friendly governments and which would involve very
> large appropriations to establish and maintain. It is hoped, however,
> that information collected during the International Geophysical Year
> will perhaps assist in deciding on the present and potential value of
> various parts of the continent.
>   In view of all the considerations discussed above it is not consid-
> ered advisable for the United States to advance an official claim at
> the present time. . . . We shall, however, follow developments
> carefully and take or recommend such steps, including the advanc-
> ing of official claims, as are required to protect the national
> interest.[97]

True to its word, the Antarctic Working Group of the Operations
Coordinating Board meeting in July 1957 "had two main problems
before it: (1) U.S. claims to territory, and (2) the scope of future
operations."[98] The National Security Council, having involved the
United States in enormous expense ostensibly in behalf of the IGY,
now wanted the scope of future operations "to be the minimum
essential to support U.S. interests."[99] Presumably, it was the task
of the Working Group to determine what this meant. As to the
perennial question of a U.S. claim to Antarctic territory, the
advantages in making one seemed to be waning. The arguments in
favor were that it would put the United States on an equal footing
with the other claimants, would increase its leverage in finding a
solution to the claims problem, and would forestall a possible

Soviet claim to the segment no one had yet spoken for. On the other hand, it could as well be argued that a U.S. claim would provoke a Soviet counterclaim. Since most countries active in Antarctica fervently hoped that the Soviet Union would pack up and go home after the IGY, perhaps the best policy for the United States was to lie low—at least for the present. Although some felt the United States was entitled to claim at least two-thirds of Antarctica, as a practical matter the alternatives were by now more restricted, unless the United States was prepared to outrage important allies.[100] Most obviously, the United States could claim the sector no one had spoken for—between 90°W and 150°W—an area that the United States almost alone had explored.[101] But the sector had a physical liability that had always caused the United States to hesitate: It was virtually unapproachable from the sea. Nowhere around the continent's periphery was the pack ice more impenetrable. The many traverses Americans had made through Marie Byrd Land and Ellsworth Land had started either from the Ross Ice Shelf (New Zealand) or from the disputed peninsula area, including the ice shelves of the Weddell Sea.

Some people also felt strongly that since the unclaimed sector was not strictly continental, but rather an ill-defined archipelago, a territorial claim would be absurd. But possibly the most compelling argument against making a claim was that it would restrict the cherished right to move freely anywhere on the continent. The United States could hardly assert a claim without recognizing the claims of others, thus relinquishing open access and accepting a segmented continent.

Yet the United States was under pressure to stake a claim not only from its citizens but also from its allies. "All the present claimants," Walter Sullivan wrote, "are anxious to persuade the United States to thrust its finger into the Antarctic pie, since this would bring the might of the United States into the informal alliance that seeks to keep out unwelcome visitors."[102] Since the United States and New Zealand increased their cooperation during the IGY, when the major U.S. base was established on territory claimed by New Zealand, it was suggested that the two countries make a joint claim over the sector from 90°W to the western boundary of the Ross Dependency at 160°E. Many New Zealanders felt that this would strengthen their position and ease the burden of a small country trying to administer a territory many times its size.[103] A New Zealand writer asserted that "the present situation in the Dependency constitutes an undeclared United States/New Zealand condominium. Recognition of this fact would appear to provide the only presently available solution to New Zealand problems in the Dependency."[104] Although these words were written considerably later, a similar attitude was encountered in the 1950s.

Many Australians likewise believed that a U.S. claim would enhance the political position of the claimant states. Sir Douglas Mawson wrote Laurence Gould expressing regret that the United States had not asserted a claim. His wish, he said, was that Antarctica should be controlled by "a limited number of sovereignties of good repute and mutual regard" so that it "could be administered on good lines conjointly for the benefit of all."[105] When the Soviets established all their stations in Australian Antarctic Territory, the Australians were seriously alarmed. Their newspapers gave front-page treatment to every move of the Soviets in Antarctica. The comment of an international law scholar was relatively restrained: "Posts originally established under the sheep's clothing of scientific research may subsequently be revealed in their wolf reality of political and military gains."[106]

Admiral George Dufek and Paul Siple, who cordially disliked each other and disagreed in most things, were among those who thought a condominium with New Zealand and Australia desirable and probably feasible politically.[107] Under the urging of Admiral Dufek, the Antarctic Working Group in the summer of 1957 reached a consensus that went considerably further.

> Condominium discussions [it was decided] could be taken up in phases as the situation might require. In the first phase, the U.S. would carry on discussions with Australia and New Zealand; in the second phase, Norway and France might be added; and in the third phase, all other claimants would be brought in and a condominium for the entire continent considered.[108]

In the event, not even phase one was reached, primarily because, for different reasons, it was difficult for any of the three countries to take the initiative. If members of the Antarctic Working Group seriously believed that phase three would ever be reached, they were deluding themselves.[109]

So, as the IGY came to a close, the positions of the superpowers were similar. Both would remain in Antarctica and pursue science on a considerable scale. Both recognized no claims and both had refrained from making a claim but reserved the right to do so. Both maintained stations in territory claimed by others; and while the United States had fewer and less scattered stations, it had the distinction of sitting astride six claims where they converge at the South Pole.[110] Whether in fact this is an exploitable political asset—a point of leverage on the claims issue—remains unclear, but it is symbolically important and will be denied to anyone else, even at considerable financial cost. The Soviet Union, of course, had no basis for any Antarctic claim comparable to that of the United States; the lands sighted by Bellingshausen already had three claimants, and during the IGY, the Soviets had ignored the unclaimed sector. While many claimant states sought to strengthen their claims both during and after the IGY, the arguments against a claims policy for the superpowers remained compelling. In the minds of some, this might well change if it is confirmed that the quadrant no one wanted now promises oil.

Even as the United States appeared most indecisive in its Antarctic policy, a decision was reached in Washington that would unalterably change the pattern of events in the frozen continent.

CHAPTER

V

The Antarctic Treaty

. . . there are many implications of this treaty that we will
return to twenty years from today.

—*Senator Wayne Morse in 1960*

In the early autumn of 1957, Washington and other Western
capitals were held by conflicting sentiments regarding the Antarctic. On the one hand, they were impressed by the Soviet Union's
unprecedented cooperation there and wanted to preserve it beyond the International Geophysical Year; on the other hand, they
felt acute anxiety about the continued presence of the Soviets in
Antarctica. The Australian press was speculating that Mirnyi, the
principal Soviet station, would be converted to a submarine base
after the IGY.[1] There were other reasons—those stemming from
conflicting territorial claims—for fearing that intensified political
rivalry might follow the mild euphoria brought on by the IGY.
Also, the gentlemen's agreement to suspend all political activity
during the IGY was to expire at the end of 1958.

Secretary of State John Foster Dulles recalled to Washington a
retired Foreign Service officer and named him special adviser on
Antarctica. Paul C. Daniels knew little about the Antarctic, but he
was experienced in Latin America, especially the disputes among
Argentina, Chile, and Great Britain. His instructions were impre-
cise because the Department of State had no clear concept of what

it wanted except to continue the amicable state of affairs in Antarctica.[2]

While Daniels was sounding out various interest groups in Washington, Britain was already conducting a comprehensive policy review and reconsidering the earlier U.S. proposal (1948) for an international consortium. Within a few months, this led to quiet consultations within the Commonwealth. In February 1958, Prime Minister Macmillan visited Australia. At a press conference Mr. Macmillan acknowledged under questioning, that he had been holding discussions with prime ministers Menzies of Australia and Nash of New Zealand and called for internationalization and demilitarization of Antarctica. Macmillan proposed two essential principles for an international settlement of Antarctic questions: that "there should be free trade in science" and that Antarctica "should not be allowed to develop" into an area "used for military purposes."[3] The Times (London) reported that Macmillan's Commonwealth tour had "greatly increased interest in the establishment of an international regime or authority for Antarctica."[4] But when the prime minister was questioned in Parliament, he denied any intention of entering into negotiations with other interested nations.

Although the reaction of Chile and Argentina to these developments was predictably negative, the United States now sought actively to persuade all the involved nations that it was time for some form of international agreement to ensure that Antarctica "shall be used only for peaceful purposes." The words are those of President Eisenhower announcing on May 3, 1958, that notes had been simultaneously delivered to eleven nations, including the Soviet Union, proposing "that the interests of mankind would best be served, in consonance with the high ideals of the Charter of the United Nations, if the countries which have a direct interest in Antarctica were to join together in the conclusion of a treaty. . . ."[5]

To win any possibility of acceptance by Chile and Argentina, the note stated:

> It is believed that such a treaty can be concluded without requiring any participating nation to renounce whatever basic historic rights it may have in Antarctica, or whatever claims of sovereignty it may have asserted. It could be specifically provided that such basic rights and such claims would remain unaffected while the treaty is in force,

and that no new rights would be acquired and no new claims made by any country during the duration of the treaty.

This freezing of the legal status quo was a major difference from the U.S. plan of 1948. Although made out of necessity, it was widely believed at the time—and not in Washington alone—that the sovereignty issue would waste away over one or two decades if a treaty could be successfully negotiated.

The other new principle incorporated in the American proposal of 1958 (although it was not spelled out in the note) was the coupling of nonmilitarization with an inspection system. In 1957–58, military/strategic concerns about Antarctica were very real and represented one of the principal motivations for negotiating the Antarctic Treaty. It was pointed out that an occupier, once entrenched in Antarctica, could not be dislodged, because there are virtually no beaches and every approach is hazardous. For the nations surrounding the Southern Ocean, the thought of Antarctica in the hands of hostile forces was profoundly disturbing. For major maritime nations such as the United States and Britain, the possibility of hostile submarines hiding under Antarctic ice to prey on Allied shipping—perhaps after destruction of the Panama or Suez canals—aroused fears partly justified by experience in two wars. And with the dawn of the missile age, it seemed not unlikely that Antarctica might become a launching site for intercontinental ballistic missiles. Admiral Dufek, who had commanded the forces that built the seven U.S. stations for the IGY, himself drew up a contingency plan, dated August 26, 1957, proposing a "course of action in Antarctica in the event of hostilities."[6]

A characteristic comment was that of *New York Times* columnist Cy Sulzberger in a story filed from the South Pole:

> It is in our interest to insure that this vast region should never be turned by the Russians into a kind of Antarctic Albania. Moscow now threatens Greece and Turkey from rocket ramps in that Adriatic land. Similar launching pads, operated by a handful of men, could be used by the U.S.S.R. to blackmail the entire Southern Hemisphere from here.[7]

The annual global review by the Carnegie Endowment for International Peace said that interest in Antarctica "has been steadily increasing . . . most of all, because of strategic considerations."[8]

No doubt to reassure the hardliners in Congress, the U.S. note included, as if by rote, the usual proviso:

> The United States for many years has had, and at the present time continues to have, direct and substantial rights and interests in Antarctica. . . . In view of the activities of the United States and its nationals . . . my government reserves all of the rights of the United States with respect to the Antarctic region, including the right to assert a territorial claim or claims.

It is significant that nearly all the important provisions of the Antarctic Treaty were proposed in the original U.S. note and that within one month all eleven nations had responded favorably— although in the case of Chile and Argentina very reluctantly. Nevertheless, another year would pass before the conference was called for October 15, 1959, in Washington. In the full interval of fifteen months, approximately sixty meetings were held among the twelve nations. All were tightly closed, and most were held in the boardroom of the National Academy of Sciences, with the result that few people knew of their existence. No formal minutes were kept, but either Alan Neidle or Earl Luboeansky of Ambassador Daniels' staff prepared fairly detailed memoranda after each meeting. These were classified progressively as "official use only," "confidential," and finally "secret," as minor leaks occurred and as a working text took shape. A request by this writer under the Freedom of Information Act to see these memoranda was turned down, and they remain classified after nearly a quarter of a century. The reason offered (and expected) is that the United States cannot unilaterally abrogate the agreement of the participating countries to conduct all their deliberations in private. However, memoranda for the meetings held in 1958 were found in an open, private collection of papers, and they provide a better idea than has heretofore been available of how the treaty was negotiated and why the process took so long.[9]

When the first meeting of the so-called Informal Working Group on Antarctica was held on June 13, 1958, it was fully expected that the Treaty Conference would be held within a few months—in September or October. In due course, October 23, 1958, was agreed upon for the opening of the conference; indeed, the date was very nearly announced publicly and was not actually abandoned until October 2—roughly a year before the conference was actually held. The reason for the delay was the total failure to break down the obstruction of the Soviet Union, which was alone in insisting that (1) the working group should not involve itself in substantive discussion and should confine itself to agreeing on time and place for the conference and rules of procedure; (2) the conference should be open to any nation wishing to participate; (3) the only proper topics for inclusion in the proposed treaty were scientific cooperation and peaceful uses of Antarctica; and (4) specifically, any reference to territorial claims was unacceptable. The Soviet Union had not the slightest chance of winning any of these points, and the more stubbornly it persisted, the more the other nations became progressively convinced that without substantive preparatory work and large areas of agreement, a conference would be fruitless. Clearly the Soviet representative, Andrei Ledovski, was being kept on a short tether, without adequate instructions to respond to any new initiative.

Despite its opposition, the Soviet Union could not prevent the circulation of documents, and many draft paragraphs were considered. At the meeting of November 18, 1958, the United States submitted drafts of twelve articles that are strikingly similar in substance and language to those adopted more than a year later. The most substantial changes made thereafter were rejection of compulsory arbitration by the International Court of Justice, extensive elaboration of the articles on jurisdiction, review of the treaty in thirty years after ratification rather than ten years, and elimination of any reference to *"administrative* measures"—since the idea of international administration was unacceptable to most of the claimant states. Also by November 1958, the Working Group —including the Soviet Union—had agreed on rules of procedure for the conference.

Eleven of the twelve nations continued to thrash their way toward substantial agreement without significant change in the Soviet position. In March 1959, Ambassador Daniels reported to a meeting of the Planning Board of the National Security Council that he saw only "a 50-50 chance that the Treaty Conference would come into being."[10] But the following month, Daniels was invited to lunch by the Soviet ambassador to Washington, Mikhail Menshikov. The Russian conveyed little but prodded Daniels with questions in an atmosphere of cordiality. A week or so later, the

Soviet position at the preparatory meetings altered completely to one of active participation and flexibility.[11] Rapid progress was made thereafter, and in June, the opening date of the conference was announced: October 15, 1959.

PROVISIONS OF THE TREATY

While the Soviet Union was alone in refusing for so long to discuss substantive matters, the negotiations were difficult enough under any circumstances. It was relatively easy to agree on the preservation of Antarctica for peaceful purposes, freedom of scientific investigation, and exchange of information and personnel (the first three Articles of the Antarctic Treaty, printed in Appendix A). These had been accepted objectives from the start. After that, controversy surrounded almost every point. Even the nonmilitarization decision was not entered into with enthusiasm by all, especially as it was tied to inspection. Britain and France advocated international inspection machinery. The United States proposed instead an unlimited right of unilateral inspection and its view prevailed. Under Article VII, observers "have complete freedom of access at any time to any or all areas . . . including all stations, installations . . . ships and aircraft." Although there is no enforcement provision—a practical impossibility—this system of inspection is simple, unbureaucratic, and unqualified. That the Soviet Union submitted without protest to such unconditional inspection rights caused no small surprise, but the Soviet delegate said his government had no problem agreeing "where inspections cannot be used against national security."[12]

Significantly, the Soviet Union has never exercised its right of inspection. Indeed, only five countries have conducted inspections: New Zealand in 1963; Australia and Britain jointly in 1963; Argentina in 1966 and 1977; and the United States in 1964, 1967, 1971, 1975, 1977,[13] and 1980. The smaller powers feel it is an unnecessary expense since no treaty violations have ever been discovered, and the frequent exchange of scientists may be more informative. Nevertheless, Tucker Scully of the Department of State, who led the U.S. inspection team in 1979–80, believes the process is useful in ways not contemplated by the drafters of the treaty. Inspectors, he says, can check not only on nonmilitarization but also on adherence to the Agreed Measures for the Conservation of Antarctic Fauna and Flora and the Code of Conduct for Antarctic Expeditions and Station Activities (see below). Beyond this, Scully believes, a team with adequate technical and linguistic expertise serves a representational function, provides a special opportunity for the exchange of information, and, by hauling mail and people from station to station, helps to replace suspicion with amity.[14]

Another purpose of inspection is to monitor the agreement to ban all nuclear explosions in Antarctica and to prohibit dumping of radioactive material (Article V). Understandably, Chile and Argentina, as well as other Southern Hemisphere countries, lobbied energetically for this provision. A second paragraph was added to keep open the possibility that someday, under broader international agreements, peaceful uses of atomic energy might be permitted—perhaps in mining. But since the expectations of Project Ploughshare expired, that possibility is extremely remote, and the prohibition in the Antarctic remains total except for nuclear power reactors, of which none is any longer in existence or planned. This was one of the relatively few issues left to the Washington Conference itself. According to Ambassador Alfred van der Essen, a member of the Belgian delegation in 1959 and head of delegation at many Consultative Meetings, the most time-consuming matters at the formal conference were whether peaceful uses of nuclear energy would be permitted and conditions and procedures for new consultative memberships.[15] Neither of these issues has received much attention since, although the latter may come alive soon.

On many crucial issues, the range of opinion was broad. New Zealand was prepared to surrender its claim in the interest of a genuinely international regime within—or closely associated with —the United Nations.[16] Argentina and Chile wanted no part of the United Nations. The head of the Chilean delegation said it would be unconstitutional "to accept any formula that might imply internationalization" because "the Chilean Antarctic territory does not have the character of a colonial possession but is part of its metropolitan territory and forms part of its southernmost province."[17] The representative of Argentina took a similar position and further told the delegates: "This Conference . . . has not been convened to institute regimes or to create structures. It is not its mission to change or alter anything."[18]

The United States was not particularly concerned about the relationship of the treaty structure to the United Nations, but from the beginning, it believed membership should be limited to the twelve most active members of the Antarctic segment of the IGY. As we have seen, the Soviet Union (and less adamantly Japan) favored the widest possible participation; the lines were drawn when Poland formally applied for inclusion and was denied. The compromise worked out is somewhat less straightforward than the language of the treaty suggests. Ostensibly, membership is covered in Article XIII, which states that the treaty "shall be open for accession by any State which is a Member of the United Nations, or by any other State which may be invited to accede to the Treaty with the consent of all the Contracting Parties whose representatives are entitled to participate in the meetings provided for under Article IX of the Treaty."[19]

This is the sheeps-and-goats paragraph that translated means: Everyone is welcome and encouraged to accede to the treaty but only the original twelve will participate in making decisions—plus such other nations as, in the unanimous judgment of the original contracting parties, have demonstrated an interest in Antarctica "by conducting substantial scientific research activity there" (Article IX). So far, two nations—Poland in 1976 and West Germany in 1981—have been invited to join as "Consultative Parties." To the disappointment of many, only eleven other nations have acceded to the treaty—Czechoslovakia (1962), Denmark (1965), the Netherlands (1967), Romania (1971), German Democratic Republic (1974), Brazil (1975), Bulgaria (1978), Uruguay (1980), Peru, Italy, and Papua New Guinea (1981).[20]

While the idea of freezing territorial claims (Article IV) was a premise without which the Washington Conference could not have been held, finding the words to satisfy all parties was predictably difficult. Nevertheless, a U.S. draft was adopted almost unchanged. But the sovereignty question was by no means laid to rest and continued to impinge on the most difficult issues.

The "joint administrative arrangements" foreseen in the original U.S. note and intentionally left vague proved impossible to define in acceptable terms. For the claimant states, it was hard enough to allow scientists unrestrained access to their sovereign territory; to create an international administrative body with authority to make decisions bearing on their territories seemed to compromise their claims too far. Hence, to this day, the treaty has no organization as such, no secretariat, not even a central depository for relevant documents.

This caution by the claimant states had some justification. For despite what is said in Article IV ("Nothing contained in the present Treaty shall be interpreted as . . . a diminution . . . of any basis of claim," etc.), many observers feel that the freedom of movement across boundaries of national claims, the obligation to cooperate and to share knowledge, and the unlimited right of unilateral inspection all tend over time to weaken claims and to strengthen internationalism.[21]

Despite the resistance to any form of organization, the treaty does provide for continuing consultations "on matters of common interest pertaining to Antarctica, and formulating, considering, and recommending to their Governments, measures in further-ance of the principles and objectives of the Treaty" (Article IX). This provision has been admirably fulfilled; it has meant the difference between a rigid document, frozen in time and circum-stance, and an evolving system with the capacity for change. Many consider Article IX the treaty's most important and innovative provision. The same article required that the first consultative meeting be held (in Canberra) within two months of the treaty's coming into force. The treaty does not say with what frequency meetings should be held thereafter, but two years has become the norm, excluding occasional special sessions.

Another issue profoundly affected by claims to sovereignty was that of jurisdiction, one of the weakest aspects of the treaty and one that was by no means settled prior to the Washington Conference. The compromise struck in Article VIII provides that scientists and officially designated observers, as well as their staffs, remain under the jurisdiction of the country of which they are nationals, regardless of where they may be in Antarctica. Although this represented a concession by the claimant states, it is a very untidy solution and goes some way toward recognizing territorial claims. For if any nation allows one of its citizens to be arrested and tried by another country, it is at least implicitly acknowledging the sovereign authority of that country. As to the untidiness, imagine an American tourist or businessman arrested in the Antarctic Peninsula, where jurisdiction is contested. Theoretically, he would be subject to three different criminal codes—those of Argentina, Britain, and Chile—although in practice the arresting country would no doubt control the situation. To maintain friendly international relations, the arresting country *might* turn the alleged criminal over to the United States, but it would be under no obligation to do so.

Although no other conclusion can be reached from reading the text of Article VIII, the head of the U.S. delegation, testifying on the treaty before the Foreign Relations Committee, declared that "by virtue of recognizing that there is no sovereignty over Antarctica we retain jurisdiction over our citizens who go down there and we would deny the right of the other claimants to try that citizen." He conceded that such flouting of Article VIII would lead to "an international controversy."[22]

The seven claimant states have either specifically enacted legislation governing criminal conduct in Antarctica or consider their domestic criminal legislation applicable to the areas they claim.[23] Since the United States claims no territorial sovereignty in Antarctica, such criminal statutes as exist are not applicable. The U.S. military in Antarctica is covered by the Uniform Code of Military Justice.[24] But civilians, a body that includes not only scientists but also an increasing number of employees of private contractors, are in a legal limbo. Civilians have been asked to sign waivers subjecting themselves to the same rules as the military, but the constitutionality of this practice is dubious and untested.[25] There have been numerous bills in Congress since the 1960s designed to clarify these ambiguities, but none has been acted upon, apparently because of entanglement with the broader effort to revise the U.S. criminal code.

The permutations of this issue of jurisdiction are almost endless and are fascinating to legal scholars and old Antarctic hands alike. As a Norwegian writer put it: Imagine a French tourist who arrives at the U.S. McMurdo Station on board a Norwegian ship on a tour arranged by a British agency and is the victim of a serious crime committed by a person of unknown nationality in the New Zealand sector.[26] When Rear Admiral David F. Welch, then commander at

McMurdo, was asked what kept him awake at night, he replied:
the uncertainty of legal jurisdiction.[27] Here is one of the major
"loose ends" of the Antarctic Treaty system.

The geographical scope of the treaty proved more difficult to
negotiate than might have been imagined, because the decision
affected about a dozen islands and island groups, and because
complex questions involving the legal status of ice were involved.
Article VI states that "the provisions of the Treaty shall apply to the
area south of 60° South Latitude, including all ice shelves. . . ."
The more or less permanent ice shelves had to be included, not
only because they resemble land more than water, but also because
they are the site of many research stations. Quite properly, the
treaty specifically excluded the high seas south of 60°, leaving this
huge domain under existing international law. This one-sentence
article, as we shall see, is now weighty with political overtones
arising out of the Convention on the Law of the Sea.

The only briefer article in the treaty is that in which the
contracting parties appear to agree that no outsider will rock their
boat if they can help it. In the language of Article X, each signatory
"undertakes to exert appropriate efforts . . . to the end that no one
engages in any activity in Antarctica contrary to the principles or
purposes of the present Treaty." The possibility of a nonsignatory
state or states becoming active in Antarctica and refusing to abide
by the rules is of continuing, indeed growing, concern to the
consultative members.

Dispute settlement is nonbinding. The U.S. delegation joined
those favoring compulsory jurisdiction of the International Court
of Justice. It did so in spite of the Connally amendment, which
preserves for the United States the option of accepting or rejecting
the Court's jurisdiction. Since, in the U.S. view, Antarctic issues
were (and are) patently international, the Connally reservation,
designed to prevent interference in American domestic affairs, did
not apply.[28] But Chile, Argentina, and the Soviet Union refused
binding arbitration.[29] Thus, Article XI merely urges the peaceful
settlement of disputes by any means possible, including application to the International Court of Justice. So far there have been no
disputes that did not exist prior to the treaty, and no formal
dispute settlement has been required.

Finally, the treaty has no terminal date. However, thirty years
after the treaty has come into force (*i.e.*, 1991) any consultative

member may call for a review conference wherein changes in the treaty can be made by simple majority (Article XII). Meanwhile, modifications or amendments can be made only by unanimous agreement.

RECEPTION AND RATIFICATION

It has sometimes been said that the Antarctic Treaty was a modest achievement at best because it merely codified what had already been tacitly agreed upon; that it was made possible by the similarity of U.S. and Soviet interests; and that with regard to the really difficult issues it postponed one (territorial claims) and was silent on the other (resources). The last point is indisputable: There was no possibility of settling the sovereignty issue, and this in turn prevented any resolution of resource questions, although discussion was protracted. It is also probable (and irrelevant) that if the United States and the Soviet Union had been on opposite sides of every issue there would have been no treaty. But the point about tacit agreements already reached does not hold up under examination. The gentlemen's agreement to exchange scientific information and to hold political issues in abeyance for eighteen months was initiated by scientists within the nongovernmental International Committee for the IGY. No doubt the tacit acceptance of governments was needed, but there is a world of difference between toleration of a short-term arrangement and a formal and legal commitment for a minimum of thirty years. The agreement to keep armaments and military installations out of Antarctica, to ban nuclear explosions and radioactive material, and to permit unlimited unilateral inspection perpetuated conditions very unlikely to endure in the absence of a treaty. Only the naive could believe that the international ambience existing in the IGY could last indefinitely. This must include the scientists in large numbers who opposed the idea of a treaty because they feared the intervention of diplomats and politicians where scientists (they believed) should be in control.[30] Perforce this attitude changed after the treaty had been negotiated, and ratification appeared preferable to rejection. Yet again, in 1963, when the United States made plans to exercise its right of inspection, American scientists fought the decision vehemently. They argued that formal inspection would destroy cooperation and was unnecessary because American scientists serving at other stations could confirm adherence to the treaty by all parties. But the Department of State felt that a commitment had been made to the Senate during the ratification hearings. Also, there was something to be said for establishing a precedent *before* a violation was suspected. So controversial was the issue that the final decision to proceed with the inspection had to be made by President Kennedy.[31]

The Antarctic Treaty was well received by press and public almost everywhere. *The Economist* (London) called it "the first truly self-denying ordinance to be signed by, among others, all the nuclear powers."[32] Yet in the United States, it was uncertain to the very end whether the Senate would produce the necessary two-thirds majority. Opposition to the treaty centered on the U.S. failure to assert its rightful claim and on "what is considered a gratuitous invitation to the USSR to enter the Antarctic on a basis of equality with nations possessing legitimate rights in the area."[33] A single day of hearings before the Senate Foreign Relations Committee sufficed for all parties to be heard, and nine days later the bill was reported out:

> The Committee . . . considers that the Antarctic Treaty is a notable instance of U.S. initiative, preceded by careful planning and followed by patient and skillful negotiation. . . . [O]pponents did not offer any feasible alternative method of preventing disputes and national aggrandizement, and of insuring cooperative access to the scientific data of the entire continent.[34]

But Senator Thomas Dodd, in language that was often repeated in three days of floor debate, called the treaty a giveaway of American rights and for the Soviet Union "a completely unexpected and unlooked-for bonanza."[35] While opponents argued that the treaty legitimized the presence of those who had no right to be in Antarctica, the proponents pointed out that "the Russians are already there." Apparently no one asked, however, whether the IGY was a political mistake or whether it was a graceful way of letting the Soviet Union onto a continent where they soon would have been anyway. In either case, the IGY made the treaty both possible—by setting a precedent for cooperation and restraint— and necessary—because if activity in Antarctica was to continue indefinitely, nations involved elsewhere in a cold war needed ground rules.

If Senator Dodd was not the most effective critic, he was one of the most quotable. The twelve-power agreement amounts, he said, "to putting the free world and the slave world on the same footing by treaty arrangement."[36] "Do we want to spread the disease of communism even to the penguins?" he asked.[37] Senator Clair Engle felt that "for the United States to give up the sovereign rights it has earned in Antarctica would be as great a folly as it would have been many years ago to forgo the purchase of Alaska."[38] Since the consultative powers can act only in unanimity, "the Soviet Union could veto measures agreed upon by all the other signatories."[39] Senator Engle and Senator Russell Long suspected that, since the treaty could not bind nonsignatories, the Soviets would order their East European satellites to Antarctica to flout the rules whenever and however it might be in the Soviet interest.[40]

In striving to prevent a two-thirds majority, opponents of the treaty could count on some exceptionally influential members, considered to have special qualifications. Senator Ernest Gruening of Alaska, who had been one of the four directors of the short-lived United States Antarctic Service, spoke forcefully against the treaty. Senator Harry E. Byrd of Virginia joined other senators in suggesting that the treaty was in effect a betrayal of his brother, Admiral Byrd, and all he had accomplished.[41] On the third and last day of debate on the Senate floor, the principal speaker in opposition was Senator Richard B. Russell, who said that the treaty was "diametrically opposed" to the best interests of the United States and "represents a dim conclusion to one of the brightest, proudest chapters in American history."[42]

Nevertheless, on August 10, 1960, the U.S. Senate ratified the Antarctic Treaty by a vote of sixty-six to twenty-one. One of those who voted in the minority was Barry Goldwater, who would be the Republican presidential candidate just four years later.[43] In 1971–72, Senator Goldwater visited Antarctica and upon his return wrote a rhapsodic piece for *The New York Times* about the "relaxed and unsuspicious freedom" in which nations were working together in Antarctica. He speculated that "the pattern of cooperation among nations which is working out here in the Antarctic, I believe, could become a pattern for harmonizing the relationships between nations in all areas of the world at some later date."[44]

Within a year of the signing of the treaty, nine countries had ratified. The British House of Commons did not even debate the treaty; in the Lords, there were a few speeches by old Antarctic hands, all of them praising the treaty.[45] Of the three remaining countries, Australia was a slow mover, as always, because of the nature of its federal system; the outcome was never in doubt. Argentina and Chile, however, had serious political problems. Argentina was in one of its rare periods of democracy, under President Arturo Frondizi; approval was required by both houses of the legislature, where the government's support was shaky. In Chile, the Congress had not even begun consideration of the treaty as late as March 1961. Nevertheless, on June 23, 1961, all three of the holdouts deposited instruments of ratification in Washington, and the treaty entered into force.

While the treaty was being hailed everywhere as an important precedent and a breakthrough in the Cold War, its weaknesses and limitations were spelled out by its friends as a warning not to expect too much. Robert Hayton, one of the leading political students of Antarctica, pointed out that "the crucial processes of disputes settlement and decision-making provided by the treaty are *very* weak, permissive, and add little, if anything, to the present opportunities and obligations of the nations involved."[46] Howard Taubenfeld concluded that the treaty "represents a lost opportunity for settling the Antarctic question definitively . . . [and for] a creative experiment which might have been a useful precedent for the peaceful administration of more difficult areas."[47] Somewhat later, Finn Sollie, director of Norway's Nansen Foundation, called the treaty "a non-solution, a . . . constructive evasion."[48] No serious analyst failed to point out how the treaty might have been improved upon.

Nevertheless, the Antarctic Treaty spawned a large literature in which it was analyzed as a precedent for the administration of other environments. Taubenfeld himself joined with Philip Jessup in a book-length study entitled *Controls for Outer Space and the Antarctic Analogy*, written even before the treaty was signed.[49] Senator Hubert Humphrey spoke for many when, at the treaty hearings, he said: "[W]e are possibly pioneering as we reach into the faraway places of the Antarctic, into the outer stretches of outer space."[50] Although the treaty was generally recognized to be *sui generis*, it was carefully dissected for its possible relevance to disarmament, a nuclear test ban, nonproliferation, the Arctic, outer space, and the moon. But the outcome was always the same: Either the analogous environments were perceived to involve more vital national interests, or they required greater universality than obtained in Antarctica.

EVOLUTION OF THE TREATY SYSTEM

The real test of the treaty rested on the operation of Article IX—the provision for continuing consultation on matters of mutual interest.

Since the Antarctic Treaty was ratified, there have been eleven consultative meetings at which 130 recommendations have been adopted.[51] Almost all have subsequently received formal approval of the member governments. (This is not surprising since all delegates to consultative meetings are instructed by their governments.) Although theoretically recommendations cannot take effect until all governments have given formal approval, they are considered guidelines and in practice become operative immediately. The recommendations have dealt with such topics as how and what information will be exchanged; cooperation with the United Nations and other international bodies, especially in the field of meteorology; improvements in telecommunications; cooperation in logistics, transport, postal matters, and emergencies; the problems created by tourism; and the designation of forty-three historic monuments.[52] The dates and places of Antarctic Treaty consultative meetings have been as follows:

> 1961—Canberra
> 1962—Buenos Aires
> 1964—Brussels
> 1966—Santiago
> 1968—Paris
> 1970—Tokyo
> 1972—Wellington
> 1975—Oslo
> 1977—London
> 1979—Washington
> 1981—Buenos Aires

Setting aside Poland and West Germany, which attained consultative membership only recently, it will be noted that two capitals are missing—Moscow and Johannesburg. Several members are not eager about going to these cities, and the Soviet Union is adamant in refusing to meet in South Africa. Chile and the Soviet Union have not had diplomatic relations for decades, and some were surprised that the Soviets were willing to attend the Santiago meeting in 1966. Thus, on a shortened list of hosts, Argentina appears for the second time, starting the alphabetical cycle again. The cost of consultative and special meetings is high and is borne entirely by the host country, which must provide a temporary secretariat and simultaneous translation in English, French, Spanish, and Russian. The unequal burden is increasingly resented by the majority, but the Soviet Union has resisted all proposals for a more equitable sharing of the costs of meetings.

At the early meetings of the consultative parties, one of the most controversial issues was Australia's desire to have a secretariat established at Canberra. The United States was opposed to the measure on the grounds that it would involve unnecessary expense. But two other reasons were also given privately: "We felt any Secretariat created would require Soviet representatives"; and "We also want to avoid getting Antarctic Treaty problems mixed up with the United Nations and its sub-bodies. . . ."[53] The recommendation was killed without the United States having to speak against it, largely because of the eloquence of the French delegate on the evils of bureaucracy. After more than two decades, however, the absence of a secretariat becomes increasingly awkward (and not only for scholars); the rotation of personnel through foreign offices causes an absence of continuity and ensures that preparation for each consultative meeting becomes an on-the-job training program. It may be time to reconsider the need for some central organization, even if its function is only archival.

Other matters causing friction at the early meetings were the question of jurisdiction, discussion of which was blocked by Argentina and Chile, and the relationship of the treaty powers to the Scientific Committee on Antarctic Research. The awkward wording of Recommendation I-4 is due to the difference of opinion among those who wanted to make SCAR an official scientific body serving the treaty members, those who wanted to reduce dependence on SCAR, and those who wanted to maintain

SCAR as an independent, nongovernmental body responsive to requests for study and information.[54] The last concept of SCAR is the one that has prevailed, although obviously different nations are in a position to exert different degrees of control over their nationals serving in SCAR.

By far the largest number of recommendations, as well as those of greatest substance, have dealt with protection of the Antarctic environment and conservation of living resources. The treaty members have adopted Agreed Measures for the Conservation of Antarctic Fauna and Flora and designated seventeen Specially Protected Areas and nine Sites of Special Scientific Interest where access is limited.[55] They have taken the first steps to regulate tourism and have adopted a sealing convention, although strictly speaking this was not negotiated within the treaty structure.[56] After considering "man's impact on the Antarctic environment" at several meetings, they adopted a Code of Conduct for Antarctic Expeditions and Station Activities. The code recommends procedures for waste disposal and urges that environmental impact statements be prepared for major Antarctic projects.

The Agreed Measures for the Conservation of Antarctic Fauna and Flora were adopted at the Brussels meeting in 1964. They provide that animals and plants shall be taken from the Antarctic only by permit and as necessary for scientific research and education; offer special protection for certain species and certain areas; designate activities that are harmful to birds or seals; obligate governments to do everything possible to reduce pollution of coastal waters; and prohibit the introduction of animals or plants not indigenous to the Antarctic, except under license.

The Agreed Measures are indeed so sweeping and place such severe constraints on the citizens of democracies that most of the participating nations had to enact special legislation to bring themselves into legal compliance. The United States, while effectually complying with the Agreed Measures, dawdled for fourteen years before the Antarctic Conservation Act of 1978 was adopted.[57] Although the law has not been challenged, some believe it is unconstitutional. The most severe operative paragraph reads as follows:

> It is unlawful for any United States citizen, unless authorized by regulations prescribed under this Act or a permit issued under section 5—

(A) to take within Antarctica any native mammal or native bird,

(B) to collect within any specially protected area any native plant,

(C) to introduce into Antarctica any animal or plant that is not indigenous to Antarctica,

(D) to enter any specially protected area or site of special scientific interest, or

(E) to discharge, or otherwise to dispose of, any pollutant within Antarctica.[58]

For those countries that claimed sovereignty in Antarctica, compliance was not especially difficult; legal regimes already existed. For others, it was politically or constitutionally awkward to place constraints on their citizens beyond national borders in a realm deemed to belong to no one. Japan in particular, operating under an American-drafted constitution, had constitutional difficulties in enforcing the provisions of the Agreed Measures on persons other than its civil servants. For Belgium, too, the Agreed Measures presented constitutional problems.

The political effort involved in achieving compliance with the Agreed Measures illustrates as well as anything the seriousness with which the consultative members take their obligation to protect the Antarctic environment. Of the more than thirty recommendations dealing with conservation and the environment, one in particular deserves to be quoted. Recommendation VIII-13, adopted at Oslo in 1975, reads in part:

> In exercising their responsibility for the wise use and protection of the Antarctic environment, [the member governments] shall have regard to the following:
>
> (a) that in considering measures for the wise use and protection of the Antarctic environment they shall act in accordance with their responsibility for ensuring that such measures are consistent with the interests of all mankind;
>
> (b) that no act or activity having an inherent tendency to modify the environment over wide areas within the Antarctic Treaty Area should be undertaken unless appropriate steps have been taken to foresee the probable modifications and to exercise appropriate controls with respect to the harmful environmental effects such uses of the Antarctic Treaty Area may have;
>
> (c) that in co-operation with SCAR and other relevant agencies they continue, within the capabilities of their Antarctic scientific

programmes, to monitor changes in the environment, irrespective of their cause, and to exercise their responsibility for informing the world community of any significant changes caused by man's activities outside the Antarctic Treaty Area; . . .

Recommendation IX-5, adopted in London only two years later, took essentially the same ideas and cast them in the form of a declaration.

Thus, in word certainly, and in deed generally, the treaty powers have behaved responsibly and fulfilled their obligation to use Antarctica exclusively for peaceful purposes, to ensure freedom of scientific investigation, and to protect the Antarctic environment "in the interest of all mankind." The question is whether these admirable objectives will survive the discovery of exploitable resources.

As the treaty system enters a more difficult phase involving decisions on resource management and sharing of benefits, a few minor changes in the treaty and its operation would be advantageous. These would strengthen the consultative parties' position vis-à-vis the rest of the world as well as in their own internal relationships.

For example, the principle that authorized scientists and official observers, wherever they may be in Antarctica, are subject only to the jurisdiction of their own government (Article VIII of the treaty) must be extended to all. That is, no one should be subject to the laws of another nation simply because he is in a part of Antarctica over which sovereignty is claimed. This has already been recognized by Britain, a claimant state that incorporated the concept in its Antarctic Treaty Act of 1967.[59] On this issue, the United States has been immobilized by the inability of Congress to pass a new criminal code that has been pending for years. But in principle, there appears to be no obstacle to fourteen-nation agreement on this commonsense measure. And it is significant that "questions relating to the exercise of jurisdiction in Antarctica" are specifically mentioned in Article IX of the treaty as one of the topics most appropriate for consideration and the formulation of recommendations. That a serious crisis has not arisen over this issue of jurisdiction may be due more to good luck than to good management. It constitutes a hazard that the parties should not be exposed to.

The treaty system should be practiced with less secrecy and less vulnerability to the charge of operating an exclusive club. Surprise and disappointment have been expressed by some of the original signers of the Antarctic Treaty that so few countries have acceded to the treaty. Small wonder. They have virtually no incentive; they get nothing in return. It has been suggested that nations acceding to the treaty are "fully entitled to receive automatically all the information which Consultative Parties exchange annually."[60] Whether this would be an adequate incentive for other states to join is difficult to judge. Ambassador Keith Brennan of Australia, who takes a very tough position on most issues involving the treaty, believes that acceding nations should be invited to attend the consultative meetings as observers.[61] If activities in Antarctica are to be controlled and the environment protected, wider acceptance of Antarctic Treaty obligations becomes increasingly important. Every effort should be made to gain additional accessions, even if some cost is involved.

Further, while continuing to conduct their deliberations behind closed doors, the consultative parties should permit wider circulation of documentary material. Reports of meetings might well be more detailed. There has been some progress in this direction, but it has been excessively slow. Where publicity would adversely affect negotiations, confidentiality must be maintained. But greater openness wherever possible would reduce the suspicion that secrecy generates. In the years ahead, the treaty powers will need, if not allies, at least neutrals who will allow the consultative parties to continue in their self-elected role.

Both the "public availability of documents" and "matters relating to the appointment of observers" were on the agenda of the Eleventh Consultative Meeting in mid-1981. Although they were debated at great length, no consensus was reached, and therefore no recommendation was forthcoming. Among the consultative members, there is a sense of unease about operating a closed system, but some felt it might be dangerous to involve the acceding nations before 1991, the date of the optional treaty review. Despite efforts of the United States to permit greater openness, the Soviet Union, Chile, and Argentina are opposed. Under the present rules, member nations are not even allowed to circulate publicly such working papers that they themselves have prepared. This is an unconscionable restraint on democratic government and totally unwarranted by the nature of the topics under consideration.

These matters qualify the implicit claim of the consultative parties to have earned the rights they assume on the basis of responsible performance over two decades.

The treaty and the system that has evolved from it are unquestionably notable achievements. Oscar Pinochet de la Barra, the uncompromising articulator of Chile's territorial sovereignty in the 1950s, said in 1980 that "the Antarctic Treaty is synonymous with peace and international common sense."[62] In the judgment of an American law scholar:

> In the two decades since the Antarctic Treaty was concluded, the treaty regime has been remarkably successful. . . . Moreover, the parties, through their actions under the treaty during this period, have created a distinctive legal and political regime, more substantive and far-reaching than the text of the treaty itself might suggest. The treaty framework has now been supplemented by established ways of working together, a broad network of informal arrangements and cooperative practices . . . and the gradual emergence among the parties of a sense of commitment to and pride in the unique system they have created.[63]

How astonishing that a group of countries with so much fear, antagonism, and resentment among them can have managed so well. Clearly, the treaty is seen to serve their individual interests more effectively than any conceivable alternative and therefore they feel it must be preserved even at the cost of difficult compromises. The rising expectation of resources is, of course, putting the treaty system under more severe internal stress than ever before. And today, everything the consultative parties do is watched with far greater attention by other countries concerned that they not be left out if there are riches to be had.

To establish the rules under which resource exploitation might proceed, the process of recommendation and approval under the treaty system was not adequate. New agreements and new instrumentalities were needed to compensate for the limitations of the treaty and to recognize that the global community had rights in the Southern Ocean. The international context in which this difficult task was undertaken is the subject of the next chapter.

VI

Outside Interests

The way to obtain the acceptance of the community of nations is not through a sort of self-coronation.

—Alvaro de Soto of Peru

ANTARCTICA AND THE UNITED NATIONS

The United Nations was only two years old when the suggestion was made in the Trusteeship Council that polar regimes be created under U.N. aegis.[1] At that time, all the world—even Western governments—loved the United Nations, and the proposal as applied to the Antarctic might have taken hold if it had not been linked with the North Polar region, where the Eastern and Western blocs were already glaring fearfully at each other. Earlier in 1947, *The New York Times* had come out in favor of U.N. trusteeship, saying that Antarctica should "be held in trust for the peoples of all the world."[2] The same year, the Commission to Study the Organization of the Peace, a continuing body formed by Americans after World War I, recommended "an international regime for the Antarctic continent . . . with direct administration by the United Nations."[3] In late 1948, just weeks after the United States had called for a conference of interested parties, Dr. Julian Huxley urged upon UNESCO the organization of an International Antarctic Research Institute, financed and controlled by the United

Nations.[4] The next year, Edward Shackleton, son of the famous explorer, a member of Parliament, and later a Lord, argued that "there is no problem in the world which the United Nations is better suited to handle."[5] The argument that the trusteeship system was designed to protect people, not penguins, he contended, "is an academic quibble."[6]

Meanwhile, the Tenth Report of the Commission to Study the Organization of the Peace appeared (1957), reiterating in greater detail its argument for the internationalization of Antarctica under the United Nations.[7] Describing the region as "a strategic center from which air and naval fleets may control vital seaways," the report averred that "the world does not need another strategic area to be struggled for, and such a struggle between the United States and the Soviet Union would appear to be inevitable if the continent is to be divided up by occupying powers as Africa once was."[8] After describing its concept of a U.N. administration, the report concluded: "Effective occupation in terms of international law has not yet taken place. Thus Antarctica is a continent in search of a sovereign. The United Nations ought to establish its sovereignty there."[9]

Of the nations that would soon negotiate the Antarctic Treaty, only one was prepared for internationalization under the United Nations. In January 1956, Prime Minister Walter Nash of New Zealand made the first of his proposals for a U.N. trusteeship and the establishment of Antarctica as a "world territory" under the control of the United Nations.[10] In one form or another, this suggestion was repeated frequently, notably at the Washington Conference in 1959,[11] and for the last time at the Seventh Consultative Meeting in Wellington in 1972. The idea has never received any official support from other treaty powers.

Only a month after Nash initially proposed U.N. trusteeship, the United Nations was, for the first time, requested to take up the issue of Antarctica. Arthur S. Lall, permanent representative of India, asked that "The Question of Antarctica" be inscribed on the agenda of the Eleventh General Assembly.[12] The proposal met considerable opposition, led by Argentina and Chile, and was withdrawn. In July 1958, Ambassador Lall tried again, attaching an Explanatory Memorandum that read in part:

[Antarctica's] mineral wealth . . . is believed to be considerable and its coastal waters contain important food resources. With the development of rapid communications, the area is coming to have practical significance to the welfare and progress of all nations. . . .

In view of the growing interest in and knowledge about the area, and in view of the fact that many countries including India are particularly interested in the meteorological aspects and implications of all that happens in Antarctica, it would be appropriate and timely now for all nations to agree and affirm that the area will be utilized entirely for peaceful purposes and for the welfare of the whole world.[13]

Then he added a point not mentioned two years earlier: "The Government of India believes that this limited purpose can be achieved without any nation renouncing such rights as it may claim in Antarctica, or claims of sovereignty or other rights consistent with the Charter."[14] Whether or not this made his proposal more palatable to the claimant states, the ambassador's timing was bad; preparatory meetings for the Antarctic Treaty Conference were already under way, and again India was persuaded to withdraw its request. Although India has not since acceded to the treaty nor made any official effort to involve the Third World in Antarctic affairs, the subject has been of continuing interest to Indian scholars. One, writing soon after the treaty was negotiated, praised the agreement, but concluded that India and other developing countries will ultimately want "full internationalization of Antarctica."[15] Another, writing more recently, found "glaring drawbacks" in the treaty, hoped that the resources of Antarctica would someday "boost the United Nations' finances," and concluded that the Antarctic "should be controlled by the United Nations in conformity with the wider community expectations."[16]

If Antarctica were to be internationalized under the United Nations, some argued, the nations capable of conducting valuable scientific research there would lose interest. To get around this and other objections of the claimant states, it was proposed that transfer of authority to the United Nations might be gradual. Its principal function would be to ensure orderliness in the development of Antarctica. Initially the United Nations would serve as a Land Registry Office, leasing development rights and offering first refusal to claimant states.[17] This idea, too, was preempted by the Washington Conference, then in the preparatory stage.

In recent times, the subject of Antarctica has been raised in at least four bodies of the United Nations. In January 1971, the Committee on Natural Resources of the Economic and Social Council was advised by the secretary-general that "clearly the era of systematic exploration" for Antarctic resources had arrived. Bearing in mind the committee's "own specific mission concerning the preparation of summaries and evaluations of the World's natural resources," U Thant said that all its work "would be incomplete and unrealistic if any significant portion of the globe went unreported and excluded."[18] Although the secretary-general was somewhat premature, his point was both well taken and extremely unattractive to the treaty powers. The idea appears to have died on the spot and never to have been revived in that committee.[19]

In 1975, the United Nations Environmental Program (UNEP) proposed to involve itself in the protection of the Antarctic environment and the establishment of ecologically sound guidelines for exploration and exploitation of resources. The treaty powers succeeded in blocking any consideration of the proposal by the Governing Council.[20] This seemed entirely warranted since the treaty powers have been particularly conscientious in this regard, and UNEP already had on its agenda rather more than it could manage.

In contrast, it seems appropriate that the prospects for krill be discussed in FAO's Committee on Fisheries. Starting in 1974, the subject arose quite regularly, and there were differences of opinion as to how active FAO should be in research in the Southern Ocean and in representing the interests of nontreaty members. Guinea was perhaps the most aggressive proponent of the idea that the resources of the Southern Ocean should contribute to the New International Economic Order, but no one offered any specific suggestion as to how this could be accomplished.[21]

The subject of Antarctica was broached in the General Assembly in 1975 by the late Shirley Amerasinghe of Sri Lanka, who was then president of the Law of the Sea Conference:

> There are still areas of this planet [he said] where opportunities remain for constructive and peaceful cooperation on the part of the international community for the common good of all rather than the benefit of a few. Such an area is the Antarctic continent. . . . There can be no doubt that there are vast possibilities for a new initiative

that would redound to the benefit of all mankind. Antarctica is an area where the now widely accepted ideas and concepts relating to international economic cooperation, with their special stress on the principle of equitable sharing of the world's resources, can find ample scope for application, given the cooperation and goodwill of those who have so far been active in this area. . . . The mention of this subject will not, I hope, create a flutter in any dovecotes.[22]

The ambassador must have known his statement would create a substantial flutter, for Amerasinghe was a statesman of considerable stature and influence who was much respected for his skill in managing the Law of the Sea Conference and who became President of the General Assembly the following year. His remarks could easily be interpreted as the start of a systematic campaign by the Group of 77 (the developing countries) to obtain a voice in Antarctic affairs. That this did not prove to be the case was primarily due to the adamant stand of Argentina and Chile, but also Ambassador Amerasinghe felt increasingly constrained from speaking out, and no one of comparable stature emerged to take his place.[23]

Strangely, all subsequent public statements in a similar vein by representatives of Third World countries have been under the auspices of the London-based International Institute for Environment and Development (IIED) and its affiliate, Earthscan, which provides material on environment/development issues for the press and radio. In conjunction with the Ninth and Tenth Consultative Meetings, Earthscan held press conferences providing platforms for Third World spokesmen who had not otherwise been heard from. In 1977, the principal speaker was another Sri Lankan, Christopher Pinto, then ambassador to the Federal Republic of Germany. He said in part:

> All states and international organizations with relevant responsibilities should cooperate in measures to ensure that . . . exploration, exploitation and conservation of the resources . . . are carried out in such a manner as to reflect adequately the undoubted and continuing interest of the international community in such areas and [that] those resources will be made subject to a regime of rational management and utilization to secure optimum benefits for mankind as a whole and, in particular, for the developing countries, in accordance

with appropriate global international arrangements, and within the framework of the new international economic order.[24]

In 1979, the principal performer was Alvaro de Soto, a Peruvian who became a principal spokesman for the Group of 77 at the Law of the Sea Conference. In the course of his remarks, he said:

> The silence of the [international] community regarding [the Antarctic] Treaty can hardly be understood as a form of acquiescence. Nor is it possible to say that there is any statute of limitation in respect of the options open to the rest of mankind.
>
>   . . . I feel that although the participation of the international community as a whole in the negotiation of a question of global interest presents difficulties of a methodological and procedural character which sometimes seem gargantuan, on the other hand the results obtained from those negotiations must necessarily produce far more solid results, and more acceptable to a truly universal community.
>
>   . . . I am under the impression that a comprehensive political debate on the question of Antarctica is inevitable and that it may well be desirable. . . . I find it surprising that some sort of démarche, whether individual or collective, is not yet forthcoming from the African continent with respect to Antarctica. I should not be surprised if, when this happens, Antarctica becomes a glaring banner similar to Namibia or Zimbabwe, capable of rallying the Continent around it, *en bloc*. It is hard to imagine individual African countries seeking Consultative Status in the Treaty subject to the veto of South Africa. And the second class citizenship of non-consultative partyhood may easily smack of an international version of apartheid.[25]

It is entirely consistent with the objectives of the International Institute for Environment and Development to encourage and publicize such viewpoints.[26] Without its efforts, there would have been in recent years an almost eerie silence on the subject, imposed by the unspoken understanding that if Antarctica were introduced in the Law of the Sea negotiations, the conference would collapse. But no one expects this appearance of indifference to last beyond the conclusion of a Law of the Sea Convention. However, one may hope—perhaps fruitlessly—that arguments comparing uninhabited Antarctica with southern Africa and suggesting the treaty powers are practicing apartheid will be replaced with arguments of greater logic and more compelling substance. There are many to be made.

Ambassador Pinto, who was later one of the principal candidates to succeed Amerasinghe as president of the Law of the Sea Conference, subsequently spelled out his ideas for the internationalization of Antarctica in a scholarly article.[27] He wrote that "the Antarctic is ripe for conflict" and proposed that the matter be brought before the United Nations "for a comprehensive study of the economic potential of Antarctica."[28] The General Assembly should establish a committee to "make recommendations . . . on how best to reconcile the interests of the world community with the interests of individual countries." The committee would consist of "the Antarctic Treaty parties, together with fifteen other states," thereby ensuring that the experienced nations would be outvoted. The idea is not without merit, but the rationale offered for other nations being involved in the administration of Antarctica shows how far certain fixations at the Law of the Sea Conference are likely to be projected into the Antarctic. Nonsignatory states, Pinto wrote, "will want to ensure that their own specific interests are protected. For example, oil exporting countries will be particularly concerned with ensuring that the oil resources of Antarctica are rationally exploited."[29] OPEC need not fear; Antarctica will not produce a flood of cheap oil. Nontreaty powers can surely marshal better arguments than this.[30]

Finally, Pinto wrote that, if his approach to the Antarctic problem were followed, "this remote region could become the first area to witness the abandonment of international rivalries, the celebration of interdependence, and the fulfillment of the aims of the Charter of the United Nations."[31] The treaty parties, of course, feel that they have already achieved precisely this, and that expanding the decision-making body to include nations without demonstrated interest or experience would ignite new rivalries and reenact old failures of the United Nations.

By 1981, Sri Lanka had lost its taste for this fray and only Peru, which has periodically threatened to assert a claim in Antarctica, was aggressively seeking to involve the Group of 77 in Antarctica.

THE LAW OF THE SEA

The Antarctic Treaty powers, in their efforts to establish ground rules for the development of marine and mineral resources, have been influenced in many ways by the United Nations Conference on the Law of the Sea and the decisions hammered out there after years of negotiation. The treaty powers have been strengthened in their conviction that they want no part of the United Nations and the difficulties of conducting negotiations among more than 150 nations.[32] They have also been looking over their shoulders, hoping to complete their own resource arrangements before a Law of the Sea Treaty is adopted. They feared that once the LOS Conference came to an end a battalion of international lawyers would have nothing better to occupy them than to challenge the exclusive rights of the Antarctic Treaty powers. And if national sovereignties have not been convincingly established in Antarctica after three-quarters of a century, why should it not too be "the common heritage of mankind," like the floor of the sea or the moon or space? Or put another way, if the United States and other nonclaimant nations support a seabed authority for areas of the seabed outside national jurisdiction, and if they assert that no national jurisdiction exists in Antarctica, it would seem to justify the international seabed authority's right to claim responsibility for Antarctic resources from the shoreline outward.[33] None of the consultative parties to the treaty would look kindly on such an initiative.

But more immediately, the Antarctic Treaty powers have been profoundly influenced by the consensus reached early in the Law of the Sea negotiations that coastal states should be the beneficiary of the marine and mineral resources up to 200 miles from shore— the so-called exclusive economic zone (EEZ).[34] This was a profound change from what was contemplated a decade ago, when planning started on the Third Law of the Sea Conference. A U.S. draft presented to the United Nations Seabed Committee in 1970 proposed that the limit of national jurisdiction be drawn where the water depth reached 200 meters; beyond that, to the limit of the continental margin, would be a trusteeship zone administered by the coastal state, but with revenues shared with the international community.[35] The United Kingdom, Canada, and others endorsed the proposal.[36] But on the whole, little enthusiasm for the idea was shown, and after the oil crisis of 1973, the United States pushed its revenue-sharing suggestion no further.[37] Under the dominance of Third World coastal states, the so-called Group of 77 agreed to EEZs without revenue sharing in the 200-mile zone, but with certain limited rights for landlocked and other geographically disadvantaged states.[38] Also coastal states that do not fish their waters up to the "maximum sustainable yield" are obligated to license others to do so.[39] But an even more drastic reduction in the common heritage was effected by the decision to grant coastal states exclusive jurisdiction beyond the 200-mile EEZ in some instances. More than forty nations whose continental margins extend beyond 200 miles will have mineral rights in the seabed up to 350 miles. However, a portion of whatever is extracted from this region is to be paid in kind to the international community for distribution to the poorest nations—up to a maximum of 7 percent.[40]

The decision to create EEZs of 200 miles or more means that coastal states control 99 percent of the fish in the sea and virtually all of the offshore oil and gas.[41] Although this expansion of the economic zone was pushed by the less-developed nations, primarily those of Latin America, on balance the developed nations were the biggest gainers. If all U.S. territories, including Micronesia, are added in, the largest single beneficiary is the United States.[42]

From the standpoint of the Antarctic Treaty powers, the first consequence of the anticipated decision to form EEZs was to heighten interest in the Southern Ocean. Without waiting for completion of a treaty, a majority of coastal nations—including the United States—declared exclusive fishing rights off their shores, generally to a distance of 200 miles. As a result, traditionally long-distance fishing nations such as the Soviet Union and Japan were excluded from waters they had long exploited. Seeking alternative hunting grounds, they and others turned with new interest to the Southern Ocean, thus posing a potential threat to the marine ecosystem. The need for a regime to protect Antarctic marine living resources became more apparent.

The second consequence of the Law of the Sea Conference was to add a further and more dangerous dimension to the territorial claims issue in Antarctica. If coastal states were to be granted exclusive economic zones 200 miles off their shores, then the claimant states in Antarctica must claim their EEZs or forfeit their credibility. On the other hand, if no effective sovereignty had been established on land, then no EEZ could be claimed. In any case, would not staking out an EEZ constitute an enlargement of an existing claim—an act prohibited by the Antarctic Treaty? Chile declared its jurisdiction to 200 miles in 1947; hence, it could assert that an EEZ was part of its claim when the treaty was adopted.[43] Argentina laid claim to a 200-mile zone after the Antarctic Treaty was signed but before the Third Law of the Sea Conference began. Australia and New Zealand approached the problem in different ways. In 1979, Australia simply announced that its 200-mile zone included the Australian Antarctic Territory but that for the present the Fisheries Act would not be applied there.[44] New Zealand passed a Territorial Sea and Exclusive Economic Zone Act, empowering the governor-general to apply its provisions to the Ross Dependency at his pleasure.[45] Thus, both countries asserted their right to an EEZ off their Antarctic claims, and both refrained from exercising it.

In the long run, the most important consequence of the Law of the Sea Conference—and treaty—with respect to the Antarctic may be psychological. It puts further pressure on the treaty powers to deal with resource issues with "the interest of all mankind" in mind. Revenue sharing may now be enough; if indeed exploitable minerals do exist in Antarctica, the Group of 77 will almost surely demand a voice in their management and distribution. An Antarctic Treaty Working Group on the minerals regime reported laconically in 1979, "representatives were mindful of developments likely to result from the Third United Nations Conference on the Law of the Sea."[46]

Another link between the Law of the Sea Convention and Antarctica has quite possibly been forged unwittingly by the Reagan administration. Unless the United States reconsiders its vote in opposition to the convention, the resentment of the Third World may focus on the Antarctic on the defensible grounds that its resources, like those of the seabed, should be the common heritage of mankind. This perception may be inevitable, but the year's delay in completing the LOS Convention while Washington decided what its policy should be, the apparent inflexibility of the United States on seabed issues, and U.S. refusal to adopt the convention by consensus have angered the Group of 77. Concerted refusal to accept the legitimacy of the Antarctic Treaty system, the questioning of every premise on which the treaty powers have been acting, would be troublesome at best and possibly destructive. A lingering fear among the consultative parties is that, when and if the Antarctic Treaty is opened for review in 1991, every nation in the Third World will show up, demanding a seat. Clearly, the continued viability of the treaty system and its successful adaptation to new circumstances require at least the toleration of the developing countries.[47]

THE MOON/SPACE ANALOGY

Whatever the shortcomings of the Antarctic Treaty, its adoption was almost universally hailed as an important precedent —especially for outer space, which was then emerging as a realm of immense interest and concern. "The signing on Tuesday of a twelve-nation treaty on Antarctica," Walter Sullivan wrote in *The New York Times*, "has given new courage to those seeking agreement on the peaceful exploration of outer space."[48] By 1967, a treaty on outer space had been successfully negotiated in the United Nations.[49] In three particulars, it followed the Antarctic Treaty: (1) it ensured the nonmilitarization of outer space, "including the moon and other celestial bodies" (a phrase that recurs in almost every article) and prohibited weapons testing in space; (2) it called for the exchange of information and the free availability of scientific knowledge; and (3) it provided for inspection by making "all stations, installations, equipment and space vehicles . . . open to representatives of other States . . ." (Article XII).

But the differences were at least as interesting as the similarities. Article I of the Outer Space Treaty reads in part: "The exploration and use of outer space, including the moon and other celestial bodies, shall be carried out for the benefit and in the interest of all countries, irrespective of their degree of economic or scientific development, and shall be the province of all mankind." Article II spells out the point further: "Outer space, including the moon and other celestial bodies, is not subject to national appropriation by claim of sovereignty, by means of use or occupation, or by any other means."

In December 1979, the U.N. General Assembly adopted without

a dissenting vote a more detailed convention on outer space known as the Moon Treaty.[50] The United States played a leading role in the drafting, which took seven years. Although adding little of substance to the earlier treaty, which had been swiftly ratified by the United States, the Moon Treaty was not signed by President Carter nor sent to the Senate for its consent. With the change in administration and given the political complexion of the new Senate at the start of 1981, the Moon Treaty lost all hope of ratification. The principal sticking point is in Article XI: "The moon and its natural resources are the common heritage of mankind." It was Soviet objection to this provision that stalled treaty negotiations for three years. But is there any substantive difference between this sentence and those quoted above from the Outer Space Treaty of 1967? If national appropriation is prohibited, then resources of the moon or other celestial bodies must belong to all. Yet so effective has been the lobbying against the Moon Treaty that the majority and minority leaders of the Senate Foreign Relations Committee were induced in late 1979 to cast aspersions on a policy that the Department of State had been pursuing diligently since 1969 in the Law of the Sea Conference and since 1972 in negotiating the Moon Treaty.[51]

The reason the Moon Treaty is relevant here is simply that analogies between outer space and Antarctica have been drawn since the first Earth satellite was placed in orbit in 1957.[52] The manner in which the Moon Treaty has been presented and misrepresented by opponents in the United States has created a climate in which it will be very difficult to show flexibility regarding the control of resources in what, for lack of a better term, are called "nonstate areas." Furthermore, the Moon Treaty has been so willfully entangled and confused with the Law of the Sea Treaty that both may fail to achieve the universality they require for success. And finally, if these conventions, so laboriously negotiated over so many years, are not ratified by the United States, the political climate surrounding Antarctica will surely sour. However ineffectually, the Third World will more aggressively seek to restrict or eliminate the special privileges of the treaty powers in Antarctica.

In the letter cited above, Senators Church and Javits wrote the secretary of state:

We remain skeptical of further efforts to extend the concept of the
common heritage when the understanding of this principle on the
part of many countries of the world is so contrary to our own
interests. In this regard, suggestions by some participants in the
[Law of the Sea] negotiations that Antarctica also be declared the
common heritage of mankind are indications of the general trend we
are confronting in international forums.

Orchestrating the opposition to the Moon Treaty was Leigh S.
Ratiner, described in *Science* as "a high-powered Washington
lobbyist."[53] Some years ago, Ratiner represented the United States
on the key seabed committee at the Law of the Sea Conference. He
resigned to take a job with Kennecott Copper, perhaps the most
active of all U.S. corporations lobbying for Law of the Sea provisions more favorable to the American mining industry. In late
1981, Ratiner was retained by the State Department as a consultant
who, having charged the government a controversial hundred-
thousand-dollar fee, was hired to be deputy chairman of the U.S.
delegation to the March/April 1982 session of the Law of the Sea
Conference.

Before his second incarnation in the Department of State, Ratiner
was retained by the L-5 Society, the extraordinary alliance of scientists, industrialists, and idealistic young people who hope to
build a habitat in space. "The L is for libration, a point at which
the gravitational pulls of Earth, moon and sun are equalized. L-5
is the fifth libration point, where the society would park a space
platform to manufacture all sorts of handy articles out of sunlight
and moon dust. . . ."[54]

In language quite similar to that in the Antarctic Treaty, the
Moon Treaty permits each state to conduct its own inspection to
ensure compliance with the convention. This provision, which was
considered one of the most admirable features of the Antarctic
Treaty, has been interpreted by opponents of the Moon Treaty as
an invasion of privacy. "It is a major step in eliminating the civil
liberties for those who go into space," says Carolyn Henson,
president and co-founder of L-5. "No warrants are needed. Considering what our own police sometimes do, I doubt a KGB search
would leave any air in a habitat."[55]

The opponents of the Moon Treaty believe that it would doom
free enterprise in space and delay indefinitely the exploitation of its

resources. Although L-5 has fewer than four thousand members, it has powerful friends. A large Connecticut-based conglomerate, United Technologies, ran ads in a number of newspapers, saying that

> through the Moon Treaty, Third World Nations supported by the Soviet Union are seeking to exploit the U.N. to create a new order in which free enterprises of the industrialized West would be subordinated to the wishes of so-called non-aligned nations, guided by the Eastern bloc. The basic goal is redistribution of the world's wealth.[56]

It is of some interest that the president of United Technologies at that time was Alexander Haig, secretary of state under the Reagan administration.[57]

Opponents of the Moon Treaty are correct in one respect: A universally accepted definition of "the common heritage of mankind" is lacking. In U.S. government parlance, the term is virtually synonymous with "the commons"—defined as

> those areas beyond the jurisdiction of any state which are available for the use of all. . . . These commons are: first, the oceans, including the bottom of the oceans, that is the seabeds, beyond the limit of national jurisdiction; second, outer space, above the limits of national jurisdiction (wherever that may be); and third, Antarctica, although one must note that some states have still preserved their territorial claims to parts of Antarctica under the Antarctic Treaty regime. . . .

The quotation is from a paper prepared by the then deputy head of the U.S. delegation to the Law of the Sea Conference, George H. Aldrich, at the request of Senator Adlai Stevenson.[58] Note especially that the seabeds beyond national jurisdiction, which by U.N. consensus are declared "the common heritage of mankind," are here included in "the commons." According to Ambassador Aldrich, if the mining companies had been willing to take nodules as one harvests fish, there would have been no need for prolonged seabed negotiations in the Law of the Sea Conference. But exclusive right to sectors of the seabed, which the companies felt were necessary, could be conferred only by international agreement.[59] This is an essential point that many conservative critics of the draft Law of the Sea Convention fail to comprehend.[60] It is precisely the mining companies that need the treaty; they alone cannot, they believe, get along without it if they are going to mine the sea floor. But so determinedly did they seek to have their cake and eat it that they later had to explain to a confused Congress and administration why the treaty should not be scuttled entirely.[61]

Most nations of the world, certainly the Group of 77, place a very different interpretation on "the common heritage of mankind." To them, it is not a commons where resources are up for grabs by the most technologically advanced, but an area where all share equally or in proportion to need. Aldrich does concede that "the use of these areas should normally be preceded by good faith negotiations aimed at creating an agreed legal regime prior to any unilateral action," but this obligation cannot be used to impose a moratorium on resource exploitation.[62] The difference in perception of what "the common heritage" means will become increasingly troublesome when and if Antarctic resources become significant.[63]

The high seas of the Southern Ocean are an undoubted commons. It is of great concern to many that unless exceptional measures are taken, the beneficiaries of its presumed riches will be the few and the advantaged. How the marine living resources surrounding Antarctica might be shared and used to improve nutrition where it is poorest may be questions without answers. But they are being asked by, among others, the same people who are concerned with environment and conservation.

THE ROLE OF THE ENVIRONMENTALISTS

A substantial difference in perspective among the treaty powers is created by the varying degrees of influence exerted on their governments by environmentalists/conservationists. Where there is no strong tradition of nongovernmental organizations, there is incomprehension that the U.S. and British governments, especially, can be so responsive to them. While Australia, New Zealand, Norway, and France also have environmental lobbies with varying degrees of influence on government, only the United States includes leaders of private conservation organizations on its delegation to meetings of consultative parties to the Antarctic Treaty.

The conservationists learned about Antarctica through their

interest in whales, and their concern for the Antarctic ecosystem is proportional to their passionate concern for these threatened and endangered species. Significant numbers of conservationists have made themselves expert and have contributed importantly to policy. The degree of their influence is partly attributable to the absence of any countervailing force: In the United States especially, the public has been unaware of the Antarctic for at least two decades, and there are as yet no organized commercial interests.

While showing proper respect for conservationists in public, officials involved in Antarctic affairs in the United States and Britain particularly are in a state of more or less perpetual irritation with the environmentalists for what is often seen as their demand for absolutes, their unwillingness or inability to comprehend the reality of international politics, and the processes of negotiation among sovereign states. And inevitably, for every well-informed conservationist there are ten whose ignorance can confound issues. Also inevitably, the singlemindedness of conservationists, even when they are knowledgeable, is bound to grate on those who must reconcile varied domestic and foreign interests.

An environmental and public-interest lawyer who has had an unequaled opportunity to observe the Antarctic Treaty system in action has proposed seven requirements for "a legal and equitable solution" of the Antarctic problem, knowing full well that probably all, certainly a majority, are unacceptable to the treaty powers.[64] These conditions include renunciation of all territorial claims, present or future; all deliberations to be conducted in public (a dubious benefit); and the Southern Ocean and the continent of Antarctica to be declared a common heritage area. This is not the first time that, by asking for everything, environmentalists have obtained less than they could have.

A high official in the British Foreign Office complained that he spent a good part of the summer of 1980 replying to letters demanding that Her Majesty's Government refuse to ratify the Living Marine Resources Convention[65] because it was not strong enough. He believed that the write-in campaign was organized and originated in the United States. He pointed out that certain provisions of the convention to which conservationists objected could have been avoided if they had not insisted on perfection at earlier negotiating sessions.

A pamphlet published by the Friends of the Earth in Sydney

concluded that Australia should aim for the dissolution of the
Antarctic Treaty and for the internationalization of the Antarctic,

> with control of it vested in the U.N. as a part of the common heritage
> of mankind. However, instead of the common heritage being seen as
> yet another area for exploitation, it should be preserved as a natural
> wilderness, thereby excluding the exploitation of the Antarctic for its
> living and non-living resources, as well as excluding the Antarctic's
> development as a tourist attraction.[66]

It was not made clear how these unrelated political and conservation objectives were to be reconciled, or why designation of
Antarctica as a permanent wilderness would be more easily
achieved with 150 nations to be persuaded rather than 14.

A ranking official in the National Science Foundation, asked
whether economics was subverting science in Antarctica, replied
that the principal threat came not from those who want to discover
resources but from those who do not. "Some environmentalists,"
he said with feeling, "don't want us to exhale in Antarctica." It is
true that many environmentalists fear scientists will discover
resources, which then inevitably will be exploited; they would like
to restrict science to activities that cannot possibly lead to economic
development. At least in the Carter administration, this attitude
was found at high levels within the U.S. government as well as
among its critics.

Ideally, what most conservationists want is the establishment of
Antarctica as a world park in perpetuity. The idea was first given
concrete form in 1972 at the Second World Conference on National
Parks, where a resolution to this effect was adopted without
objection.[67] The proposal was submitted to the consultative treaty
powers by New Zealand at the 1972 meeting in Wellington, but was
not warmly received.[68] The idea was taken up and promoted by the
executive director of the United Nations Environment Program,
Maurice Strong, speaking at the Pacific Science Congress in Van-
couver. Strong said, "The surest course might well be to make the
whole Antarctic region into a truly international park or reserve
which would permit continuation of its exclusive use as the site of
important scientific research."[69]

When it became apparent that this idea was going nowhere, the
conservationists advocated an extended moratorium. In the United

States, officers of twenty leading environmental and conservation organizations addressed a letter to President Carter, saying:

> We believe that a World Preserve for the Antarctic continent, prohibiting all mineral exploitation until such time as the resources can be obtained without danger to the Antarctic terrestrial and marine ecosystems, is in the best interests of both the United States and the world on environmental, political, economic, and military grounds.[70]

Suggesting that "the ban on exploitation might be permanent, or for a significant term of years," the conservationists asked for a halt to the United States' pursuit of a minerals regime.

More than seventeen months elapsed before a reply was received—over the signature of a deputy assistant secretary of state. "Our concept of a regime," wrote Morris D. Busby, ". . . in no way presumes that mineral resource development will take place." He said that the department did not entirely exclude the possibility of a world preserve, but he felt the careful approach being taken "assures that we will be able to implement and sustain necessary protection of the Antarctic environment equal to or greater than that reflected in the 'world preserve' concept."[71] The quite legitimate fears of environmentalists that, if oil *can* be economically taken from Antarctica, it *will* be, were implicitly dismissed. But the environmental ethic that has pervaded the Department of State's Bureau of Oceans and International Environmental and Scientific Affairs is not characteristic of all other treaty nations nor of all other departments and agencies of the U.S. government.

Using the concept of a world preserve to forestall mineral development in Antarctica did not appeal to all conservation organizations. The International Union for Conservation of Nature and Natural Resources (IUCN) responded, "In our view the term [world preserve] should apply only with respect to an area of the highest importance at large and whose ecological integrity must be safeguarded in the interest of all mankind. Anything less surely demeans that concept." IUCN questioned the adequacy and acceptability of the Antarctic Treaty system as custodian.[72] Implicit in this criticism is the obligation of IUCN to see that dedication of land or water as a park or preserve, whether national or world,

represents a lasting commitment. And IUCN knows that pressure
to develop Antarctica will be as nothing compared to the pressure
to exploit existing national parks or preserves in tropical and
temperate lands.

It is apparent that U.S. environmentalists have appreciably less
influence in the Reagan administration than they had through
1980. But even without a change of government, there has historically been a movement to the right with respect to specific issues as
they moved from the abstract to the concrete, from distant possibility to present reality. Policy positions formulated by the Department of State in liberal internationalist terms have gradually been
eroded as Treasury, Commerce, and other departments and agencies began to take notice and feel the pressure of special interests.
This shift can be observed in the progress of the Law of the Sea
Conference and the Moon Treaty discussed above. It is likely to
happen with U.S. policy toward an Antarctic minerals regime as
more players participate in an exercise that has until now gone
forward with a relatively small number of participants.

CHAPTER

VII

In Anticipation of Riches

For all we know now, [Antarctica] may also be a great reservoir of raw materials capable some day of being exploited in the service of man.

—Howard Beale, Australia,
Treaty Conference, 1959

THE MARINE LIVING RESOURCES CONVENTION

At least since 1975, when they met in Oslo, the consultative parties to the Antarctic Treaty realized that some special approach would be needed to protect the living resources of the Southern Ocean. They acknowledged the need for more "detailed studies of the biology, distribution, biomass and population dynamics and the ecology of Antarctic marine living resources" (VIII-10). Interest in krill was becoming intense, and far greater knowledge was (and is) needed before intelligent decisions can be made. Yet the baleen whales and other species could not wait until all the data were in to receive protection from the danger of overfishing. In London in 1977, the consultative parties called for "a definitive regime for the Conservation of Antarctic Marine Living Resources" to be concluded before the end of 1978 (IX.2). Moreover, the recommendation spelled out in some detail how the regime should be negotiated, what it should contain, and some very generalized guidelines for the interim period until the regime should take effect.

183

The consultative parties were faced with several dilemmas. First, the ocean ecosystem with which they were concerned was larger than the treaty area; it extended to the Antarctic Convergence, which in some areas lay north of 60° south latitude and therefore outside the treaty's zone of application. More important, the Antarctic Treaty properly excludes the high seas in the following language of Article VI: "[N]othing in the present Treaty shall prejudice or in any way affect the rights, or the exercise of the rights, of any State under international law with regard to the high seas within that area." To exclude the high seas from a conservation regime for the protection of Antarctic marine living resources would obviously be an absurdity. But the treaty powers could not legally dictate the terms on which the world could fish the Southern Ocean. Already, there were a number of countries fishing the Southern Ocean who were not consultative members, and no doubt there would be more in the future. How could these countries be compelled to abide by the rules unless they had a part in making them? On the other hand, how could the treaty powers compromise their privileged position by admitting other nations to roles of equality? The proposed solution was a two-stage process in which a special consultative meeting would be called to prepare a draft and to decide which other countries "actively engaged in research and exploitation of Antarctic Marine Living Resources" would receive an invitation to "the decisive meeting" at which the convention would be "negotiated." The special meeting would also determine which international organizations were entitled to attend "on an observer basis."[1]

The negotiations proved far more difficult than had been anticipated. By the end of 1978, no convention had been completed, but in three negotiating sessions—in Canberra, Buenos Aires, and Washington—the substantive issues had been largely agreed upon. What delayed the convention for another eighteen months were two matters that to an outsider might seem inconsequential. The first was France's insistence that its islands of Kerguélen and Crozet be excluded from the application of the convention.[2] France is not alone in holding unquestioned sovereignty over islands within the region—or islands whose exclusive economic zones extend into the region. Its demand thus drew attention to one of the flaws in the concept of protecting the entire Antarctic marine ecosystem—namely, that several countries with island possessions south of the Convergence could, if they chose, remove their exclusive economic zones from the application of the convention. Worse, France's insistence endangered a delicate compromise on which the whole structure of the draft convention was based. This involved a way around the ever-present problem of claims and the added difficulties imposed by the two-hundred-mile EEZs. Article IV of the convention (as of the Antarctic Treaty) is designed to ensure that nothing alters the status of claims. It speaks of "coastal state jurisdiction" with calculated ambiguity: Nonclaimant states can interpret the phrase as referring only to the islands where national sovereignties have long been accepted, while claimant states can read the phrase to include coasts of the Antarctic continent where sovereignty is indeed in question. France's adamant position threatened to upset this ingenious obfuscation, which came to be called the "bifocal approach." Although the delegates of other nations were never able to understand the French argument, a compromise was finally reached in a series of convoluted paragraphs inserted in the Final Act of the conference. They are not part of the convention and do not alter the convention in any way. (The text of the convention is to be found in Appendix B.)

The second and more complicated problem involved the position of the European Community (EC) in relation to the convention. In the original 1978 draft, the EC had been ignored—one rationale being that British and French Antarctic territories are specifically excluded from the EC. When the EC insisted on being a participant, the Soviet Union took the position that it was willing to include the community or its individual members with interests in the Antarctic, but not both. The compromise finally worked out recognized that the EC had mixed competence—that is, while it has no uniform policy on scientific research and conducts no research in the Southern Ocean, it does have a common policy on fishing. Thus, the EC will be allowed to participate in making decisions on some issues but not others. It will not have an additional vote (Article XII). A further compromise provides that the Community will not be an original signatory but will become a participating member as soon as the convention comes into force.

The Convention on the Conservation of Antarctic Marine Living Resources was adopted at Canberra on May 20, 1980.[3] It followed the precedent set by the Convention for the Conservation of

Antarctic Seals, signed in 1972, in that it sought to lay down plans for management of a fishery *before* the target resource was already in danger of overexploitation. It was negotiated because the creatures at greatest risk are whales, which have a remarkably active and vocal constituency throughout much of the world. The convention is distinctive if not unique in treating the Antarctic marine ecosystem as a single management area, where conservation principles will reflect concern for all species and their interrelationships. Thus, among the convention's thirty-three articles and an annex providing for an arbitral tribunal, the most notable feature is the statement of purpose in Article II, which defines conservation to include "rational use," but then prescribes fairly rigorous principles to guide "any harvesting or associated activities."[4]

Executive authority resides in a commission composed of representatives of each contracting party and acceding parties "engaged in research or harvesting." The convention also provides for a scientific committee to advise the commission and an executive secretary and secretariat, which are to be based in Hobart, Tasmania, where the Australians are planning an eight-million-dollar headquarters including a conference center, museum, library, and scientific laboratories. The creation of a secretariat by the consultative treaty parties, even though in a different context, is a precedent of considerable significance. At the Washington conference and for twenty years thereafter, the idea of any organizational structure was rejected, generally on the grounds that it would become an unnecessary, expensive, interfering bureaucracy. For a fishing convention, it became unavoidable. The same will be true of a minerals regime.

The functions of the commission, which is to meet annually, are spelled out in detail (Article IX) and are extremely broad, although at least one chief delegate contends that the commission does not have power to allocate resources—*i.e.*, establish national quotas.[5] Clearly, the convention is only what the commission makes of it, for—as the convention states (IX.1)—"The function of the Commission shall be to give effect to the objectives and principles set out in Article II. . . ." One promising requirement is that the commission must publish data on which its conservation measures are based as well as the reports of its scientific committee (IX.1.[b], [c], and [d]).

As in the Antarctic Treaty system, voting is by consensus; U.S. advocacy of a two-thirds or three-quarters majority vote on all issues was forcefully supported only by Norway and New Zealand.[6] The article as adopted is probably the most criticized feature of the convention, for it is widely seen as favoring the fishing nations. However, some have identified a possible advantage in that "a decision reached by consensus would be less likely to invoke use of the objection procedures,"[7] by which a nation can escape a conservation measure simply by notifying the commission that it is unacceptable (IX. 6). This is known as the double veto or what might be called the "include me out" provision: After participating in a consensus decision, one can ignore it. This unsatisfactory arrangement presumably arises from the unusual fact that a majority of the commission, at least as initially constituted, will be composed of nations whose interest is confined to conservation, rather than commercial fishing. "The harvesters, naturally, saw their own willingness to participate in a negotiation where they were outnumbered two to one by conservers as a considerable concession. . . ."[8]

The weakness of inspection and enforcement is another aspect of the convention that troubles conservationists. Each nation is responsible for its own compliance (Article XXI). In this respect, the convention conspicuously fails to meet one of the five elements that the United States had previously said were essential to a conservation regime.[9] A "system of observation and inspection" is to be established by the commission; the convention merely provides some principles on which the system will be based— among them that observers and inspectors shall be responsible only to their own governments (Article XXIV). On the positive side, there is a requirement that "any activity contrary to the objective of this Convention" be reported to the commission for further dissemination (Article XXII).

The United States hoped for a commitment that the nations taking most of the krill from the Southern Ocean would bear most of the operating costs of the bodies called for in the convention. It failed. Article XIX provides that for the first five years "the contribution of each Member of the Commission shall be equal. Thereafter the contribution shall be determined in accordance with two criteria: the amount harvested and an equal sharing among all Members of the Commission. The Commission shall determine by

consensus the proportion in which these two criteria shall apply."
This is just one of several loose ends that remain to be resolved,
and it may finally place an unreasonable burden on the smaller
countries such as Belgium that have no distant-water fishing fleets.

The convention came into force in March 1982 with the ratification of the eighth contracting party, producing a simple majority
that included the United States. Initially, conservationists were
concerned that the convention might not come into force for four
or five years, during which serious damage might be done to the
Antarctic marine ecosystem. Now it appears that the institutions
called for in the convention may be in place by the end of 1982. The
scientists will contend that they still lack knowledge on which to
base sensible quotas, but fortunately, it now appears that krill
harvesting will grow less rapidly than had been generally assumed. Some of the factors deterring expansion are the increased
fuel costs to such distant fishing grounds; the slow growth of
markets; the failure of an expected breakthrough in technology for
shelling krill; the discovery of high levels of fluoride in krill; and
the tendency for ships' processing capacity to be either over-
whelmed with a surfeit of krill brought on deck or underutilized
when nets drag empty. Also, according to one estimate, if all the
existing oceangoing fleets of the world were devoted to Antarctic
krill fishing, they could collectively harvest less than ten million
tons annually.[10] Nevertheless, experience shows that, with various
government subsidies and other inducements, excess capacity can
build up very rapidly. When there are too many specialized fishing
vessels pursuing too few fish, the conditions for establishing
quotas or otherwise limiting the harvest are the most difficult.[11] To
guard against this, some conservationists have suggested that the
krill harvest should be limited not only by setting overall and
national quotas but also by placing limitations on national efforts at
the start.[12] That is, to avoid upward pressure on quotas later,
fishing nations would be limited at the start in the number or
tonnage of vessels harvesting krill.

By the time the convention was initialed in the spring of 1980,
concern for immediate catch limitations was less pronounced.
Most conservationists seemed satisfied with an admonition in the
final act "to show the greatest possible care and concern . . . in
any harvesting of Antarctic marine living resources in the period
prior to entry into force of the Convention. . . ." In their preoccu-

pation with krill and whales, too many conservationists have forgotten their own doctrine of ecosystem management. It is not krill that are immediately at risk but fish.[13] Fin fish in the Southern Ocean are not nearly so productive as krill and are already being harvested in what experts fear are unsustainable quantities. Fish are being exploited partly to offset the costs of experimental harvesting of krill. As much as 450,000 tons of fish were taken in one season from the waters around South Georgia alone. Although this was exceptional, it does appear quite likely that in the process of learning more about krill and how to catch them efficiently, fin fish will pay the price.

Today there is widespread awareness of the need for expanded research on krill and its predators, but whether budgets will be adequate is in serious doubt. Also, while the importance of exchanging data is recognized, information may be treated as privileged until the convention comes into effect. The Soviet Union contended at Canberra that it was constitutionally prohibited from exchanging information on krill until relieved of this restraint by a convention, ratified and in force.[14] Several other countries with serious commercial interests in the Southern Ocean fishery may withhold at least some information.

ASSESSMENT OF THE CONVENTION

Although the completed convention is far less desirable than the draft proposed by the United States in 1978,[15] it is probably the best that could be obtained and better than conservationists contend. What can be seriously questioned is the manner in which the convention was negotiated and the requirement that parties to the convention be bound by the Antarctic Treaty. "It is unclear," James Barnes has written with exceptional restraint, "on what basis the Parties felt they had the right to negotiate in secret a treaty regarding high seas resources, and then to present the document for the rest of the world to endorse as a *fait accompli*."[16] The so-called two-stage process climaxed by a "decisive" negotiating session was largely a fiction. As had been intended from the beginning, the convention was drafted entirely by the consultative treaty powers; by the time of the final conference, ostensibly open to other nations fishing the Southern Ocean, there was little left to negotiate and no substantive changes were to be tolerated. The final conference was preceded by a Special Meeting of the Antarctic

Treaty Consultative Parties whose agenda included "confirmation of the invitations extended to the diplomatic conference by the Government of Australia; and adoption of draft rules of procedure for the Conference."[17]

Conferences, of course, usually adopt their own rules of procedure, and two days before the conference was to begin seemed a bit late to be discussing invitations. In fact, the only outsiders invited were East and West Germany, both of which were looking forward to full membership in the club and therefore not disposed to make waves.[18] To have invited South Korea and Taiwan would obviously have been awkward politically, so they were excluded on the grounds that neither actively engaged in research *and* exploitation at the time the rules were first drawn. These requirements, of course, did not apply to the consultative treaty members, some of whom engage neither in research *nor* fishing in Antarctic waters. Obviously, being a signatory of the Antarctic Treaty did not ensure an invitation to the conference on any basis. The Netherlands, which acceded to the treaty in 1967, and the Republic of Korea were refused observer status, as was the Antarctic and Southern Ocean Coalition (ASOC), representing more than a hundred environmental organizations claiming a total membership of more than two million. The United States led a majority favoring the accreditation of all three, while the Soviet Union led the opposition. ASOC was not entirely excluded, since its executive head was a member of the U.S. delegation. Organizations that were accredited as observers, in addition to the European Community, were FAO, the International Whaling Commission (IWC), SCAR, SCOR, and IUCN. These showed their estimation of the conference's importance by sending very junior people or simply their resident representative in Australia.

This convention must surely be the first wherein a majority of the drafters and charter members cast no nets in the fishery covered by the agreement. When the convention takes effect and the commission begins to make the important decisions, it may be an advantage to have representation by a group of nations (including the United States) that do not have a financial stake in the fishery. It may help to make good the assurance that the parties' first concern is conservation and the protection of the total ecosystem. But it may increasingly raise the question why some nations are clearly more equal than others, even on the high seas.

The convention as it was presented to the final conference provided that only consultative treaty members could propose amendments—a clear assertion of privilege by the club. Fortunately, in the course of discussing the rights of the European Community under the convention, this condition was removed—the only change of substance permitted in the text finally adopted.

Particularly galling to some was the secrecy not only of the negotiations but also of the several drafts of the convention itself—one with acknowledged implications for the entire world. While the farce of confidentiality was being played out, articles criticizing the draft appeared in many countries.[19] U.S. officials described the draft convention in detail to Congress in open hearing,[20] and finally, the full text was published in Europe in early 1979.[21]

Although the United States has been less rigid, less inclined to exclusivity than most other treaty powers, the Department of State deceived Congress by cultivating the illusion that nontreaty nations would play a significant part in negotiating the convention. At a Senate hearing in 1978, Patsy Mink, then assistant secretary for Oceans and International Environmental and Scientific Affairs, fostered this impression in her prepared statement and again under hard questioning from the subcommittee chairman, Claiborne Pell: "[P]erhaps it would be the preference of the consultative parties," she said, "if they could keep the matter within themselves and within their exclusive management. But the realities are that the rest of the nations of the world and many international organizations are insistent upon having a say, having a role, having a part. . . ."[22] These "realities" are what have so far been successfully evaded.

Similarly, the language by which provisions of the Antarctic Treaty are imposed on parties to the fishing convention is arbitrary if not arrogant. Articles III and IV of the convention require that participants be "bound" by specified articles of the treaty, while Article V requires that "Contracting Parties which are not Parties to the Antarctic Treaty acknowledge the special obligations and responsibilities of the Antarctic Treaty Consultative Parties for the protection and preservation of the environment of the Antarctic Treaty area." These impositions seem unnecessary and offer fishing nations an excuse, based on politics or principle, to ignore the convention.[23] However desirable the objective, it is inappropriate to use the Antarctic Treaty, which specifically excludes the high seas, as the basis for rulemaking in another context. The language employed by the consultative powers to assert their ascendancy reflects attitudes that spell future trouble.[24]

A final peculiarity of the convention is its somewhat ambiguous relation to the International Whaling Commission and the Convention for the Conservation of Antarctic Seals. Since the preservation of whales was perhaps the chief motive for the Living Marine Resources Convention, and since this convention calls for the management of the entire ecosystem as a single entity, it is odd—even if inescapable—that whales and seals should be, in effect, excluded. The province of the IWC is, of course, all the waters of the world, although the Southern Ocean is now the most important whaling ground. The Sealing Convention was adopted only in 1972 and came into effect in 1978. It, too, was negotiated entirely by the consultative treaty powers (although formally outside the framework of the treaty), and when the convention was signed, no other nations were even present.[25] The Marine Resources Convention lacks adequate provision for coordination with these and other bodies. As an example of the need for close liaison, if krill are to be harvested without adversely affecting the recovery of whale populations, it may be necessary to cull some species of seals and minke whales, which have benefited from the decline in the great whales.

And yet no one can be sure. The Ad Hoc Scientific Committee on Antarctica of the National Oceanic and Atmospheric Administration concluded in 1979 that "available information on the biology and ecology of Antarctic marine living resources was insufficient to identify the precise measures needed to achieve the conservation objectives set forth in the draft Convention."[26] After much delay, a committee of the Polar Research Board was convened to assess the state of ecological studies of the Southern Ocean and to identify areas of urgent need for expanded research. The committee, headed by John H. Steele, director of the Woods Hole Oceanographic Institution, completed its report in the summer of 1981. In its recommendations, the committee emphasized the need for a coordinated, multidisciplinary research program to find out why krill swarm and to better understand the biological and physical processes that occur at the edge of the pack ice. It also made

Antarctic marine scientists happy by urging the construction of at least one new ice-strengthened research vessel.[27]

As called for in the final act of the conference, the signatories held a preliminary meeting in Hobart, Tasmania, in September 1981 "for the purpose of considering steps which might be taken to facilitate the early operation of the Commission, the Scientific and the Executive secretariat when these bodies are established." Largely as a result of initiatives taken by the Marine Mammal Commission, the United States was well prepared.[28] No decisions were made or intended, but progress was made toward rules of procedure, a headquarters agreement, and agendas for the first meeting of the commission and the scientific committee in mid-1982.

Arguments for greater openness in the Antarctic Treaty system are even more compelling with respect to the Convention on the Conservation of Antarctic Marine Living Resources. The convention has no comparable rationale for confidentiality. Its purpose is more narrowly defined than that of the Antarctic Treaty, it embraces the high seas—an unquestioned commons—and its concerns are universal in nature. Therefore, nongovernmental organizations with legitimate interests should be allowed to attend meetings of the commission as observers, with access to all documentation made available to the delegates. At the second Canberra meeting, where the convention was adopted, the Antarctic and Southern Ocean Coalition petitioned unsuccessfully for such a right, including the right to make formal submissions.[29] However, nothing in the convention prevents the commission, when it is constituted, from opening its doors to accredited nongovernmental organizations.

A MINERAL RESOURCES REGIME

With a mixture of high expectation and uneasiness, the treaty powers began in the early 1970s to anticipate the day when mineral exploration and exploitation would begin in Antarctica. The expectation had increasingly to do with the possibility that the Antarctic might yield oil to lessen the crisis brought on by OPEC. The unease stemmed from the probability that the discovery of minerals would add grave stresses to the treaty system, reopen the issue of territorial claims in the most explosive context, and rouse the Third World to demand its share. There was also the serious question of what mineral exploitation might do to the environment. And finally, each member country feared that others might get a headstart in exploration.[30]

As early as 1972—that is, before the oil crisis—the Seventh Consultative Meeting adopted a recommendation "that the subject 'Antarctic Resources—Effects of Mineral Exploration' be carefully studied" and included on the agenda of the next meeting (VII-6). Most of the discussion at that next meeting (1975) was devoted to the mineral resources issue. A majority favored a moratorium on exploration until the technical, environmental, and political problems could be resolved. Only the United States was overtly opposed. Later, a State Department spokesman would explain: "There was a feeling on our side at that time, that a moratorium was not so much a delay to permit rational consideration as a decision not to examine the issue at all, at a time when perceptions of resource scarcity and hydrocarbon scarcity were dawning."[31]

Nevertheless, tacit agreement was reached among the treaty powers to refrain from exploration and exploitation until some ground rules had been agreed upon. While this policy of "voluntary restraint" was in force, the parties would attempt to negotiate "a minerals regime."[32] A special group was assembled by SCAR to make a preliminary assessment of the environmental hazards of mineral exploration and exploitation for the Ninth Consultative Meeting in 1977. A special preparatory meeting, held in Paris in 1976, could not get much beyond the enunciation of four principles:

   (i) the Consultative Parties will continue to play an active and
       responsible role in dealing with the question of the mineral
       resources of Antarctica;
  (ii) the Antarctic Treaty must be maintained in its entirety;
 (iii) protection of the unique Antarctic environment and of its depen-
       dent ecosystems should be a basic consideration;
  (iv) the Consultative Parties, in dealing with the question of mineral
       resources in Antarctica, should not prejudice the interests of all
       mankind in Antarctica.[33]

Just what this last clause implied was obviously subject to interpretation and has been a matter of speculation ever since. All four principles were incorporated in the first recommendation of the Ninth Consultative Meeting and, for lack of anything more concrete to say, were repeated by yet another group of experts assembled in the early summer of 1979.[34] The most quoted passage from the recommendations of the 1977 meeting is the paragraph from IX-1 articulating the agreement on a moratorium while avoiding the word. It was recommended that governments:

> . . . urge their nationals and other States to refrain from all exploration and exploitation of Antarctic mineral resources while making progress towards the timely adoption of an agreed regime concerning Antarctic mineral resource activities. They will thus endeavor to ensure that, pending the timely adoption of agreed solutions pertaining to exploration and exploitation of mineral resources, no activity shall be conducted to explore or exploit such resources. They will keep these matters under continuing examination. . . .

The first sentence is a useful reminder that only suasion can keep Country X or Corporation Y from digging in Antarctica. For despite the exclusivity of the club, the Antarctic Treaty provides that the continent is open to all. The only restraint on nationals of the consultative parties is that they are subject to domestic law or regulation designed to implement the Agreed Measures for the Conservation of Antarctic Fauna and Flora. Thus far, only a few corporations have asked for exploration rights in Antarctica, and they have easily been dissuaded by their governments. In the United States, according to NSF's representative in the Antarctic Policy Group, only twice have exploring companies taken an initiative in the Southern Ocean. In 1975, the Aquatic Exploration Company of Houston, Texas, sought to form an international consortium of twenty companies in Australia, France, Great Britain, Japan, the Soviet Union, and the United States. It proposed a circumpolar seismic study to be called Operation Deep South, with each company putting up $120,000, for a total of $24 million.[35] It is not entirely clear whether there was insufficient interest or whether the Houston firm drew back when it learned belatedly the implications of the enterprise. In any event, the project came to nothing. More recently, the Gulf Oil Corporation—or its exploring subsidiary—has sought official U.S. blessing for, and participation in, a consortium for the purpose of conducting seismic studies. The initial proposal of July 1978 was turned down; at that time

Washington wanted to appear purer than Caesar's wife with respect to oil exploration, but now that a majority of treaty members are making geophysical surveys of one kind or another on Antarctic shelves, a revised proposal by Gulf will probably go forward.

Through 1979 and early 1980, it was apparent that until a Convention on Marine Living Resources was successfully concluded, discussion of a minerals regime would be ritualistic. For on one point everyone is agreed: A minerals regime is far more difficult to negotiate than a marine regime. Nothing makes nations so covetous as oil. Moreover, while the resources of the Southern Ocean are in constant flux and are renewable, mineral resources are fixed and finite. The clever evasion that permitted agreement on the fishing convention will not work when the subject is oil down a hole at a specific site in a specific "sovereign territory." If the treaty powers could not agree on a marine resources regime, there was no hope for a minerals regime.

Indeed, a majority of the treaty powers have become more aggressive in pursuit of national interests more narrowly defined. They include some particularly energy-dependent nations for whom Antarctica appears to be the last best hope of slaking their thirst for oil. New Zealand feels itself in a permanent depression, and its mood is reflected in a net decline in population through emigration. South Africa has felt acutely vulnerable to an oil cutoff much longer than other nations. Japan's energy predicament is without parallel. An Australian spokesman has been quoted as saying that every drop of oil that may be found in its claimed territorial waters belongs to Australia.[36] The spokesman was Ambassador Keith Brennan, perennial representative at consultative treaty meetings, who maintains that "the Treaty did not freeze territorial claims; it merely put them on the back burner to keep warm."[37] He argues further that the claims issue is postponed only for those matters specified in the treaty—a position supported by at least some experts in international law.[38] Hence, in the Australian view, unilateral exploration and exploitation of resources by claimant states are entirely legal, subject only to voluntary and temporary restraints. At least this is Australia's bargaining position, and it is shared, at a minimum, by Chile and Argentina.[39] "The validity of a claim does not depend on recognition," Ambassador Brennan contends. "The *existence* of a claim is a reality. You cannot extinguish sovereignty by vote."[40] Other claimant states, especially Chile and Argentina, have appeared no less adamant. For example, at the Tenth Consultative Meeting in the fall of 1979, the head of the Argentine delegation distributed recent legislation entitled "Risk Contracts for Exploration and Exploitation of Hydrocarbons."[41] In his prepared, on-the-record remarks, he made clear that the Argentine government considers the law applicable "in the sector of Antarctica over which it has reserved sovereign rights."[42]

The United States, in contrast, has adhered to the principle of "free non-discriminatory access." As with science, anyone should have the right to go anywhere, and the spoils will go first and fastest to the nation(s) with the most advanced technology. Since the Soviet Union lacks the technology for the extraction of offshore oil, it appeared uninterested. Taking a stance very appealing to conservationists, the Soviets held that concern for the environment should be paramount and mineral exploitation postponed indefinitely.

By the time serious discussions started in Washington in December 1980, continuing in March 1981 in Buenos Aires, almost all of these positions had subtly changed. To some extent, the shift was from a public stance to a private one where delegates were exchanging views without instructions and without commitment. But more than this, the change was compounded of several considerations that caused a growing sense of urgency: Accommodation among the consultative parties was preferable to any conceivable alternative; if the Group of 14 did not have their act together before the Law of the Sea Convention was concluded, the Group of 77 would cause all kinds of trouble; in the absence of a minerals regime, the discovery of economically recoverable oil in Antarctica might easily wreck the treaty. The Soviets may have become more cooperative simply because, with Afghanistan and Poland to concern them, the creation of further antagonism seemed ill-advised. The United States did not abandon its demand for equality of opportunity but conceded that which nation(s) produced or received Antarctic oil might be less important than that any significant increase in hydrocarbon production, now or in the future, would relieve pressure on world supplies and moderate the power of OPEC.

None of this would make agreement easy to achieve, but by 1981

something approaching a consensus had emerged on several
points:

1. A minerals regime must be in place before the technical capacity
   exists for oil extraction in Antarctic conditions; otherwise the
   possibility of precipitous unilateral action may put the environment and the treaty at risk.
2. Development must proceed by degrees, with assurance at each
   step that the environment will not be seriously endangered by
   advancing to the next one. Thus, for example, a green light to
   explore will not necessarily ensure a license to produce.
   (Whether commercial firms will assume the high costs of
   exploration without promise of reward is a matter of debate; yet
   offshore oil exploration is taking place all over the world,
   including the United States, without any assurance that exploitation will be permitted on acceptable terms.)
3. Even though the extraction of hard minerals now seems distant,
   the regime must cover this eventuality as well as the drilling for
   oil.
4. The claimant states must derive some tangible benefit from any
   mineral extraction on "their territory," over and above what
   others may gain, although it might be disguised in a variety of
   ways, such as a contribution to environmental protection.
5. Revenue sharing with the Third World is unavoidable.

Although this seems like a substantial beginning, the issue has
been on the agenda since 1972, and the most difficult questions lie
ahead. It was not until the Eleventh Consultative Meeting, June/
July 1981 in Buenos Aires, that the treaty parties decided to open
formal negotiations beginning in 1982, with the first session to be
in New Zealand. Indeed, the meeting was so preoccupied with the
minerals issue that almost nothing else was accomplished. Only
three recommendations emerged from the two-week meetings,
and of these two were of little or no significance. But Recommendation XI-1 agreed that "a regime on Antarctic mineral resources
should be concluded as a matter of urgency." In language very
similar to the recommendation calling for negotiations of a regime
for marine living resources, the treaty parties set forth in broad
terms some principles and purposes. Agreement was most difficult

to achieve on the principle that "any agreement . . . should be acceptable and be without prejudice" to both claimant and non-claimant states. Mildly surprising was the consensus—so soon— that adhering states would be "eligible to participate in mineral resource activities under the regime."[43] In other words, the club would permit outsiders to dig in Antarctica—but not to share in decision-making—provided they bound themselves to the basic provisions of the Antarctic Treaty.

At the Eleventh Meeting, the division between claimant and nonclaimant states was even sharper than some longtime observers had expected. The claimant states caucused each morning in an effort to achieve a unified position, and there was every indication that the negotiations will be long and difficult. What ingenious solution can be found that will not irrevocably compromise the positions of those nations that claim territorial sovereignty and those that do not? Are the United States, the Soviet Union, and other nonclaimant states prepared to concede any special status to the claimant states? How, in short, can the Antarctic Treaty's Article IV, which suspends such questions, be reconciled with an equitable plan to develop mineral resources? Every conceivable procedure is being explored: leases, licenses, joint ventures, consortia, and public/private corporations. What seems likely to emerge is some limited form of condominium (although the word will be avoided) with an authority to issue licenses or conduct exploration and exploitation in behalf of all the treaty powers. One suggestion is that, at least initially, any revenues should be used to expand scientific research in Antarctica—the idea being, presumably, that this would take the sting out of demands by outsiders for sharing of benefits.

An ingenious proposal discussed in Washington prior to the first formal negotiating session seeks both to evade the territorial claims issue and to avoid the formality of a treaty. Antarctica would be divided into four regions (actually quadrants, starting at 30°E) drawn in such a way that at least three of the four regions contain promising areas for exploration. Each region would have a panel composed of parties to the regime to serve as resource manager in accordance with the standards set forth in the regime. No party to the regime could be a member of more than two panels and no panel would include more than 50 percent of the parties to the regime. A decision to open an area for exploration and development would be made by the regional panel by consensus, but it could be reviewed at the next full meeting of the parties. The suggestion has been thought out in considerable detail. In the somewhat unlikely event that its principal provisions are acceptable to all the parties, a solution may have been found to some of the most difficult issues.

A matter of concern to some is that the development of mineral resources in Antarctica will seriously compromise Article III of the Antarctic Treaty calling for the full and free exchange of scientific information. If there is to be serious exploration, the information obtained must be privileged—especially if private industry is to participate, as it must. Thus, confidentiality will replace openness in Antarctica, and difficult questions will arise as to what data can be exchanged and what withheld. Others contend that this appears to be a problem only from our present perspective; that once principles of sharing have been adopted and the machinery for administering an agreement is in place, the need for privileged information becomes academic. It is then all for one and one for all. This happy outcome, if achieved, is unlikely to come quickly. But neither, perhaps, is exploratory drilling by commercial firms. Meanwhile, nations are proceeding with seismic studies—the Japanese most vigorously—and promising to make their data available as called for in the Antarctic Treaty.

It is well to remember, too, that even if oil is found in quantity, it may never be extracted because of the high cost or the inability to ensure adequate environmental protection. A close observer has written: "Thus far, at least, there is considerable indication that the parties will treat environmental concerns as more important than resource development concerns."[44] Whether this is true for all the parties seems doubtful. But certainly the United States has been emphatic that the treaty powers must proceed in measured stages, without assurance that exploration will be ultimately permitted.

Although the claims issue is widely seen as the principal obstacle to agreement, what has historically seemed to be the most stubborn facet of this problem—the overlapping claims—may now be seen as contributing to a settlement. One of the two most promising areas for offshore oil exploration is the peninsula, claimed by Britain, Chile, and Argentina. If a substantial deposit were found and any one of these powers began unilaterally to drill production wells, the result would quite probably be war. Since this outcome is recognized and since a resolution of the overlapping claims seems beyond the wit of man, adaptation, adjustment, and compromise are the only alternatives.

The possibility that these qualities may be forthcoming has clearly been jeopardized by the war over the Falklands. Indeed, one must conclude that the burning antagonism between Britain and Argentina cannot help but delay the already difficult talks of formulating a minerals regime acceptable to fourteen nations.

VIII

A Commons in Trust

If the treaty shall remain a useful instrument, . . . we may, in fact, have to develop new concepts for international cooperation.

—*Edvard Hambro, Oslo, 1975*

A White House directive of October 13, 1970, which is still in effect, states as one of the objectives of U.S. Antarctic policy, "To . . . develop appropriate measures to ensure the equitable and wise use of living and non-living resources."[1] What does "equitable" mean in this context? That nonclaimant states shall get no less than claimant states? Or that everyone shall have equal access? Or that the Third World should share in any resources obtained from Antarctica and the surrounding ocean? And when has government managed to see that resources are used wisely? Many officials are unaware that this directive exists; they certainly are not eager to offer an interpretation of what it means. One can be reasonably sure, however, that when this passage was drafted, "equitable use" did not have a global reach.

The Antarctic Treaty consultative powers have regularly cited their contribution to the greater good of all—by maintaining peace and disarmament in a considerable sector of the world and by making available the findings of science. This was stated perhaps most eloquently by the Soviet delegate at the Ninth Consultative

Meeting in 1977. "The investigation of Antarctica, which requires colossal effort and the application of substantial material resources, thus acquires the character of a noble mission bringing benefits to all the peoples of the earth."[2]

The treaty members have not been insensitive to world opinion, although they vary greatly in their willingness to take it into account. That the club has obligations going beyond the spread of scientific knowledge has been best articulated by the British. At the opening of the Washington Conference in 1959, Sir Esler Dening said:

> The . . . question is how to safeguard the interests of countries other than those represented at this Conference. We are concerned that no misunderstanding should arise as to the motives of the Twelve Powers; we should not wish our deliberations to raise doubts in the minds of other nations, and particularly of those who, although hitherto not actively interested in the Antarctic, may question the right of any single group of countries even to give the appearance of legislating on a matter of worldwide concern.[3]

Again, in 1977, Ted Rowlands, minister of state for Foreign and Commonwealth Affairs, said in opening the Ninth Consultative Meeting in London:

> Whether we like it or not, one of the tests of the obligation imposed on us by our possession of knowledge is whether the decisions we reach are acceptable to the wider world community. The test of that acceptability will largely depend on the clarity with which we are seen, as we were in 1959, to be serving the long term interests of the Antarctic and the world community rather than short term illusions of national advantage.
>
> The world will not give us long to see if we can pass these tests. If we fail them, the obligation to come up with answers to Antarctic problems will inevitably devolve on the wider community. . . .[4]

Similar thoughts have been expressed from time to time by New Zealand, Australia, and Norway. It is noteworthy, though, that these sentiments generally betray a concern to maintain the treaty members' advantageous position. It is only now, with the question of resource benefits coming to the fore, that the parties have to decide with precision what they owe the rest of the world—

whether, for example, sharing is an obligation, a tactical necessity, or something to be avoided. Before pursuing this further, it will be useful to review briefly the principal proposals that have been made for the political and organizational future of Antarctica.

PROPOSED POLITICAL SOLUTIONS

One of the first writers to examine in some depth the possible alternatives for the political future of Antarctica was international law scholar C. Wilfred Jenks. Writing shortly before the Antarctic Treaty negotiations began in 1958, he implicitly rejected both territorial sovereignty and trusteeship and contended that "government by a consortium of Powers would tend to project political problems into Antarctica in a most undesirable manner."[5] Believing that form should follow function, he saw the problem as one "of organizing a limited number of world services in an Antarctic waste." Most of these services—meteorological, telecommunications, aviation—could be provided by existing international organizations. Jenks foresaw the exploitation of mineral resources as extremely remote, even unlikely, but offered several alternative methods of arranging concessions, leases, or licenses. He seemed to expect no serious political problems or demands from outsiders for a share. But he did argue that an important function of an international regime would be to prohibit any exclusive claim to offshore resources.[6]

To the extent that the Antarctic Treaty created a limited consortium, it is remarkable how little political tensions elsewhere have intruded into the Antarctic. Since the demise of détente, relations between the United States and the Soviet Union could hardly have been worse. The Soviet Union and Chile do not recognize each other. In other fora, South Africa has been excoriated by all its colleagues in the treaty system. On the issue of human rights, the United States has been outspokenly critical of Chile and Argentina, which at various times in recent years have been on the brink of war with each other. Yet negotiations involving Antarctica have consistently gone forward in an atmosphere that, if not always amicable, has been eminently correct. As to Jenks's belief that a few international services would suffice, this surely is no longer true if it ever was.

Writing at almost the same time, Philip Jessup and Howard Taubenfeld took into consideration the interest of the world community and foresaw that "if and when Antarctic mineral resources prove economically attractive . . . we may come to a critical period for the successful continuation of a purely functional approach to Antarctica."[7] They proposed an international stock company to be established by treaty. Shares in the Company for the Exploitation of the Minerals of Antarctica would be allocated according to the time and extent of each country's "exploration and development of the continent or parts of it."[8] "Some provision could be made for participation by other states at later dates if they showed adequate reason or exerted sufficient pressure."[9] The treaty "might also provide certain guarantees of an economic or scientific nature for the benefit of the international community," but these were not spelled out.[10]

The idea of an international stock company has merit. One wishes that Jessup and Taubenfeld had elaborated on their proposal, but as lawyers are wont, they seemed more concerned to prove that there were precedents for their idea. Surely the hard part would be to determine what factors should be weighed in allocating shares. Presumably, these would include the size of each country's scientific effort and/or its claim. How would the large scientific effort of the United States equate with New Zealand's potentially valuable claim? Would Australia's shares exceed France's by the relative size of their territorial claims? It is this kind of detail that, in the view of some of the present negotiators of a minerals regime, could be fatal. If the agreement is not relatively simple, they contend, it may not be reached at all.

In 1974, Edvard Hambro, representative of Norway to the United Nations and chairman of the Eighth Consultative Treaty Meeting in Oslo, appeared to hope that the adaptations required in order to develop the resources of Antarctica would encourage the formation of a de facto condominium in which the issue of territorial claims would be laid to rest. He implicitly urged that the parties act together in granting mining concessions and that royalties be paid into a common fund.[11] A de facto condominium of some kind does indeed seem to be the direction that the consultative parties are taking, but it will be a long time before territorial claims are laid to rest. The opportunity for a de jure condominium may have been lost, if only for tactical reasons: It would tend to emphasize the appearance of exclusivity. Hambro was silent on how royalties should be divided.

After leaving the British Foreign and Commonwealth Office, where he was in charge of Antarctic affairs for many years, the late Brian Roberts proposed in 1978 that the consultative parties establish "a joint licensing authority" and a regime for protecting the environment. Remarkably, for a long-time representative of a claimant state, Roberts favored "non-discriminatory access under license to the minerals of the *whole* area."[12] He noted "the growing body of opinion" holding that "all nations have equal rights in the Antarctic"[13] and observed that the consultative parties "will no longer be able to make effective decisions about the peaceful development of the Antarctic without steadily growing opposition."[14] Licensed access, he believed, must be open to all.[15] He hoped, however, that the consultative parties would ultimately "be recognized by the United Nations as responsible trustees acting on behalf of a much wider group of nations."[16]

All these points are well taken, and his contention that licensed access must be open to all appears to have been already accepted by the treaty members. But again, one wishes this much respected scholar/diplomat of perhaps unequaled experience had spelled out his ideas as to how the consultative parties could win the full confidence of the United Nations.

The most comprehensive analysis of the legal and political implications of resource exploitation in Antarctica is by Steven J. Burton, a law professor formerly in the Department of State. In order to proceed with the orderly development of Antarctic resources, he proposes "a conditional regime" based on "Antarctic Community Principles," building on "the common interests of states active in Antarctic affairs."[17] Its aim would be to create a stable investment climate while retaining the capacity to issue a "stop-work" order if environmental risks prove too great. "Neither the principle of territorial sovereignty nor the principle of open use," he believes, "can serve as a basis for establishing an effective conditional regime."[18] He contends that "the juridical dispute over sovereignty is illusory. . . . All participants will therefore pursue their national economic interests from a position of juridical equality."[19] However, he believes that as "substantial economic interests are at stake," the parties will have to abandon consensus voting; otherwise there will be very high risk of deadlock between those whose primary interest is economic development and those who stress environmental protection.[20] Burton offers several alternatives to the principle of unanimity, but as the Marine Living Resources Convention has shown, some of the treaty powers seem unbreakably wedded to consensus. It will be difficult to persuade them that their vital interests can otherwise be protected. As for sharing, Burton holds that there is no obligation, but that a voluntary contribution to the United Nations Development Program or the World Bank might be sensible.[21]

Frank C. Alexander, Jr., is both more and less specific. He is silent on the voting issue but proposes that the consultative parties form a Joint Antarctic Resource Jurisdiction over the continent and its shelves. After a five-year moratorium to permit study of the environmental impact of offshore oil exploitation, the most promising areas would be divided into concession blocks on which all interested states could bid. Revenues from permits to explore would be divided equally among the consultative parties. Royalties on oil actually extracted would be similarly shared but with "a new United Nations trust fund" as an additional recipient. All provisions of the Antarctic Treaty would remain unchanged.[22]

Another young law scholar mocks the pretensions of the consultative powers, "who purport to provide all law and authority for Antarctica." He denigrates "the stalemated Treaty structure" for its "frailty" and advocates an international regime based on "the law of common spaces." It would replicate all the machinery of the United Nations—"a bicameral legislative system . . . a strong executive body with a staff of international civil servants."[23] Except to fulfill some idealistic concept of universalism, there is very little to be said for this solution. For as far as anyone can see into the future, the resources of the Antarctic would not even cover the costs of such a bureaucracy. The mere thought of 150 sovereign nations being involved in making decisions critical to an environment of which they know nothing is unacceptable to those who have been concerned with Antarctica.

TOWARD A RECONCILIATION OF INTERESTS

There are two principles in conflict regarding Antarctica. One is that a universalist regime for Antarctica, while desirable in theory, would be practically disastrous and politically impossible. The other is that exclusive rights in Antarctica cannot justifiably be claimed by any nation or group of nations. The objective must be to achieve a reasonable trade-off between responsible trusteeship by the few and equitable sharing among many. The treaty powers are simply unwilling to share decision-making and administrative responsibility widely. They have not been prepared to abandon consensus voting within the present club; unless pushed, they are not likely to add members who would make unanimity more difficult to achieve. And outsiders have no direct leverage. To apply pressure, the developing countries will have to seek indirect avenues of influence or retaliation.

To what end would the Third World apply pressure? If access remains open to all, and if revenue sharing is institutionalized as a matter of right, not of buying acquiescence—and it must be—then it will be very difficult to argue that global interests will be served by diluting responsibility. The decisions that need to be made over the coming decades both to protect the Antarctic environment and to create a stable climate for investment in exploration will be difficult enough as it is. Too many cooks, most of them inexperienced, could be fatal. The present members of the club will have to act with an exceptional sense of responsibility, but on the basis of their record over two decades, they deserve the cautious confidence of the world community. As for those who wish to keep the Antarctic permanently locked up as a scientific laboratory, they are simply not being realistic. The way to protect the Antarctic environment is to anticipate development, not to halt it, and to ensure that *parts* of Antarctica are protected in perpetuity as world parks or wilderness areas.

Although it can be argued that, consistent with its principles, the Group of 77 *must* demand a role in Antarctica, its members know full well they cannot dictate terms. Also, they have learned a lot from eight years of sea-law negotiations, including the fact that there are no El Dorados on the sea floor—or in Antarctica. If it is doubtful that the Antarctic will ever yield minerals, it is even more doubtful that it will generate significant revenues. Nevertheless, a formula for sharing must be negotiated among the consultative parties and must become a permanent obligation, with sufficient attraction to remove the Antarctic from the agenda of North-South issues. Politically, it should be far easier for the consultative parties to obligate themselves to share revenues that are, at best, distant than to increase foreign aid in current budgets. Such shared profits, if they occur, will fall in the category of "automatic revenues" so persuasively advocated by the Brandt commission. Because it is as yet undeveloped, the Antarctic and its surrounding ocean are well suited to initiatives "in making aid continuous and predictable," even if not, in this case, immediate. As the Brandt commission wrote, "Those who argue that the concept of international taxation is unrealistic in the light of public opinion should recall that the same was said about national income tax in nearly all western countries a century ago."[24]

Many have hoped that the principle of international taxation on use of the commons might be introduced in the Southern Ocean. Because it is as yet an undeveloped resource, the idea might in theory be more palatable than if it were applied to an established fishery. The difficulty is that the economics of krill fishing are at present so marginal, if not negative, that a use tax might kill it entirely. A tax on profits would be strongly resisted, would be difficult to apply, and might yield no return for many years. A more practical approach might be to involve developing countries of the Southern Hemisphere in joint enterprises for the exploitation of the Southern Ocean. Assuming a gradual growth of a krill fishery, it is possible to conceive of mutual benefits in having home ports and processing plants in, say, Namibia and Mozambique. Economies in fuel and crews might be effected by keeping the fishing vessels in the Southern Hemisphere year-round, using them in the off-season to develop coastal fisheries of developing countries.[25] A country with the resources of Nigeria might in time develop its own long-distance fishing fleet.

An idea being discussed in the minerals regime negotiations is that initially, at least, any revenues from the issuance of leases and licenses to explore be reinvested in Antarctic scientific research or used to defray the cost of ensuring that exploration and exploitation do not damage the environment. Since there could be no assurance that such funds would in every case represent an addition to present budgets, the parties might agree to pool the revenues in a fund especially for research on the environmental impact of proposed activities. In any case, the funds are not likely to be large, and by applying them to the further study of the Antarctic region, the question of equitable distribution both inside and outside the treaty system would begin only when and if profitable exploitation occurred.

What happens if promises of future revenue sharing do not suffice to defuse pressure from the Group of 77? Perhaps the most convenient step would be to establish a relationship with the Seabed Authority, when it has been created under the Law of the Sea Convention, assisting it to explore in Antarctica on the same terms worked out for the consultative parties. The United States seems already prepared for this modest concession.

The difficulty of obtaining a consensus will make it troublesome for the consultative parties to make concessions before they are forced to. But there is much to be said for keeping the goodwill of outsiders by signaling flexibility and a willingness to seek compromises between exclusivity and universalism. One way to give outsiders a sense of participation at relatively small cost would be to reconsider the basis of consultative status under the Antarctic Treaty.

Among the charter members of the club, it must be of some embarrassment that neither Belgium nor, more recently, Norway conducts research in Antarctica. Since this is the qualification for consultative membership required of nations other than the original signatories, the noninvolvement of two of them weakens the treaty parties' case. Article IX.2 of the treaty provides that such countries as Poland and West Germany, which first acceded to the treaty and then were granted consultative status, can be dropped from the club whenever they cease to demonstrate their "interest in Antarctica by conducting substantial scientific research activity there. . . ."[26] But the so-called contracting parties—those that negotiated the treaty—are immune from disqualification. In the long run, there can be no justification for this kind of discrimination. Contracting parties that become inactive in Antarctica and contribute nothing to the common fund of knowledge over a period of years should not continue to enjoy consultative status. Their departure would strengthen the argument for earned responsibility and informed trusteeship.

It is by no means out of the question that a small, inactive country like Belgium might resign for financial reasons. In the future, real costs are likely to be associated with consultative status; after doing without a secretariat for two decades, the need for some organizational structure is apparent and already called for by the Convention on the Conservation of Antarctic Marine Living Resources. Belgium's turn to host a consultative meeting is at hand—a surprisingly costly operation. For a country with little expectation of a return on its investment, these expenses may seem unjustifiable.

Norway is a more complicated case, for it *has* conducted research in Antarctica from time to time since the IGY, it *is* a long-distance fishing nation, and moreover it is a claimant state. But Norway has always been more interested in the Arctic and has seemed uncomfortable with its Antarctic claim, which was made primarily to forestall Nazi Germany and to protect its now-defunct whaling industry. The Labor party, until very recently the dominant party in Norway, favors giving up the claim, but it never pushed the issue, partly in deference to other claimant states. Especially now that Norway possesses North Sea oil more than adequate for its own needs, it should not be politically difficult to surrender its claim if it were seen to be in the general interest to do so.

It is true that the calm and disinterested voices of Belgium and Norway would be missed. They will not be forced out, and their withdrawal is not essential. But it would help the consultative parties to move toward uniform qualifications for membership, and it would provide an opportunity to offer representation to outsiders without increasing the size of the decision-making body.

It is suggested that the consultative parties might well invite two other countries to join their deliberations on a rotating basis. A term of four years would ensure participation in at least two consultative meetings as voting members. Even if the new members obstructed a consensus, they could postpone action only briefly.[27] It would be appropriate to start the cycle with nations that have acceded to the treaty but have not become consultative parties.[28] Selection of the rotating members could temporarily be retained by the club, but ultimately should be placed in the hands of a body of the United Nations—perhaps the Trusteeship Council —with the clear understanding that there would be genuine rotation of geographic and political representation.

Unless one assumes that this proposal would constitute an irresistible foot-in-the-door leading to a Group of 77 takeover of decision-making, the consultative parties would be giving away very little and gaining much. They would anticipate the demand of outsiders for a voice in making decisions, forestall pressures that may prove very divisive even if ineffectual, defuse the charge of arbitrarily assuming powers that should be shared, and overcome some of the ill effects of secrecy while keeping actual deliberations off the record. (Despite demands for openness, discussion behind closed doors is essential if anything is to be accomplished by countries with such varied interests and perspectives.) The original signatories would retain control and maintain all the provisions of the Antarctic Treaty unchanged except for paragraph 2 of Article IX, which in any case needs greater precision. When the benefits of membership in the club exceed the obligations, what constitutes "substantial scientific research activity" is going to be an increasingly troublesome question. Already the question arises whether South Africa is conducting "substantial scientific research activity." If the term were defined, South Africa would have to do more or ultimately lose its consultative status—a possibility that South Africa would resist at whatever price was necessary. To replace Belgium or Norway with one or more representatives of the Group of 77 will not be easy and will almost certainly be resisted by Chile and Argentina especially. But the proposal does represent a compromise of the conflicting principles of universalism and exclusivity, and it is one that both sides should be able to live with. By temporarily controlling the selection of outside representatives, the transition would be eased and a possible crisis avoided in 1991.

Many people assume that the treaty system will come apart of its own accord, either on the resource issue or in 1991, when a review conference can be called at the behest of even a single consultative party. At that time, changes in the treaty can then be made by simple majority. But the treaty system has proved remarkably adaptable, and its members are held together by powerful interests in common. As far as one can foretell, the consultative parties will be no more inclined to break up the treaty system in 1991 than they are now. If this is so, then the provision for majority vote is without significance. Indeed, the parties are quite likely not to call for a review conference at all lest outsiders try to take it over. In any event, the consultative members will not demand changes that others cannot live with; hence, in effect, consensus voting will apply then as now.

The situation would not be fundamentally altered if the review conference contained one or two nations determined to destroy the

Antarctic Treaty system, but it would certainly be awkward. The newcomers would presumably be outvoted by a simple majority. The minority would then have no alternative but to approve the proposed amendment(s) or withdraw. The difficulty is that under the terms of Article XII this process could take four years—two years for ratification plus two years before notice of withdrawal takes effect—or until 1995. These could be very unconstructive years if the rotating representatives were hostile. Therefore, it would seem sensible and politically feasible to maintain control of the selection process until after 1991.

U.S. POLICY AND PRACTICE

In the spring of 1975, Senator Claiborne Pell summoned to the Hill Dr. Dixy Lee Ray, then assistant secretary of state for Oceans and International Environmental and Scientific Affairs (OES), to probe the Department of State's thinking on mineral exploration and exploitation in the Antarctic. Secretary Ray, who was new in the office, was accompanied by a quartet of able young lawyers and aides: Steven J. Burton, Peter Bernhardt, Addison Richmond, and Theodore Sellin. When the executive hearing was printed eight weeks later, some of the more interesting exchanges read as follows:

SENATOR PELL: Is there any thought that the Antarctic resources might be considered as the heritage of all mankind similar to the seabed resources in the Law of the Sea negotiations?

DR. RAY: [Deleted.]

MR. BURTON: [Deleted.]

SENATOR PELL: Has anybody opposed it? And if so, who?

DR. RAY: [Deleted.]

SENATOR PELL: Has the United States taken a position in this regard one way or the other?

MR. BURTON: [Deleted.]

MR. BERNHARDT: [Deleted.][29]

And later:

SENATOR PELL: What are the alternatives available to the United States as we develop a policy on this issue?

DR. RAY: [Deleted.]

SENATOR PELL: We should recess for a few moments.

[*Brief recess.*]

SENATOR PELL: [*Deleted.*] What course of action has the Antarctic Policy Group recommended to the NSC?
DR. RAY: [*Deleted.*][30]

And finally, still speaking of mineral exploitation in Antarctica:

SENATOR PELL: Would you have any objection to the issue being raised within the U.N. or Law of the Sea Conference?
MR. BURTON: [*Deleted.*]
DR. RAY: [*Deleted.*]
MR. BURTON: [*Deleted.*]
MR. BERNHARDT: [*Deleted.*]
MR. RICHMOND: [*Deleted.*][31]

Now these are good and reasonable questions. The answers were censored not because of any justified need for confidentiality but because the United States at that time had no policy on these issues. Since World War II, Antarctic affairs have been in four different bureaus of the Department of State, and in each Antarctica has been a stepchild. When the Bureau of Oceans and International Environmental and Scientific Affairs was created in 1973, the announcement did not even mention that the bureau included Antarctica.[32] In its first five years, the OES was headed by a succession of three inexperienced assistant secretaries, and for thirty-one months the post was vacant.[33] OES is a grab bag of leftover missions that have not found a home elsewhere. One of the more important is nuclear nonproliferation. Thus it was that Dixy Lee Ray, recently come from the Atomic Energy Commission, had her mind on other things when she appeared before Senator Pell's committee. And thus it is that President Reagan's choice for assistant secretary was James Malone, a lawyer whose only experience relevant to his bureau was in nuclear matters. In regard to international nuclear issues, the Department of Energy and the Arms Control and Disarmament Agency have been downgraded, and added responsibility has been given to the Department of State. There may be sound rationale for doing so, but it is one indication that inattention to Antarctica will be perpetuated. Oddly, within a year Malone had been removed from his job and made chairman of the U.S. delegation to the Law of the Sea Conference.

The Antarctic Policy Group (APG), established April 10, 1965, remains the responsible body for setting objectives in Antarctica and seeing that they are effectively pursued. Its permanent members are representatives of the Department of State (acting as chairman), the NSF, and the Department of Defense. Other departments and agencies, such as Commerce, Interior, Transportation, and National Oceanic and Atmospheric Administration, may participate as appropriate, especially on working groups of the APG focusing on particular issues. But the Department of State has the primary responsibility.

So cavalierly has this obligation been taken that, through the early 1970s, U.S. position papers for the treaty consultative meetings were prepared by the NSF.[34] Neither Dixy Lee Ray nor her deputy attended the Oslo meeting in 1975; the U.S. delegation was headed by Robert Hughes of NSF. In the more recent period, when the Marine Living Resources Convention was being negotiated, when the Tenth Consultative Meeting was being planned and conducted in Washington, and when negotiations on a mineral resources regime were beginning, the deputy assistant secretary for Oceans and Fisheries Affairs—the responsible officer for Antarctic affairs—changed four times in less than three years. Knowledge, experience, and continuity essentially resided in a single Foreign Service officer, who required special dispensation to remain in Washington beyond the prescribed eight-year limit.[35]

No other nation with interests in the Antarctic manages its affairs in so haphazard a manner. Many of the delegates to consultative meetings have been involved with Antarctic affairs for years—some since the treaty was adopted. Often they feel intense frustration in not knowing whom to deal with in Washington and whether anyone is in charge. In the British Foreign and Commonwealth Office, the head of the Polar Regions Section is a career assignment, and this is not exceptional.

More assured continuity of organization and personnel within the Department of State is now a matter of urgency, as Antarctic issues become more pressing and technical. While recognizing that the issue involves fundamental, indeed philosophical, questions about how best to man and operate the nation's foreign relations, the principle that Foreign Service officers should have broad experience at a variety of stations and posts has been carried to ridiculous extremes in the case of Antarctica. No doubt that unpopulated, cultureless continent may have seemed especially easy to ignore; no crises, no urgent demands have emanated from the ice. But things are obviously changing, and we need a stronger corps of experts at more senior ranks and with greater promise that Antarctica is a professional stepping-stone rather than a dead end. It is the more necessary because the Department of Defense has lost all interest in the Antarctic since its responsibility was confined to providing support at the behest of the National Science Foundation. Defense now altogether lacks the few politically knowledgeable experts it had a decade ago.

One of the issues with which the United States may need to be first among equals will arise if significant petroleum deposits are found in West Antarctica in the unclaimed sector explored and studied primarily by Americans. Depending on policy decisions, this eventuality could be instrumental either in strengthening the treaty system or in tearing it apart after 1991. If a firm decision is not made in advance, and oil is found in, say, Marie Byrd Land, the domestic political pressure to assert a claim may be overwhelming. On the other hand, because U.S. primacy in the unclaimed sector is generally acknowledged, the United States might exploit the situation to strengthen the treaty and to weaken the territorial claims of others. By exercising such restraint, Washington could exert leverage in moving the consultative parties toward a genuine consortium in which none could assert a privileged position. Discovery of oil in West Antarctica could present the United States and the treaty parties with a more severe test than any yet encountered. We should be better prepared.

The Division of Polar Programs of the National Science Foundation could also use an overhaul. In recent years, it has become increasingly slack and inflexible. A small indicator—perhaps insignificant in itself—is the *Antarctic Journal of the United States*, which has become nothing more than a house organ published on so erratic a schedule that it cannot even serve this limited purpose effectively. (Meanwhile the British *Polar Record* has evolved from a periodical of record to a journal of considerable substance.)

Another area of concern is the decline in international cooperation. Those who experienced the IGY in Antarctica came away with strong convictions about the value of international cooperation in science. Those who now administer the U.S. Antarctic Research Program seem skeptical of the value of multinational projects or simply find them a nuisance. To be sure, a number of international research projects can be pointed to, but they often have a kind of hands-across-the-seas artificiality or they fulfill exchange obligations. Rarer now is the selection of a foreign scientist simply because he is the most qualified person to fill a particular area of expertise on a U.S. research team. No doubt there are exceptions, but this tendency toward pro forma cooperation in international science represents a loss.

Some of the weaknesses of the Division of Polar Programs were discussed at the end of Chapter II. They all come together in the division's inability or unwillingness to adapt to changing circumstances. Until now, the NSF has resisted every effort to involve it in technical and scientific questions concerning the resources of Antarctica. Despite the directive of the National Security Council to extend scientific research in Antarctica to resource appraisal, despite pleading by other agencies that this be done, the NSF has made only a pretense of complying. No other agency has either the mandate, the money, or the qualifications to establish research priorities or to coordinate large assessment projects in Antarctica. No other agency in Washington is equipped to conduct the seismic and other geophysical studies that most treaty powers are already undertaking and that must precede even the roughest estimate of Antarctica's oil potential. Presumably, the NSF is holding out for special funding so as not to interfere in any way with its program of basic research. There is some justification for this, but the Division of Polar Programs has consistently given the lowest priority to what other agencies consider essential; and in time of high inflation and fuel costs, a low priority is tantamount to killing.[36]

Nevertheless, the need for hard decisions goes far beyond the NSF. The National Security Council has mandated "an active and influential presence" in Antarctica and "a constant level of effort." This is becoming more and more difficult to achieve despite budget increases to make some allowance for inflation. While the United States is reducing its year-round stations to three and worrying about how it can keep its C-130s flying, the Soviet Union, Japan, Australia, Argentina, and Chile are all said to be expanding their programs. West Germany has now joined the club with ambitious plans. Many believe that, without an enlarged effort, the United States will lose its ability to influence the treaty system.

This would be unfortunate. For despite lapses in attention, organizational shuffling, and inconsistencies of policy, the United States has in the broader span of time played a constructive role in the Antarctic. Even its inattention has sometimes been to advantage by avoiding acts of commission that would later have proved ill-advised. Of all the nations with interests in Antarctica, the United States on balance has been the most innovative, the most flexible, and the most inclined to seek international solutions.

Antarctica has been a pole apart not merely in its physical isolation but in its apparent immunity from the divisive issues that elsewhere make angry adversaries of the treaty members. Everything about Antarctica is sui generis—its climate, its geography, its history, its assets, its management. Analogies really do not work. The oceans are global. Space embraces us all. Antarctica has fixed dimensions, distant neighbors, a present fraternity of scientists, and a past that constitutes an emotional chapter in the history of several countries. Just as the Antarctic's unique environment must be protected from exploiters, so must its political and economic future be protected from ideologues. The Antarctic Treaty system is a continuing experiment that has served the world well. It deserves the opportunity to prove again its adaptability and the capacity of its members for adjustment and compromise, not only among themselves but with the rest of the world. If the consultative parties are realistic and avoid seeking narrow advantage in the continued exercise of their trusteeship, an era of expanding benefits is possible. If they are heedless or inflexible, then the good so far accomplished by the Antarctic Treaty may be lost forever.

A

The Antarctic Treaty

The Governments of Argentina, Australia, Belgium, Chile, the French Republic, Japan, New Zealand, Norway, the Union of South Africa, the Union of Soviet Socialist Republics, the United Kingdom of Great Britain and Northern Ireland, and the United States of America,

Recognizing that it is in the interest of all mankind that Antarctica shall continue forever to be used exclusively for peaceful purposes and shall not become the scene or object of international discord;

Acknowledging the substantial contributions to scientific knowledge resulting from international cooperation in scientific investigation in Antarctica;

Convinced that the establishment of a firm foundation for the continuation and development of such cooperation on the basis of freedom of scientific investigation in Antarctica as applied during the International Geophysical Year accords with the interests of science and the progress of all mankind;

Convinced also that a treaty ensuring the use of Antarctica for peaceful purposes only and the continuance of international harmony in Antarctica will further the purposes and principles embodied in the Charter of the United Nations;

Have agreed as follows:

Article I

1. Antarctica shall be used for peaceful purposes only. There shall be prohibited, *inter alia*, any measures of a military nature, such as the establishment of military bases and fortifications, the carrying out of military maneuvers, as well as the testing of any type of weapons.

2. The present Treaty shall not prevent the use of military personnel or equipment for scientific research or for any other peaceful purpose.

Article II

Freedom of scientific investigation in Antarctica and cooperation toward that end, as applied during the International Geophysical Year, shall continue, subject to the provisions of the present Treaty.

Article III

1. In order to promote international cooperation in scientific investigation in Antarctica, as provided for in Article II of the present Treaty, the Contracting Parties agree that, to the greatest extent feasible and practicable:

(a) information regarding plans for scientific programs in Antarctica shall be exchanged to permit maximum economy and efficiency of operations;

(b) scientific personnel shall be exchanged in Antarctica between expeditions and stations;

(c) scientific observations and results from Antarctica shall be exchanged and made freely available.

2. In implementing this Article, every encouragement shall be given to the establishment of cooperative working relations with those Specialized Agencies of the United Nations and other international organizations having a scientific or technical interest in Antarctica.

Article IV

1. Nothing contained in the present Treaty shall be interpreted as:

(a) a renunciation by any Contracting Party of previously asserted rights of or claims to territorial sovereignty in Antarctica;

(b) a renunciation or diminution by any Contracting Party of any basis of claim to territorial sovereignty in Antarctica which it may have whether as a result of its activities or those of its nationals in Antarctica, or otherwise;

(c) prejudicing the position of any Contracting Party as regards its recognition or non-recognition of any other State's right of or claim or basis of claim to territorial sovereignty in Antarctica.

2. No acts or activities taking place while the present Treaty is in force shall constitute a basis for asserting, supporting or denying a claim to

territorial sovereignty in Antarctica or create any rights of sovereignty in Antarctica. No new claim, or enlargement of an existing claim, to territorial sovereignty in Antarctica shall be asserted while the present Treaty is in force.

Article V

1. Any nuclear explosions in Antarctica and the disposal there of radioactive waste material shall be prohibited.

2. In the event of the conclusion of international agreements concerning the use of nuclear energy, including nuclear explosions and the disposal of radioactive waste material, to which all of the Contracting Parties whose representatives are entitled to participate in the meetings provided for under Article IX are parties, the rules established under such agreements shall apply in Antarctica.

Article VI

The provisions of the present Treaty shall apply to the area south of 60° South Latitude, including all ice shelves, but nothing in the present Treaty shall prejudice or in any way affect the rights, or the exercise of the rights, of any State under international law with regard to the high seas within that area.

Article VII

1. In order to promote the objectives and ensure the observance of the provisions of the present Treaty, each Contracting Party whose representatives are entitled to participate in the meetings referred to in Article IX of the Treaty shall have the right to designate observers to carry out any inspection provided for by the present Article. Observers shall be nationals of the Contracting Parties which designate them. The names of observers shall be communicated to every other Contracting Party having the right to designate observers, and like notice shall be given of the termination of their appointment.

2. Each observer designated in accordance with the provisions of paragraph 1 of this Article shall have complete freedom of access at any time to any or all areas of Antarctica.

3. All areas of Antarctica, including all stations, installations and equipment within those areas, and all ships and aircraft at points of discharging or embarking cargoes or personnel in Antarctica, shall be open at all times to inspection by any observers designated in accordance with paragraph 1 of this Article.

4. Aerial observation may be carried out at any time over any or all areas of Antarctica by any of the Contracting Parties having the right to designate observers.

5. Each Contracting Party shall, at the time when the present Treaty enters into force for it, inform the other Contracting Parties, and thereafter shall give them notice in advance, of

(a) all expeditions to and within Antarctica, on the part of its ships or nationals, and all expeditions to Antarctica organized in or proceeding from its territory;

(b) all stations in Antarctica occupied by its nationals; and

(c) any military personnel or equipment intended to be introduced by it into Antarctica subject to the conditions prescribed in paragraph 2 of Article I of the present Treaty.

Article VIII

1. In order to facilitate the exercise of their functions under the present Treaty, and without prejudice to the respective positions of the Contracting Parties relating to jurisdiction over all other persons in Antarctica, observers designated under paragraph 1 of Article VII and scientific personnel exchanged under subparagraph 1(b) of Article III of the Treaty, and members of the staffs accompanying any such persons, shall be subject only to the jurisdiction of the Contracting Party of which they are nationals in respect of all acts or omissions occurring while they are in Antarctica for the purpose of exercising their functions.

2. Without prejudice to the provisions of paragraph 1 of this Article, and pending the adoption of measures in pursuance of subparagraph 1(e) of Article IX, the Contracting Parties concerned in any case of dispute with regard to the exercise of jurisdiction in Antarctica shall immediately consult together with a view to reaching a mutually acceptable solution.

Article IX

1. Representatives of the Contracting Parties named in the preamble to the present Treaty shall meet at the City of Canberra within two months after the date of entry into force of the Treaty, and thereafter at suitable intervals and places, for the purpose of exchanging information, consulting together on matters of common interest pertaining to Antarctica, and formulating and considering, and recommending to their Governments, measures in furtherance of the principles and objectives of the Treaty, including measures regarding:

(a) use of Antarctica for peaceful purposes only;

(b) facilitation of scientific research in Antarctica;

(c) facilitation of international scientific cooperation in Antarctica;

(d) facilitation of the exercise of the rights of inspection provided for in Article VII of the Treaty;

(e) questions relating to the exercise of jurisdiction in Antarctica;

(f) preservation and conservation of living resources in Antarctica.

2. Each Contracting Party which has become a party to the present Treaty by accession under Article XIII shall be entitled to appoint representatives to participate in the meetings referred to in paragraph 1 of the present Article, during such time as that Contracting Party demonstrates its interest in Antarctica by conducting substantial scientific research activity there, such as the establishment of a scientific station or the dispatch of a scientific expedition.

3. Reports from the observers referred to in Article VII of the present Treaty shall be transmitted to the representatives of the Contracting Parties participating in the meetings referred to in paragraph 1 of the present Article.

4. The measures referred to in paragraph 1 of this Article shall become effective when approved by all the Contracting Parties whose representatives were entitled to participate in the meetings held to consider those measures.

5. Any or all of the rights established in the present Treaty may be exercised as from the date of entry into force of the Treaty whether or not any measures facilitating the exercise of such rights have been proposed, considered or approved as provided in this Article.

Article X

Each of the Contracting Parties undertakes to exert appropriate efforts, consistent with the Charter of the United Nations, to the end that no one engages in any activity in Antarctica contrary to the principles or purposes of the present Treaty.

Article XI

1. If any dispute arises between two or more of the Contracting Parties concerning the interpretation or application of the present Treaty, those Contracting Parties shall consult among themselves with a view to having the dispute resolved by negotiation, inquiry, mediation, conciliation, arbitration, judicial settlement or other peaceful means of their own choice.

2. Any dispute of this character not so resolved shall, with the consent, in each case, of all parties to the dispute, be referred to the International Court of Justice for settlement; but failure to reach agreement on reference

to the International Court shall not absolve parties to the dispute from the responsibility of continuing to seek to resolve it by any of the various peaceful means referred to in paragraph 1 of this Article.

Article XII

1. (a) The present Treaty may be modified or amended at any time by unanimous agreement of the Contracting Parties whose representatives are entitled to participate in the meetings provided for under Article IX. Any such modification or amendment shall enter into force when the depositary Government has received notice from all such Contracting Parties that they have ratified it.

(b) Such modification or amendment shall thereafter enter into force as to any other Contracting Party when notice of ratification by it has been received by the depositary Government. Any such Contracting Party from which no notice of ratification is received within a period of two years from the date of entry into force of the modification or amendment in accordance with the provisions of subparagraph 1(a) of this Article shall be deemed to have withdrawn from the present Treaty on the date of the expiration of such period.

2. (a) If after the expiration of thirty years from the date of entry into force of the present Treaty, any of the Contracting Parties whose representatives are entitled to participate in the meetings provided for under Article IX so requests by a communication addressed to the depositary Government, a Conference of all the Contracting Parties shall be held as soon as practicable to review the operation of the Treaty.

(b) Any modification or amendment to the present Treaty which is approved at such a Conference by a majority of the Contracting Parties there represented, including a majority of those whose representatives are entitled to participate in the meetings provided for under Article IX, shall be communicated by the depositary Government to all the Contracting Parties immediately after the termination of the Conference and shall enter into force in accordance with the provisions of paragraph 1 of the preent Article.

(c) If any such modification or amendment has not entered into force in accordance with the provisions of subparagraph 1(a) of this Article within a period of two years after the date of its communication to all the Contracting Parties, any Contracting Party may at any time after the expiration of that period give notice to the depositary Government of its withdrawal from the present Treaty; and such withdrawal shall take effect two years after the receipt of the notice by the depositary Government.

Article XIII

1. The present Treaty shall be subject to ratification by the signatory States. It shall be open for accession by any State which is a Member of the United Nations, or by any other State which may be invited to accede to the Treaty with the consent of all the Contracting Parties whose representatives are entitled to participate in the meetings provided for under Article IX of the Treaty.

2. Ratification of or accession to the present Treaty shall be effected by each State in accordance with its constitutional processes.

3. Instruments of ratification and instruments of accession shall be deposited with the Government of the United States of America, hereby designated as the depositary Government.

4. The depositary Government shall inform all signatory and acceding States of the date of each deposit of an instrument of ratification or accession, and the date of entry into force of the Treaty and of any modification or amendment thereto.

5. Upon the deposit of instruments of ratification by all the signatory States, the present Treaty shall enter into force for those States and for the States which have deposited instruments of accession. Thereafter the Treaty shall enter into force for any acceding State upon the deposit of its instrument of accession.

6. The present Treaty shall be registered by the depositary Government pursuant to Article 102 of the Charter of the United Nations.

Article XIV

The present Treaty, done in the English, French, Russian and Spanish languages, each version being equally authentic, shall be deposited in the archives of the Government of the United States of America, which shall transmit duly certified copies thereof to the Governments of the signatory and acceding States.

𝔹

The Convention on the Conservation of Antarctic Marine Living Resources

The Contracting Parties,

Recognising the importance of safeguarding the environment and protecting the environment and protecting the integrity of the ecosystem of the seas surrounding Antarctica;

Noting the concentration of marine living resources found in Antarctic waters and the increased interest in the possibilities offered by the utilization of these resources as a source of protein;

Conscious of the urgency of ensuring the conservation of Antarctic marine living resources;

Considering that it is essential to increase knowledge of the Antarctic marine ecosystem and its components so as to be able to base decisions on harvesting on sound scientific information;

Believing that the conservation of Antarctic marine living resources calls for international cooperation with due regard for the provisions of the Antarctic Treaty and with the active involvement of all States engaged in research or harvesting activities in Antarctic waters;

Recognising the prime responsibilities of the Antarctic Treaty Consultative Parties for the protection and preservation of the Antarctic environment and, in particular, their responsibilities under Article IX, paragraph 1(f) of the Antarctic Treaty in respect of the preservation and conservation of living resources in Antarctica;

Recalling the action already taken by the Antarctic Treaty Consultative Parties including in particular the Agreed Measures for the Conservation of Antarctic Fauna and Flora, as well as the provisions of the Convention for the Conservation of Antarctic Seals;

Bearing in mind the concern regarding the conservation of Antarctic marine living resources expressed by the Consultative Parties at the Ninth Consultative Meeting of the Antarctic Treaty and the importance of the provisions of Recommendation IX-2 which led to the establishment of the present Convention;

Believing that it is in the interest of all mankind to preserve the waters surrounding the Antarctic continent for peaceful purposes only and to prevent their becoming the scene or object of international discord;

Recognising, in the light of the foregoing, that it is desirable to establish suitable machinery for recommending, promoting, deciding upon and co-ordinating the measures and scientific studies needed to ensure the conservation of Antarctic marine living organisms;

Have agreed as follows:

Article I

1. This Convention applies to the Antarctic marine living resources of the area south of 60° South latitude and to the Antarctic marine living resources of the area between that latitude and the Antarctic Convergence which form part of the Antarctic marine ecosystem.

2. Antarctic marine living resources means the populations of fin fish, molluscs, crustaceans and all other species of living organisms, including birds, found south of the Antarctic Convergence.

3. The Antarctic marine ecosystem means the complex of relationships of Antarctic marine living resources with each other and with their physical environment.

4. The Antarctic Convergence shall be deemed to be a line joining the following points along parallels of latitude and meridians of longitude:

50°S, 0°; 50°S, 30°E; 45°S,
30°E; 45°S, 80°E; 55°S, 80°E;
55°S, 150°E; 60°S, 150°E; 60°S,
50°W; 50°S, 50°W; 50°S, 0°.

Article II

1. The objective of this Convention is the conservation of Antarctic marine living resources.

2. For the purposes of this Convention, the term "conservation" includes rational use.

3. Any harvesting and associated activities in the area to which this Convention applies shall be conducted in accordance with the provisions of this Convention and with the following principles of conservation:

(a) prevention of decrease in the size of any harvested population to levels below those which ensure its stable recruitment. For this purpose its size should not be allowed to fall below a level close to that which ensures the greatest net annual increment;

(b) maintenance of the ecological relationships between harvested, dependent and related populations of Antarctic marine living resources and the restoration of depleted populations to the levels defined in sub-paragraph (a) above:

and

(c) prevention of changes or minimization of the risk of changes in the marine ecosystem which are not potentially reversible over two or three decades, taking into account the state of available knowledge of the direct and indirect impact of harvesting, the effect of the introduction of alien species, the effects of associated activities on the marine ecosystem and of the effects of environmental changes, with the aim of making possible the sustained conservation of Antarctic marine living resources.

Article III

The Contracting Parties, whether or not they are Parties to the Antarctic Treaty, agree that they will not engage in any activities in the Antarctic Treaty area contrary to the principles and purposes of that Treaty and that, in their relations with each other, they are bound by the obligations contained in Articles I and V of the Antarctic Treaty.

Article IV

1. With respect to the Antarctic Treaty area, all Contracting Parties, whether or not they are Parties to the Antarctic Treaty, are bound by Articles IV and VI of the Antarctic Treaty in their relations with each other.

2. Nothing in this Convention and no acts or activities taking place while the present Convention is in force shall:

(a) constitute a basis for asserting, supporting or denying a claim to territorial sovereignty in the Antarctic Treaty area or create any rights of sovereignty in the Antarctic Treaty area;

(b) be interpreted as a renunciation or diminution by any Contracting Party of, or as prejudicing, any right or claim or basis of claim to exercise coastal state jurisdiction under international law within the area to which this Convention applies;

(c) be interpreted as prejudicing the position of any Contracting

Party as regards its recognition or non-recognition of any such right, claim or basis of claim;

(d) affect the provision of Article IV, paragraph 2, of the Antarctic Treaty that no new claim, or enlargement of an existing claim, to territorial sovereignty in Antarctica shall be asserted while the Antarctic Treaty is in force.

Article V

1. The Contracting Parties which are not Parties to the Antarctic Treaty acknowledge the special obligations and responsibilities of the Antarctic Treaty Consultative Parties for the protection and preservation of the environment of the Antarctic Treaty area.

2. The Contracting Parties which are not Parties to the Antarctic Treaty agree that, in their activities in the Antarctic Treaty area, they will observe as and when appropriate the Agreed Measures for the Conservation of Antarctic Fauna and Flora and such other measures as have been recommended by the Antarctic Treaty Consultative Parties in fulfillment of their responsibility for the protection of the Antarctic environment from all forms of harmful human interference.

3. For the purposes of this Convention, "Antarctic Treaty Consultative Parties" means the Contracting Parties to the Antarctic Treaty whose Representatives participate in meetings under Article IX of the Antarctic Treaty.

Article VI

Nothing in this Convention shall derogate from the rights and obligations of Contracting Parties under the International Convention for the Regulation of Whaling and the Convention for the Conservation of Antarctic Seals.

Article VII

1. The Contracting Parties hereby establish and agree to maintain the Commission for the Conservation of Antarctic Marine Living Resources (hereinafter referred to as "the Commission").

2. Membership in the Commission shall be as follows:

(a) each Contracting Party which participated in the meeting at which this Convention was adopted shall be a Member of the Commission;

(b) each State Party which has acceded to this Convention pursuant to Article XXIX shall be entitled to be a Member of the Commission during such time as that acceding party is engaged in research or harvesting activities in relation to the marine living resources to which this Convention applies;

(c) each regional economic integration organization which has acceded to this Convention pursuant to Article XXIX shall be entitled to be a Member of the Commission during such time as its States members are so entitled;

(d) a Contracting Party seeking to participate in the work of the Commission pursuant to sub-paragraphs (b) and (c) above shall notify the Depositary of the basis upon which it seeks to become a Member of the Commission and of its willingness to accept conservation measures in force. The Depositary shall communicate to each Member of the Commission such notification and accompanying information. Within two months of receipt of such communication from the Depositary, any Member of the Commission may request that a special meeting of the Commission be held to consider the matter. Upon receipt of such request, the Depositary shall call such a meeting. If there is no request for a meeting, the Contracting Party submitting the notification shall be deemed to have satisfied the requirements for Commission Membership.

3. Each Member of the Commission shall be represented by one representative who may be accompanied by alternate representatives and advisers.

Article VIII

The Commission shall have legal personality and shall enjoy in the territory of each of the States Parties such legal capacity as may be necessary to perform its function and achieve the purposes of this Convention. The privileges and immunities to be enjoyed by the Commission and its staff in the territory of a State Party shall be determined by agreement between the Commission and the State Party concerned.

Article IX

1. The function of the Commission shall be to give effect to the objective and principles set out in Article II of this Convention. To this end, it shall:

(a) facilitate research into and comprehensive studies of Antarctic marine living resources and of the Antarctic marine ecosystem;

(b) compile data on the status of and changes in population of Antarctic marine living resources and on factors affecting the distribution, abundance and productivity of harvested species and dependent or related species or populations;

(c) ensure the acquisition of catch and effort statistics on harvested populations;

(d) analyse, disseminate and publish the information referred to in sub-paragraphs (b) and (c) above and the reports of the Scientific Committee;

(e) identify conservation needs and analyse the effectiveness of conservation measures;

(f) formulate, adopt and revise conservation measures on the basis of the best scientific evidence available, subject to the provisions of paragraph 5 of this Article;

(g) implement the system of observation and inspection established under Article XXIV of this Convention;

(h) carry out such other activities as are necessary to fulfill the objective of this Convention.

2. The conservation measures referred to in paragraph 1 (f) above include the following:

(a) the designation of the quantity of any species which may be harvested in the area to which this Convention applies;

(b) the designation of regions and sub-regions based on the distribution of populations of Antarctic marine living resources;

(c) the designation of the quantity which may be harvested from the populations of regions and sub-regions;

(d) the designation of protected species;

(e) the designation of the size, age and, as appropriate, sex of species which may be harvested;

(f) the designation of open and closed seasons for harvesting;

(g) the designation of the opening and closing of areas, regions or sub-regions for purposes of scientific study or conservation, including special areas for protection and scientific study;

(h) regulation of the effort employed and methods of harvesting, including fishing gear, with a view, inter alia, to avoiding undue concentration of harvesting in any region or sub-region;

(i) the taking of such other conservation measures as the Commission considers necessary for the fulfillment of the objective of this Convention, including measures concerning the effects of harvesting and associated activities on components of the marine ecosystem other than the harvested populations.

3. The Commission shall publish and maintain a record of all conservation measures in force.

4. In exercising its functions under paragraph 1 above, the Commission shall take full account of the recommendations and advice of the Scientific Committee.

5. The Commission shall take full account of any relevant measures or regulations established or recommended by the Consultative Meetings pursuant to Article IX of the Antarctic Treaty or by existing fisheries commissions responsible for species which may enter the area to which this Convention applies, in order that there shall be no inconsistency between the rights and obligations of a Contracting Party under such regulations or measures and conservation measures which may be adopted by the Commission.

6. Conservation measures adopted by the Commission in accordance with this Convention shall be implemented by Members of the Commission in the following manner:

(a) the Commission shall notify conservation measures to all Members of the Commission;

(b) conservation measures shall become binding upon all Members of the Commission 180 days after such notification, except as provided in sub-paragraphs (c) and (d) below;

(c) if a Member of the Commission, within ninety days following the notification specified in sub-paragraph (a), notifies the Commission that it is unable to accept the conservation measure, in whole or in part, the measure shall not, to the extent stated, be binding upon that Member of the Commission;

(d) in the event that any Member of the Commission invokes the procedure set forth in sub-paragraph (c) above, the Commission shall meet at the request of any Member of the Commission to review the conservation measure. At the time of such meeting and within thirty days following the meeting, any Member of the Commission shall have the right to declare that it is no longer able to accept the conservation measure, in which case the Member shall no longer be bound by such measure.

Article X

1. The Commission shall draw the attention of any State which is not a Party to this Convention to any activity undertaken by its nationals or vessels which, in the opinion of the Commission, affects the implementation of the objective of this Convention.

2. The Commission shall draw the attention of all Contracting Parties to any activity which, in the opinion of the Commission, affects the implementation by a Contracting Party of the objective of this Convention or the compliance by that Contracting Party with its obligations under this Convention.

Article XI

The Commission shall seek to cooperate with Contracting Parties which may exercise jurisdiction in marine areas adjacent to the area to which this Convention applies in respect of the conservation of any stock or stocks of associated species which occur both within those areas and the area to which this Convention applies, with a view to harmonizing the conservation measures adopted in respect of such stocks.

Article XII

1. Decisions of the Commission on matters of substance shall be taken by consensus. The question of whether a matter is one of substance shall be treated as a matter of substance.

2. Decisions on matters other than those referred to in paragraph 1 above shall be taken by a simple majority of the Members of the Commission present and voting.

3. In Commission consideration of any item requiring a decision, it shall be made clear whether a regional economic integration organization will participate in the taking of the decision and, if so, whether any of its member States will also participate. The number of Contracting Parties so participating shall not exceed the number of member States of the regional economic integration organization which are Members of the Commission.

4. In the taking of decisions pursuant to this Article, a regional economic integration organization shall have only one vote.

Article XIII

1. The headquarters of the Commission shall be established at Hobart, Tasmania, Australia.

2. The Commission shall hold a regular annual meeting. Other meetings shall also be held at the request of one-third of its members and as otherwise provided in this Convention. The first meeting of the Commission shall be held within three months of the entry into force of this Convention, provided that among the Contracting Parties there are at least two States conducting harvesting activities within the area to which this Convention applies. The first meeting shall, in any event, be held within one year of the entry into force of this Convention. The Depositary shall consult with the signatory States regarding the first Commission meeting, taking into account that a broad representation of such States is necessary for the effective operation of the Commission.

3. The Depositary shall convene the first meeting of the Commission at

the headquarters of the Commission. Thereafter, meetings of the Commission shall be held at its headquarters, unless it decides otherwise.

4. The Commission shall elect from among its members a Chairman and Vice-Chariman, each of whom shall serve for a term of two years and shall be eligible for re-election for one additional term. The first Chairman shall, however, be elected for an initial term of three years. The Chairman and Vice-Chairman shall not be representatives of the same Contracting Party.

5. The Commission shall adopt and amend as necessary the rules of procedures for the conduct of its meetings, except with respect to the matters dealt with in Article XII of this Convention.

6. The Commission may establish such subsidiary bodies as are necessary for the performance of its functions.

Article XIV

1. The Contracting Parties hereby establish the Scientific Committee for the Conservation of Antarctic Marine Living Resources (hereinafter referred to as "the Scientific Committee") which shall be a consultative body to the Commission. The Scientific Committee shall normally meet at the headquarters of the Commission unless the Scientific Committee decides otherwise.

2. Each Member of the Commission shall be a member of the Scientific Committee and shall appoint a representative with suitable scientific qualifications who may be accompanied by other experts and advisers.

3. The Scientific Committee may seek the advice of other scientists and experts as may be required on an ad hoc basis.

Article XV

1. The Scientific Committee shall provide a forum for consultation and cooperation concerning the collection, study and exchange of information with respect to the marine living resources to which this Convention applies. It shall encourage and promote cooperation in the field of scientific research in order to extend knowledge of the marine living resources of the Antarctic marine ecosystem.

2. The Scientific Committee shall conduct such activities as the Commission may direct in pursuance of the objective of this Convention and shall:

(a) establish criteria and methods to be used for determinations concerning the conservation measures referred to in Article IX of this Convention;

(b) regularly assess the status and trends of the populations of Antarctic marine living resources;

(c) analyse data concerning the direct and indirect effects of harvesting on the populations of Antarctic marine living resources;

(d) assess the effects of proposed changes in the methods or levels of harvesting and proposed conservation measures;

(e) transmit assessments, analyses, reports and recommendations to the Commission as requested or on its own initiative regarding measures and research to implement the objective of this Convention;

(f) formulate proposals for the conduct of international and national programs of research into Antarctic marine living resources.

3. In carrying out its functions, the Scientific Committee shall have regard to the work of other relevant technical and scientific organizations and to the scientific activities conducted within the framework of the Antarctic Treaty.

Article XVI

1. The first meeting of the Scientific Committee shall be held within three months of the first meeting of the Commission. The Scientific Committee shall meet thereafter as often as may be necessary to fulfill its functions.

2. The Scientific Committee shall adopt and amend as necessary its rules of procedure. The rules and any amendments thereto shall be approved by the Commission. The rules shall include procedures for the presentation of minority reports.

3. The Scientific Committee may establish, with the approval of the Commission, such subsidiary bodies as are necessary for the performance of its functions.

Article XVII

1. The Commission shall appoint an Executive Secretary to serve the Commission and Scientific Committee according to such procedures and on such terms and conditions as the Commission may determine. His term of office shall be for four years and he shall be eligible for reappointment.

2. The Commission shall authorize such staff establishment for the Secretariat as may be necessary and the Executive Secretary shall appoint, direct and supervise such staff according to such rules and procedures and on such terms and conditions as the Commission may determine.

3. The Executive Secretary and Secretariat shall perform the functions entrusted to them by the Commission.

Article XVIII

The official languages of the Commission and of the Scientific Committee shall be English, French, Russian and Spanish.

Article XIX

1. At each annual meeting, the Commission shall adopt by consensus its budget and the budget of the Scientific Committee.

2. A draft budget for the Commission and the Scientific Committee and any subsidiary bodies shall be prepared by the Executive Secretary and submitted to the Members of the Commission at least sixty days before the annual meeting of the Commission.

3. Each Member of the Commission shall contribute to the budget. Until the expiration of five years after the entry into force of this Convention, the contribution of each Member of the Commission shall be equal. Thereafter the contribution shall be determined in accordance with two criteria: the amount harvested and an equal sharing among all Members of the Commission. The Commission shall determine by consensus the proportion in which these two criteria shall apply.

4. The financial activities of the Commission and Scientific Committee shall be conducted in accordance with financial regulations adopted by the Commission and shall be subject to an annual audit by external auditors selected by the Commission.

5. Each Member of the Commission shall meet its own expenses arising from attendance at meetings of the Commission and of the Scientific Committee.

6. A Member of the Commission that fails to pay its contributions for two consecutive years shall not, during the period of its default, have the right to participate in the taking of decisions in the Commission.

Article XX

1. The Members of the Commission shall, to the greatest extent possible, provide annually to the Commission and to the Scientific Committee such statistical, biological and other data and information as the Commission and Scientific Committee may require in the exercise of their functions.

2. The Members of the Commission shall provide, in the manner and at such intervals as may be prescribed, information about their harvesting activities, including fishing areas and vessels, so as to enable reliable catch and effort statistics to be compiled.

3. The Members of the Commission shall provide to the Commission at

such intervals as may be prescribed information on steps taken to implement the conservation measures adopted by the Commission.

4. The Members of the Commission agree that in any of their harvesting activities, advantage shall be taken of opportunities to collect data needed to assess the impact of harvesting.

Article XXI

1. Each Contracting Party shall take appropriate measures within its competence to ensure compliance with the provisions of this Convention and with conservation measures adopted by the Commission to which the Party is bound in accordance with Article IX of this Convention.

2. Each Contracting Party shall transmit to the Commission information on measures taken pursuant to paragraph 1 above, including the imposition of sanctions for any violation.

Article XXII

1. Each Contracting Party undertakes to exert appropriate efforts, consistent with the Charter of the United Nations, to the end that no one engages in any activity contrary to the objective of this Convention.

2. Each Contracting Party shall notify the Commission of any such activity which comes to its attention.

Article XXIII

1. The Commission and the Scientific Committee shall co-operate with the Antarctic Treaty Consultative Parties on matters falling within the competence of the latter.

2. The Commission and the Scientific Committee shall co-operate, as appropriate, with the Food and Agriculture Organization of the United Nations and with other Specialized Agencies.

3. The Commission and the Scientific Committee shall seek to develop co-operative working relationships, as appropriate, with inter-governmental and non-governmental organizations which could contribute to their work, including the Scientific Committee on Antarctic Research, the Scientific Committee on Oceanic Research and the International Whaling Commission.

4. The Commission may enter into agreements with the organizations referred to in this Article and with other organizations as may be appropriate. The Commission and the Scientific Committee may invite such organizations to send observers to their meetings and to meetings of their subsidiary bodies.

Article XXIV

1. In order to promote the objective and ensure observance of the provisions of this Convention, the Contracting Parties agree that a system of observation and inspection shall be established.

2. The system of observation and inspection shall be elaborated by the Commission on the basis of the following principles:

(a) Contracting Parties shall cooperate with each other to ensure the effective implementation of the system of observation and inspection, taking account of the existing international practice. This system shall include, inter alia, procedures for boarding and inspection by observers and inspectors designated by the Members of the Commission and procedures for flag state prosecution and sanctions on the basis of evidence resulting from such boarding and inspections. A report of such prosecutions and sanctions imposed shall be included in the information referred to in Article XXI of this Convention;

(b) in order to verify compliance with measures adopted under this Convention, observation and inspection shall be carried out on board vessels engaged in scientific research or harvesting of marine living resources in the area to which this Convention applies, through observers and inspectors designated by the Members of the Commission and operating under terms and conditions to be established by the Commission;

(c) designated observers and inspectors shall remain subject to the jurisdiction of the Contracting Party of which they are nationals. They shall report to the Member of the Commission by which they have been designated which in turn shall report to the Commission.

3. Pending the establishment of the system of observation and inspection, the Members of the Commission shall seek to establish interim arrangements to designate observers and inspectors and such designated observers and inspectors shall be entitled to carry out inspections in accordance with the principles set out in paragraph 2 above.

Article XXV

1. If any dispute arises between two or more of the Contracting Parties concerning the interpretation or application of this Convention, those Contracting Parties shall consult among themselves with a view to having the dispute resolved by negotiation, inquiry, mediation, conciliation, arbitration, judicial settlement or other peaceful means of their own choice.

2. Any dispute of this character not so resolved shall, with the consent in each case of all Parties to the dispute, be referred for settlement to the

International Court of Justice or to arbitration; but failure to reach agreement on reference to the International Court or to arbitration shall not absolve Parties to the dispute from the responsibility of continuing to seek to resolve it by any of the various peaceful means referred to in paragraph 1 above.

3. In cases where the dispute is referred to arbitration, the arbitral tribunal shall be constituted as provided in the Annex to this Convention.

Article XXVI

1. This Convention shall be open for signature at Canberra from 1 August to 31 December 1980 by the States participating in the Conference on the Conservation of Antarctic Marine Living Resources held at Canberra from 7 to 20 May 1980.

2. The States which so sign will be the original signatory States of the Convention.

Article XXVII

1. This Convention is subject to ratification, acceptance or approval by signatory States.

2. Instruments of ratification, acceptance or approval shall be deposited with the Government of Australia, hereby designated as the Depositary.

Article XXVIII

1. This Convention shall enter into force on the thirtieth day following the date of deposit of the eighth instrument of ratification, acceptance or approval by States referred to in paragraph 1 of Article XXVI of this Convention.

2. With respect to each State or regional economic integration organization which subsequent to the date of entry into force of this Convention deposits an instrument of ratification, acceptance, approval or accession, the Convention shall enter into force on the thirtieth day following such deposit.

Article XXIX

1. This Convention shall be open for accession by any State interested in research or harvesting activities in relation to the marine living resources to which this Convention applies.

2. This Convention shall be open for accession by regional economic integration organizations constituted by sovereign States which include

among their members one or more States Members of the Commission and to which the States members of the organization have transferred, in whole or in part, competences with regard to the matters covered by this Convention. The accession of such regional economic integration organizations shall be the subject of consultations among Members of the Commission.

Article XXX

1. This Convention may be amended at any time.

2. If one-third of the Members of the Commission request a meeting to discuss a proposed amendment the Depositary shall call such a meeting.

3. An amendment shall enter into force when the Depositary has received instruments of ratification, acceptance or approval thereof from all the Members of the Commission.

4. Such amendment shall thereafter enter into force as to any other Contracting Party when notice of ratification, acceptance or approval by it has been received by the Depositary. Any such Contracting Party from which no such notice has been received within a period of one year from the date of entry into force of the amendment in accordance with paragraph 3 above shall be deemed to have withdrawn from this Convention.

Article XXXI

1. Any Contracting Party may withdraw from this Convention on 30 June of any year, by giving written notice not later than 1 January of the same year to the Depositary, which, upon receipt of such a notice, shall communicate it forthwith to the other Contracting Parties.

2. Any other Contracting Party may, within sixty days of the receipt of a copy of such a notice from the Depositary, give written notice of withdrawal to the Depositary in which case the Convention shall cease to be in force on 30 June of the same year with respect to the Contracting Party giving such notice.

3. Withdrawal from this Convention by any Member of the Commission shall not affect its financial obligations under this Convention.

Article XXXII

The Depositary shall notify all Contracting Parties of the following:

(a) signatures of this Convention and the deposit of instruments of ratification, acceptance, approval or accession;

(b) the date of entry into force of this Convention and of any amendment thereto.

Article XXXIII

1. This Convention, of which the English, French, Russian and Spanish texts are equally authentic, shall be deposited with the Government of Australia which shall transmit duly certified copies thereof to all signatory and acceding Parties.

2. This Convention shall be registered by the Depositary pursuant to Article 102 of the Charter of the United Nations.

Drawn up at Canberra this twentieth day of May 1980.

IN WITNESS WHEREOF the undersigned, being duly authorized, have signed this Convention.

Annex for an Arbitral Tribunal

The arbitral tribunal referred to in paragraph 3 of Article XXV shall be composed of three arbitrators who shall be appointed as follows:

The Party commencing proceedings shall communicate the name of an arbitrator to the other Party which, in turn, within a period of forty days following such notification, shall communicate the name of the second arbitrator. The Parties shall, within a period of sixty days following the appointment of the second arbitrator, appoint the third arbitrator, who shall not be a national of either Party and shall not be of the same nationality as either of the first two arbitrators. The third arbitrator shall preside over the tribunal.

If the second arbitrator has not been appointed within the prescribed period, or if the Parties have not reached agreement within the prescribed period on the appointment of the third arbitrator, that arbitrator shall be appointed, at the request of either Party, by the Secretary-General of the Permanent Court of Arbitration, from among persons of international standing not having the nationality of a State which is a Party to this Convention.

The arbitral tribunal shall decide where its headquarters will be located and shall adopt its own rules of procedure.

The award of the arbitral tribunal shall be made by a majority of its members, who may not abstain from voting.

Any Contracting Party which is not a Party to the dispute may intervene in the proceedings with the consent of the arbitral tribunal.

The award of the arbitral tribunal shall be final and binding on all Parties to the dispute and on any Party which intervenes in the proceedings and shall be complied with without delay. The arbitral tribunal shall interpret the award at the request of one of the Parties to the dispute or of any intervening Party.

Unless the arbitral tribunal determines otherwise because of the particular circumstances of the case, the expenses of the tribunal, including the remuneration of its members, shall be borne by the Parties to the dispute in equal shares.

Notes

CHAPTER I

1. Explorers—and not only expedition leaders—are prolific diarists and writers. A sampling of the generally spare, sometimes poetic prose of those who have explored Antarctica can be found in Charles Neider, ed., *Antarctica* (New York: Random House, 1972). The most scholarly and detailed history of Antarctic exploration is unfortunately confined to efforts by Americans. Strangely, no other country has produced as thorough a study as Kenneth J. Bertrand, *Americans in Antarctica, 1775–1948* (New York: American Geographical Society, 1971). There are at least five general and complementary histories of the era of Antarctic exploration and discovery, each of considerable merit and, sadly, all out of print. They are Walter Sullivan, *Quest for a Continent* (New York: McGraw-Hill, 1957), overly brief on the early history, but especially valuable for the later Byrd expeditions in which Sullivan took part as correspondent for *The New York Times;* L. P. Kirwan, *A History of Polar Exploration* (New York: W. W. Norton, 1960), a standard English work by the then director of the Royal Geographical Society that covers both poles; Frank Debenham, *Antarctica: The Story of a Continent* (New York: Macmillan, 1961), which benefits from its author's dual role as active explorer (with Scott's second expedition) and scholar (geologist, biographer of Bellingshausen, and founder-director of the Scott Polar Research Institute); Walter Chapman [Robert Silverberg], *The Loneliest Continent* (Greenwich, CT: New York Graphic Society Publishers, 1964), perhaps the most detached and best balanced; and Ian Cameron [Donald Gordon Payne], *Antarctica: The Last Continent* (Boston: Little Brown, 1974), which is selective in narrative but makes good use of explorers' journals and later writings. L. B. Quartermain's, *South to the Pole* (London: Oxford University Press, 1967) is an exhaustive account by a New Zealander of the early history of the Ross Sea sector. For tracing the travels of explorers, an unequaled source is Henry M. Dater, "History of

243

Antarctic Exploration and Scientific Investigation," *Antarctic Map Folio Series,*
Folio 19 (New York: American Geographical Society, 1975). This briefly
describes and depicts sixty-nine expeditions and every scientific research
season from 1954–55 to 1974–75. See also Laurence M. Gould, "Emergence of
Antarctica: The Mythical Land," in *Frozen Future: A Prophetic Report from
Antarctica,* Richard S. Lewis and Philip M. Smith, eds. (New York: Quadran-
gle Books, 1973); and John Parker, *Discovery: Developing Views of the Earth from
Ancient Times to the Voyages of Captain Cook* (New York: Scribner's, 1972).

2. Of the contemporary sources cited above, Chapman and Cameron believe
   "Southern India" was probably the island of Madagascar (now Malagasy),
   while Debenham says it was off the coast of South America.
3. Quoted in Cameron, *Antarctica: The Last Continent,* p. 33.
4. Quoted in Debenham, *Antarctica: The Story of a Continent,* p. 39.
5. Louis J. Halle, *The Sea and the Ice: A Naturalist in Antarctica* (Boston: Houghton
   Mifflin, in cooperation with the National Audubon Society, 1973), p. 3.
6. Captain James Cook, *A Voyage Towards the South Pole and Round the World,* 2
   vols. (London, 1777).
7. *Ibid.,* vol. 2, p. 239.
8. Grenfell Price, in the introduction to the facsimile edition (1970) of Cook's *A
   Voyage Towards the South Pole.*
9. Cook, *A Voyage Towards the South Pole and Round the World,* vol. 2, pp. 230–31.
10. Alan Moorehead, *The Fatal Impact* (New York: Harper & Row, 1966), p. 195.
11. Philip I. Mitterling, *America in the Antarctic to 1840* (Urbana, IL: University of
    Illinois Press, 1959), pp. 19–24.
12. Roger Tory Peterson, "Render the Penguins, Butcher the Seals," *Audubon,*
    March 1973, p. 98. When the era of steam began, it was not exceptional for
    explorers to stoke their ships' boilers with the blubber of penguins.
13. Bertrand, *Americans in Antarctica,* p. 102.
14. Quoted in Chapman, *The Loneliest Continent,* p. 37.
15. Quoted in Sullivan, *Quest for a Continent,* p. 25.
16. Chapman, *The Loneliest Continent,* p. 44.
17. Cameron, *Antarctica: The Last Continent,* pp. 68–70.
18. *Ibid.,* pp. 75–76.
19. Cameron is entirely persuaded that Bellingshausen sighted the continent on
    three occasions in 1820, the first time on January 27 (pp. 82–83). If so, the
    coast he glimpsed (Martha Coast) was not seen again for more than a
    century.
20. Bertrand, *Americans in Antarctica,* p. 72.
21. *Ibid.,* Chapter 5. The fullest use of the two logbooks has been made by
    Edouard A. Stackpole, *The Voyage of the Huron and the Huntress* (Mystic, CT:
    Marine Historical Society, 1955). Stackpole himself discovered the *Huntress*
    log in 1951 while he was curator of the Marine Historical Society at Mystic.
22. However, the body of coastal water extending from Alexander I Island four
    hundred nautical miles westward to Thurston Island was later named the
    Bellingshausen Sea.
23. Cameron here contradicts most others by stating in his prologue (p. 18) that
    Graham Land was named by Bransfield. Yet elsewhere (p. 69) Cameron

agrees that Bransfield named the land he sighted Trinity Land, a name that survives as Trinity Peninsula—the tip of the Antarctic Peninsula.

24. There is no mechanism for reconciling differences in place names among the nations that have explored Antarctica. The English-speaking countries involved in Antarctica do make an informal effort to agree and to accept the primacy of whatever country has done most of the exploring in a given area. With the exceptions of Belgium, Poland, South Africa, and the Soviet Union, each country has an official body to decide on place names. See G. Hattersley-Smith, "Current Sources of Antarctic and sub-Antarctic Place Names," *Polar Record*, January 1980, p. 72, published by the Scott Polar Research Institute in Cambridge, England. *Polar Record* has been the premier periodical in the field for half a century. The recently published *Geographic Names of the Antarctic* contains more than twelve thousand place names approved by the U.S. Board on Geographic Names. Each entry provides geographic coordinates; a description of the feature; circumstances of its discovery, mapping, and naming; the identity of the namer and the namee; and sometimes more. The volume, compiled and edited by Fred G. Alberts, runs to 959 oversized pages.

25. Bertrand, *Americans in Antarctica*, p. 164.

26. *Ibid.*, p. 159.

27. Quoted in Cameron, *Antarctica: The Last Continent*, p. 105.

28. Bertrand, *Americans in Antarctica*, p. 190.

29. Wilkes's volume on terrestrial magnetism was either lost or never completed; in any case, Congress by then had cut off funds for publication. From data in Wilkes's papers, modern scholars have computed Wilkes's estimate of the pole's position. Today the South Magnetic Pole is just off the coast to the north and east of the point designated by D'Urville. (See Bertrand, *Americans in Antarctica*, p. 167.) Maps of Antarctica showing the whole continent can be confusing because the points of the compass are not those we are accustomed to. North, of course, is any direction away from the South Pole. East is invariably in a clockwise direction. Hence, on the lower half of maps of Antarctica, east and west are the reverse of what is familiar. However, large-scale maps of parts of Antarctica may follow the usual convention, putting north at the top.

30. Irwin Ashkenazy, "The Rest of the Iceberg," *Oceans*, May–June 1977, p. 27.

31. U.S. Department of State, Historical Studies Division, *United States Policy and International Cooperation in Antarctica* (Washington, DC, 1964), p. 2. The First International Polar Year was one of the earliest concerted efforts to make a quantum leap in scientific knowledge through a multinational, multidisciplinary program.

32. Kirwan, *A History of Polar Exploration*, pp. 215–18.

33. Bertrand, *Americans in Antarctica*, pp. 198–206. See also U.S. Department of State, "Statements by Americans Favoring an International Solution to the Antarctic Question," Historical Division, Bureau of Public Affairs (Washington, DC, 1959), pp. 1–3. In addition to the United States, Maury's letter went to Austria, France, Great Britain, Italy, the Netherlands, Portugal, Russia, and Spain.

34. Kirwan, *A History of Polar Exploration*, pp. 214–16.
35. H. G. R. King, *The Antarctic* (New York: Arco, 1969), p. 236. This excellent work, by the librarian of the Scott Polar Research Institute, was not cited earlier because it is more illuminating on geography and basic science than on history.
36. An interdisciplinary scientific body advising the government and not to be confused with the Royal Geographic Society.
37. Kirwan, *A History of Polar Exploration*, pp. 218–19, 232–34.
38. Quoted in Sullivan, *Quest for a Continent*, p. 35.
39. Elspeth Huxley, *Scott of the Antarctic* (New York: Atheneum, 1978), pp. 33–35.
40. It should be added that, in a later age of sophisticated technologies, the U.S. Navy made an outstanding contribution to Antarctic exploration.
41. Lennard Bickel, *Mawson's Will* (New York: Stein and Day, 1977), pp. 130–31. Published in the British Commonwealth as *This Accursed Land*.
42. While all place names mentioned have survived to the present, some terminology has been altered, notably "Land" to "Coast." Thus, today's maps show Adélie Coast, George V Coast, Queen Mary Coast (and many more), all within Wilkes Land.
43. Roald Amundsen, *The South Pole: An Account of the Norwegian Expedition in the "Fram," 1910–1912* (New York: Harper & Row, Barnes & Noble Division, 1976). This edition is reproduced from the original two-volume work published in 1912 by John Murray, London. Volume I is devoted to preparations, including the wintering over; volume II recounts the actual trip to the pole and back.
44. Quoted in Kirwan, *A History of Polar Exploration*, pp. 287–88.
45. Not including the splendid watercolors of the chief scientist, Edward Wilson, and a truly remarkable photographic record by Herbert Ponting. See Ann Savours, ed., *Scott's Last Voyage Through the Camera of Herbert Ponting*, with an introduction by Sir Peter Scott (New York: Praeger, 1975; London: Sidgwick and Jackson, 1974).
46. *Scott's Last Expedition: the personal journals of Captain R. F. Scott, CVO, RN on his journey to the South Pole* (London: The Folio Society, 1964). The journals were first published in 1913 in two volumes. Despite Scott's many admirable qualities and his reputation for intelligence, his judgment on this expedition was inexplicably disastrous, and he appeared to have learned nothing from previous experience. As before, he underestimated the caloric intake necessary for man-hauling sledges in subzero weather, and he failed to take any preventive measures against scurvy. He disregarded Shackleton's bad experience with ponies, and for the second time ignored the advice of famous Arctic explorer Fridtjof Nansen to use Greenland huskies rather than Siberian dogs that were not even trained for the job but had been used in the Russian postal service. On this point, see statements by Sir Charles Wright, who was in the party that discovered the bodies of Scott and his companions, quoted in Charles Neider, *Edge of the World: Ross Island, Antarctica* (Garden City, NY: Doubleday, 1974), p. 283. Further, as was the case when Scott led the *Discovery* expedition, ten years earlier, no one in this expedition was competent to handle work dogs. As the last support team was returning to base, Scott made an eleventh-hour decision to take an extra man to the

pole—one who had no skis and for whom rations and tenting had not been planned. In this party of officers, Scott also included one lone enlisted man, whose separateness surely contributed to his being first to die. Only one depot had been laid the previous winter, and this one was too close to the departure point; Scott never reached it. And finally (although here it is more difficult to find fault), Scott failed to separate science and adventure, to define his objectives and establish priorities. (This judgment is unaffected by a book that denigrates Scott unremittingly, published after the foregoing was drafted: Roland Huntford, *Scott and Amundsen* [New York: G. P. Putnam's Sons, 1980].)

47. The full story of this expedition of 1914–17 is told by Shackleton with great economy of words in *South* (London: Heinemann, 1919).

48. Sullivan, *Quest for a Continent*, p. 82.

49. Quoted in Paul A. Carter, *Little America: Town at the End of the World* (New York: Columbia University Press, 1979), p. 141. A particular merit of this book is that its author had continuous access to the person and papers of Laurence M. Gould, who was a towering figure in Antarctic science for nearly half a century.

50. Laurence M. Gould, *Antarctica in World Affairs*, Foreign Policy Association, Headline Series no. 128, 1958, p. 26. This was merely one of many instances when Americans, either independently or on orders, made claims that the United States never officially accepted or endorsed. (See Chapter 4.)

51. Sullivan, *Quest for a Continent*, pp. 79–88; Carter, *Little America*, pp. 120–29, 144; Bertrand, *Americans in Antarctica*, pp. 290–312.

52. Carter, *Little America*, pp. 172–77.

53. *Ibid.*, p. 101.

54. Debenham, *Antarctica: The Story of a Continent*, p. 105.

55. Quoted in Carter, *Little America*, p. 184.

56. Sullivan, *Quest for a Continent*, pp. 90, 96–99; Bertrand, *Americans in Antarctica*, chapter 18. See especially pp. 316–19.

57. Sullivan, *Quest for a Continent*, p. 103.

58. The two Ellsworth expeditions are detailed in Bertrand, *Americans in Antarctica*, chapters 19 and 20.

59. Sullivan, *Quest for a Continent*, pp. 124–28.

60. Paul Siple, *90° South: The Story of the American South Pole Conquest* (New York: G. P. Putnam's Sons, 1959), p. 73.

61. Bertrand, *Americans in Antarctica*, p. 407.

62. Laurence M. Gould, "The Polar Regions in Their Relation to Human Affairs," Bowman Memorial Lectures (New York: The American Geographical Society, 1958), p. 1.

63. "Weather from the Ends of the Earth," *Mosaic* (published by the National Science Foundation) 9, no. 5, September/October 1978, p. 39.

64. Edward P. Todd, *U.S. Activities in Antarctica*, Hearing Before the Senate Committee on Energy and Natural Resources, April 23, 1979 (Publication no. 96–21), p. 11.

65. Central Intelligence Agency, *Polar Regions Atlas* (Washington, DC: 1978), p. 36.

66. Joseph O. Fletcher, "Polar Ice and the Global Climate Machine," in *Frozen Future*, p. 127.

67. Morton J. Rubin, "Cold Poles and Heat Balances," in *Research in the Antarctic*, Louis O. Quam, ed. (Washington, DC: American Association for the Advancement of Science, 1971), p. 426.

68. King, *The Antarctic*, p. 28.

69. For a fuller comparison of the poles by some eighteen criteria, see George A. Llano, "Polar Research: A Synthesis with Special Reference to Biology," in *Polar Research: To the Present, and the Future*, Mary A. McWhinnie, ed., published for the American Association for the Advancement of Science (Boulder, CO: Westview Press, 1978), pp. 27–31.

70. Debenham, *Antarctica: The Story of a Continent*, p. 126.

71. "Weather from the Ends of the Earth," *Mosaic*, p. 40.

72. K. B. Mather and G. S. Miller, "The Problem of the Katabatic Winds on the Coast of Terre Adélie," *Polar Record* 13, no. 85, p. 425.

73. Gould, *Antarctica in World Affairs*, p. 7.

74. King, *The Antarctic*, p. 180.

75. Walter Sullivan, *Assault on the Unknown: The International Geophysical Year* (New York: McGraw-Hill, 1961), p. 321.

76. Richard E. Byrd, *Alone* (New York: G. P. Putnam's Sons, 1938), pp. 154–55.

77. King, *The Antarctic*, p. 183. A great deal of drifting is caused by human activity—such as shoveling, building structures that alter wind flow.

78. CIA, *Polar Regions Atlas*, p. 37.

79. *Ibid.*, p. 35.

80. King, *The Antarctic*, p. 47.

81. *Ibid.*, p. 103.

82. *Ibid.*, p. 38.

83. Todd, *U.S. Activities in Antarctica*, p. 5.

84. Debenham, *Antarctica: The Story of a Continent*, p. 149.

85. Some students of the Southern Ocean prefer the term "Polar Frontal Zone" on the grounds that the mixing process is more complicated than the word "convergence" implies. See, for example, D. James Baker, Jr., "Currents, Fronts and Bottom Water," *Oceanus*, Summer 1975, p. 11. The entire issue is devoted to the Southern Ocean. See also Harm J. de Blij, "A Regional Geography of Antarctica and the Southern Ocean," *University of Miami Law Review* 33, no. 2 (December 1978), pp. 299–314.

86. Joel W. Hedgpeth, "The Antarctic Marine Ecosystem," in *Adaptations Within Antarctic Ecosystems*, George A. Llano, ed. (Houston: Gulf Publishing Company, 1977), p. 3.

87. CIA, *Polar Regions Atlas*, p. 54.

88. Vera Rich, "USSR's Polar Research," *Nature* 261, June 24, 1976, p. 625.

89. Inigo Everson, "Antarctic Fisheries," *Polar Record* 19, no. 120 (1978), p. 233.

90. King, *The Antarctic*, p. 12.

91. George A. Llano, "A Survey of Antarctic Biology: Life Below Freezing," in *Frozen Future*, p. 220.

92. Halle, *The Sea and the Ice*, p. 78.

CHAPTER TWO

1. Phillip Law, "Australia and the Antarctic," The John Murtagh Macrossan Memorial Lecture, 1960 (Brisbane, Australia: University of Queensland Press, 1962), p. 21.

2. U.S. Department of State, *The Conference on Antarctica, Washington, October 15-December 1, 1959* (Washington, DC: September 1960), p. 23. Hereafter cited as *Conference Documents*.

3. Thomas O. Jones, "Developing the U.S. Antarctic Research Program," in *Frozen Future: A Prophetic Report from Antarctica*, Richard S. Lewis and Philip M. Smith, eds. (New York: Quadrangle Books, 1973), p. 250.

4. Apsley Cherry-Garrard, *The Worst Journey in the World* (London: Chatto & Windus, 1965; first published 1922), p. 545.

5. Raymond E. Priestley, "Twentieth Century Man Against Antarctica," *Nature*, 178/4531 (September 1, 1956), p. 465.

6. Edward Wilson, *Diary of the Terra Nova Expedition to the Antarctic, 1910–1912* (New York: Humanities Press, 1972), p. 241.

7. *Scott's Last Expedition: the personal journals of Captain R. F.Scott, CVO, RN on his journey to the South Pole* (London: The Folio Society, 1964), p. 304.

8. Wilson, *Diary of the Terra Nova Expedition*, p. 142. Only by laying their eggs in the dead of winter is there time for incubation and chick-rearing to a degree of self-sufficiency that will permit survival of the young the following winter. See Louis J. Halle, *The Sea and the Ice: A Naturalist in Antarctica* (Boston: Houghton Mifflin, in cooperation with the National Audubon Society, 1973), pp. 132–43.

9. Wilson, *Diary of the Terra Nova Expedition*, p. 270 (editor's footnote).

10. Roald Amundsen, *The South Pole: An Account of the Norwegian Antarctic Expedition in the "Fram," 1910–1912* (New York: Harper & Row, Barnes & Noble Division, 1976), vol. I, p. 44.

11. *Ibid.*, vol. II, Appendices II, III, and V.

12. Grenfell Price, in the introduction to the facsimile edition (1970) of Cook's *A Voyage Towards the South Pole and Round the World* (London, 1777).

13. Ian Cameron [Donald Gordon Payne], *Antarctica: The Last Continent* (Boston: Little Brown, 1974) p. 108.

14. Priestley, "Twentieth Century Man," p. 464.

15. Frederick Mosteller, "Innovation and Evaluation," *Science*, February 27, 1981, p. 881.

16. *Ibid.*, p. 882, and E. J. C. Kendall, "Scurvy During Some British Polar Expeditions, 1875–1917," *Polar Record* 7, no. 51 (September 1955), pp. 467–68.

17. Richard S. Lewis, *A Continent for Science* (New York: Viking Press, 1965), p. 15.

18. Paul A. Carter, *Little America: Town at the End of the World* (New York: Columbia University Press, 1979), p. 17; George A. Llano, "A Survey of Antarctic Biology: Life Below Freezing," in *Frozen Future*, p. 207.

19. Kenneth J. Bertrand, *Americans in Antarctica, 1775–1948* (New York: Geographical Society, 1971), p. 159.

20. L. P. Kirwan, *A History of Polar Exploration* (New York: W. W.Norton, 1960), p. 228.

21. Walter Sullivan, *Quest for a Continent* (New York: McGraw-Hill, 1957), p. 114.
22. Richard E. Byrd, *Alone* (New York: G.P. Putnam's Sons, 1938), pp. 178–79.
23. Sullivan, *Quest for a Continent*, pp. 144–45.
24. Priestley, "Twentieth Century Man," p. 466.
25. U.S. Department of State, *Foreign Relations of the United States* (Washington, DC: 1939), vol. 2, p. 14.
26. Paul Siple, *90° South: The Story of the American South Pole Conquest* (New York: G.P. Putnam's Sons, 1959), p. 66.
27. *Ibid.*, p. 79.
28. A new account of Operation High Jump, by Lisle A. Rose, a State Department historian, is *Assault on Eternity: Richard E. Byrd and the Exploration of Antarctica, 1946–47* (Annapolis, MD: Naval Institute Press, 1980). See also Bertrand, *Americans in Antarctica*, chapter 22; Sullivan, *Quest for a Continent*, pp. 218–46; Carter, *Little America*, pp. 223–29. Much of the aerial photography was of little use because the planes were not equipped with oxygen and could not fly high enough to get pictures that would permit accurate mapping, and in any case, the necessary ground control points were not obtained.
29. Sir Vivian Fuchs, "Evolution of a Venture in Antarctic Science: Operation Tabarin and the British Antarctic Survey," in *Frozen Future*, pp. 233–37.
30. G. C. L. Bertram, "Antarctic Prospect," *International Affairs* 33, no. 2 (April 1957), p. 143.
31. Laurence M. Gould, "The Polar Regions in Their Relation to Human Affairs," Bowman Memorial Lectures (New York: The American Geographical Society, 1958), p. 24.
32. Sir Harold Spencer Jones, "The Inception and Development of the International Geophysical Year," *Annals of the International Geophysical Year* (London: Pergamon Press, 1958–69), vol. 1, p. 383. Under the aegis of Comité Spécial de l'Année Géophysique Internationale (CSAGI) of the International Council of Scientific Unions (ICSU), the record of the IGY—as well as prior instructions to participants—was published in forty-eight volumes of *Annals*, completed in 1970. Volume I consists of histories of the first and second International Polar Years and the origins of the IGY. Volume II is composed of reports of the preparatory meetings and conferences of CSAGI. The remaining volumes are scientific and technical. A more serviceable account is Walter Sullivan's *Assault on the Unknown: The International Geophysical Year* (New York: McGraw-Hill, 1961), and his briefer, more political "The International Geophysical Year," in *International Conciliation* (published by the Carnegie Endowment for International Peace), no. 521, January 1959. Lewis, *A Continent for Science*, covers a broader time period but is useful on the IGY. See also the final chapter in H. G. R. King, *The Antarctic* (New York: Arco, 1969), and the congressional testimony of the chief American scientist for the IGY, Harry Wexler, in U.S. Congress, Subcommittee of the House Appropriations Committee, *Report on the International Geophysical Year*, 85th Cong., 1st sess., May 1, 1957, pp. 116–26.
33. John Hanessian, Jr., "National Activities and Interests in Antarctica, Part II," *Polar Area Series, vol. II* (Hanover, NH: American Universities Field Staff, Report no. 6, September 1962), pp. 27–28.

34. Later, scientists from India, Canada, Switzerland, Brazil, and Italy would also serve at American stations. (U.S. Department of State, *United States Policy and International Cooperation in Antarctica*, Historical Studies Division, May 1964, pp. 5, 12, and 17.) In the 1979–80 season, about fifty scientists from ten nations, including Israel and the Soviet Union, participated in U.S. programs. ("International Participation, 1979–80," *Antarctic Journal of the United States*, published by the National Science Foundation, September 1979, p. 14.)

35. Barry Merrill Plott, "The Development of United States Antarctic Policy" (Ph.D. dissertation, Fletcher School of Law and Diplomacy, 1969), p. 172.

36. Sullivan, *IGY*, pp. 284–85 and 294.

37. Henry M. Dater, "Organizational Developments in the United States Antarctic Program, 1954–1965," *Antarctic Journal*, January–February 1966, p. 23. Dater was a staff historian in the Department of Defense, specializing in the Antarctic.

38. Laurence M. Gould, *Antarctica in World Affairs* (Foreign Policy Association, Headline Series no. 128, 1958), p. 39; Lewis, *Continent for Science*, p. 67.

39. Frank Debenham, *Antarctica: The Story of a Continent* (New York: Macmillan, 1961), p. 119.

40. A distinguished French Antarctic scientist told the writer he believed Byrd went back to the same place on the ice year after year out of a sense of tradition and a feeling that it would be *infra dig* to camp on snowless rock (as at McMurdo).

41. Debenham, *Antarctica: The Story of a Continent*, p. 122.

42. Dater, "Organizational Developments," p. 24.

43. Leigh H. Frederickson, "Hallett Station," in *Frozen Future*, pp. 416–17.

44. King, *The Antarctica*, pp. 242–46.

45. *Ibid.*, pp. 44–77.

46. Lewis, *A Continent for Science*, pp. 73–82, 98, and 100; Sullivan, *Assault*, pp. 311–12.

47. Sullivan, *Quest*, pp. 346–47.

48. Sullivan, *Assault*, p. 343.

49. King, *The Antarctic*, p. 7.

50. See testimony by Edward P. Todd in U.S. Congress, Senate Committee on Energy and Natural Resources, 96th Cong., 1st sess., *U.S. Activities in Antarctica*, April 23, 1979, p. 6 (publ. no. 96-21). Dr. Todd is director of the Division of Polar Programs of the National Science Foundation. The technique was discovered literally by accident, when several aircraft being ferried to Europe crashed on the Greenland ice sheet. At the frequencies being used by the planes' radar, the ice was transparent. See also "Tales the Ice Can Tell," *Mosaic* (published by the National Science Foundation) 9, no. 5, September/October 1978, p. 18.

51. National Science Foundation, "Antarctic Program," *Program Report*, vol. 3, no. 6, September 1979, p. 29.

52. *Annals*, vol. 48, p. 166.

53. See testimony by Robert A. Helliwell in U.S. Congress, House Subcommittee on Science, Research, and Technology, *U.S. Antarctic Program*, 96th Cong., 1st sess., May 3, 1979, pp. 128–32. Helliwell offers a more technical treatment

in *Research in Antarctica*, Louis O. Quam, ed. (Washington, DC: American Association for the Advancement of Science, 1971), pp. 493–511; Ray R. Heer, Jr., "Conjugate Phenomena," in *Research in Antarctica*, pp. 491–92; Lewis, *A Continent for Science*, chapter 8, and "Planned Field Research Projects, 1979–80: Siple Station," *Antarctic Journal*, September 1979, pp. 12–14.

54. John W. Finney, "U.S. Gives Data on Argus Tests," *The New York Times*, March 26, 1959, p. 1. The topic remains veiled in secrecy, but a recent report for the U.S. Federal Emergency Management Agency and a series of illuminating articles in *Science* indicate that the situation is even more perilous than had been previously acknowledged. The ever-increasing use of solid-state electronic equipment makes us extraordinarily vulnerable to a phenomenon called electromagnetic pulse (EMP), a high-voltage wave emanating from a nuclear explosion in space. It is now calculated that a single well-placed warhead exploding high above the United States could shut down the nation's entire power grid and knock out communications from coast to coast. (See William J. Broad, "Nuclear Pulse [I]: Wakening to the Chaos Factor," *Science*, May 29, 1981, pp. 1009–12.) The consequences of EMP are discussed by the same author in two further articles in successive issues.

55. *Antarctic Journal*, September 1980, p. 1.

56. *Annals*, vol. 2., p. 474.

57. The original name was briefly *Special* Committee on Antarctic Research.

58. Scientific Committee on Antarctic Research, *Constitution, Procedures and Structure* (Cambridge, England: 1977). (This updates the more complete SCAR *Manual*, 2nd ed., published in 1972.)

59. *Ibid.*, pp. 1–16.

60. Natural Environment Research Council, *British Antarctic Survey* (Cambridge, England: 1977), pp. 3–7.

61. John Hanessian, Jr., "Expeditions Polaires Françaises," *Polar Area Series*, vol. 1, no. 1 (Hanover, NH: American Universities Field Staff, 1960).

62. Until 1980, the private contractor was Holmes & Narver. Antarctic Services is a subsubsidiary of ITT.

63. Polar Research Board, National Academy of Sciences, *Annual Report 1978 and Future Plans*. See also Helliwell testimony, p. 128.

64. Papers of Admiral George Dufek. Part VI-I of undated report (the covering letter is dated August 31, 1959), George Arents Research Library, Syracuse University, Syracuse, New York.

65. Henry M. Dater, Memo of Record, July 20, 1959, in Dufek Papers.

66. NSF/OD General Records, RG 307, 1957–59 IGY, Center for Polar Archives in the National Archives.

67. *Ibid.*

68. *Ibid.*, letter to James R. Killian, Jr., special assistant to the President for science and technology, July 1, 1959.

69. Files of James E. Mooney, RG 330, Records of the Office of the Secretary of Defense, USAPO, Center for Polar Archives in the National Archives. Mooney was deputy to the U.S. Antarctic projects officer and a well-connected advocate of a Byrd Antarctic Commission.

70. U.S. Congress, House Subcommittee on Territorial and Insular Affairs,

Antarctica Report—1965, 89th Cong., 1st sess., April 12, 13; May 6, 7; and June 15, 1965. The hearings were on four very similar bills to create a Richard E. Byrd Antarctic Commission. Referring to the many years of hearings, Subcommittee Chairman Leo W. O'Brien said at the outset: "[W]hile I have enjoyed these little get-togethers, I intend to ask this subcommittee this year either to vote up or down . . ." (p. 17). It did.

71. Committee to Evaluate Antarctic Marine Ecosystem Research, National Research Council, *An Evaluation of Antarctic Marine Ecosystem Research* (Washington, DC: 1981), p. 54; Jones in *Frozen Future*, p. 259.

72. L. I. Dubrovin and Y. S. Korotkevich, "Twenty Years of Soviet Investigation in the Antarctic," *Polar Geography* 2, no. 2 (April–June 1978), pp. 71–72.

73. Olav Orheim, "Back to the Antarctic," *Research in Norway 1977* (Oslo, Norway: The Norwegian Polar Research Institute), pp. 2–8. See also *Research in Norway 1978*, pp. 24–25.

74. "Huge Case Injection for Bonn Antarctic Programme," *Frankfurter Allgemeine Zeitung Für Deutschland*, December 27, 1979 (printed in English in *The German Tribune*, January 13, 1980); Anatol Johansen, "German Antarctic Research Hots Up," *New Scientist*, January 24, 1980, p. 224; "New Polar Institute to Break Antarctic Ice," *Frankfurter Neue Presse*, October 11, 1978, and Horst Zimmerman, "Antarctic Base Camp Planned," *Stuttgarter Nachrichten*, February 27, 1979 (translated in *The German Tribune*, October 22, 1978, and March 11, 1979, respectively); Monika Muller, "Bonn-backed team sets up Antarctic base," *Hamburger Abendblatt*, May 8, 1980 (reprinted in translation in *The German Tribune*, May 25, 1980, p. 8).

75. Reiner Korbmann, "German Antarctic exploration gains momentum as base camp is built," *Frankfurter Rundschau*, January 31, 1981 (reprinted in translation in *The German Tribune*, February 22, 1981, p. 9) and Anatol Johansen, "German Antarctic Expedition on the Rocks," *New Scientist*, February 26, 1981, p. 518. Though West Germany is the latest nation to make a major scientific effort in Antarctica, India quietly mounted an expedition in the 1981–82 season and may establish a permanent station in Antarctica.

76. See Bruce C. Parker and Mary C. Holliman, eds., *Environmental Impact in Antarctica* (Blacksburg, VA: Virginia Polytechnic Institute and State University, 1978), especially Jere H. Lipps, "Man's Impact Along the Antarctic Peninsula," pp. 333–72.

77. "Cold Comfort for the Antarctic Environment," *New Scientist*, November 24, 1977, p. 470.

78. Paul K. Dayton and Gordon A. Robilliard, "McMurdo Sound," and Philip L. Hall, "Cleaning Up U.S. Stations," in *Frozen Future*, pp. 410–15 and 418–20.

79. National Science Foundation, *U.S. Antarctic Program: Final Environmental Impact Statement*, June 1980. Except for a page of errata, the final statement *is* the Draft Environmental Impact Statement (DEIS) issued in late August 1979; nothing of substance was changed despite sharp criticism. Having taken eight years to prepare the DEIS, the Division of Polar Programs allowed only forty-five days for comments. (The deadline was buried in the *Federal Register* rather than being announced in the DEIS itself.) Nine and a half months then elapsed before the final statement appeared, consisting of five sheets of paper. Only two federal agencies were acknowledged to have commented

on the DEIS; comments received after the deadline were ignored. The shortcomings of the impact statement need not be enumerated here, but its irrelevance is suggested by the fact that it nowhere indicates whether or to what extent the United States is in compliance with the Code of Conduct for Antarctic Expeditions and Station Activities, adopted in 1975 by all the nations conducting research in Antarctica. Instead, the EIS labors the obvious at such length as to constitute a travesty on the National Environmental Protection Act (NEPA), which it was initially intended to serve voluntarily (there being no legal commitment). Finally, the officer in the Division of Polar Programs most responsible for the EIS, summarizing the document in a journal article, concluded: "The environmental impacts discussed here apply only to the U.S. program, although many of the impacts can be generalized and extended to predict the effects of the programs which may take place in Antarctica in the future, such as mineral exploration and exploitation, commercial activities and extensive land-based tourism." (C. E. Myers *et al.*, "Environmental Assessment of Antarctic Research," *Environmental Science & Technology* 14, no. 6 [June 1980], p. 668.) This unwarranted assumption was a further affront to environmentalists.

80. See, for example, Charles Neider, *Edge of the World: Ross Island, Antarctica* (Garden City, NY: Doubleday, 1974), pp. 38 and 42; John Langone, *Life at the Bottom: The People of Antarctica* (Boston: Little Brown, 1977), p. 51; and Katherine Bouton, "South of 60 Degrees South," *The New Yorker*, March 23, 1981, p. 42.

81. Neider, *Edge of the World*, p. 38.

82. "Antarctica in a Two-Power World," *Foreign Affairs*, October 1957, p. 161.

83. *NSF Records*, Center for Polar Archives, File 71A 6662, Box 87/88 106.9 (1960).

84. Joseph M. Dukert, *This Is Antarctica* (New York: Coward-McCann, 1965), pp. 155 and 178–82.

85. Paul Siple, as reported in the *Polar Times*, December 1958, p. 15.

86. Rear Admiral G. J. Dufek, "Nuclear Power for the Polar Regions," *National Geographic Magazine*, May 1962, p. 712.

87. Law, "Australia and the Antarctic," p. 20.

88. Confidential diary note made by Jones following an interdepartmental meeting of July 26, 1960, Center for Polar Archives, File 71A 6662, Box 87/88 106.9.

89. *Ibid.*, including letter dated July 29, 1960, from Waterman to Secretary of Defense Thomas Gates. Interestingly, Jones had previously worked under Glenn Seaborg, who was then chairman of the AEC. Jones contends it was not so much the AEC that pushed for a power reactor in Antarctica as the Congress. (Interview with Thomas O. Jones, Washington, DC, May 15, 1980.)

90. Owen Wilkes and Robert Mann, "The Story of Nukey Poo," *Bulletin of the Atomic Scientists*, October 1978, p. 32. This article, by two New Zealanders, is the most comprehensive account of the McMurdo reactor to have appeared in print. Its accuracy has been confirmed in interviews with others, including Commander Joseph Renzetti of the Naval Facilities Engineering Command, who headed the dismantling operation. See also J. V. Filson, "Nuclear Power Plant Removal, Deep Freeze '75," *Antarctic Journal*, July/August 1975, p. 195.

No official account of any consequence appeared until 1980. See "McMurdo Station reactor site released for unrestricted use," *Antarctic Journal*, March 1980, pp. 1–4.

91. The safety record is presumed. A seaman on the ship that brought the used reactor vessel to the United States subsequently died of leukemia. His wife sued the government and lost.

92. Interview with Edward Todd, Washington, DC, September 17, 1979.

93. C. C. Langway, Jr., and B. Lyle Hansen, "Drilling Through the Ice Cap: Probing Climate for a Thousand Centuries," in *Frozen Future*, pp. 190 and 194. See also "Tales the Ice Can Tell," p. 19. Ice cores were first successfully extracted in 1950.

94. United Nations Environment Program, "The Carbon Dioxide/Climate Issue: A Statement—1980" (Nairobi, Kenya: Press/81/1, February 24, 1981).

95. J. Hansen *et al.*, "Climate Impact of Increasing Atmospheric Carbon Dioxide," *Science*, August 28, 1981, p. 965.

96. U.S. Department of Energy, *Carbon Dioxide Effects Research and Assessment Program: Workshop on Environmental and Societal Consequences of a Possible CO2-Induced Climate Change*, October 1980, Executive Summary, p. vi. See also T. Hughes, J. L. Fastook, and G. H. Denton, "Climatic Warming and Collapse of the West Antarctica Ice Sheet," *ibid.*, pp. 152–82. Also, William W. Kellogg and Robert Schware, *Climate Change and Society: Consequences of Increasing Atmospheric Carbon Dioxide* (Boulder, CO: Westview Press, 1981).

97. Total melting of the south polar icecap would raise the sea level nearly two hundred feet.

98. By far the best source for the layman in what is becoming a vast literature is Council on Environmental Quality, *Global Energy Futures and the Carbon Dioxide Problem* (Washington, DC: January 1981). As evidence that the topic is discussed not merely among scientists, see Charles F. Cooper, "What Might Man-Induced Climate Change Mean?" *Foreign Affairs*, April 1978, pp. 500–20.

99. See testimony by George H. Denton, in U.S. Congress, House Subcommittee on Science, Research and Technology, *U.S. Antarctic Program*, 96th Cong., 1st sess., May 3, 1979, pp. 144–45.

100. D. Q. Bowen, "Antarctic Ice Surges and Theories of Glaciation," *Nature* 283 (February 14, 1980), p. 619. See also Walter Sullivan, "Scientists Reviving Speculation on Climate and Slipping Antarctic Ice," *The New York Times*, March 9, 1980.

101. Edwin H. Colbert, "Antarctic Fossil Vertebrates and Gondwanaland," in *Research in the Antarctic*, pp. 685–99. A discussion of continental drift is postponed to the next chapter, where it has special relevance.

102. "Antarctic Fossil Find," *New Scientist*, March 16, 1978, p. 713.

103. USARP press release, July 23, 1979 (NSF PR79-53); John Noble Wilford, "Algae Are Found Thriving Under Lake Ice in Antarctica," *The New York Times*, July 25, 1979, p. A12; and E. Imre Friedmann, "Endolithic Microorganisms in the Antarctic Cold Desert," *Science*, February 26, 1982, pp. 1045–53.

104. Arthur L. DeVries, "The Physiology and Biochemistry of Low Temperature Adaptations in Polar Marine Ectotherms," in *Polar Research*, Mary A. McWhinnie, ed. (Boulder, CO: Westview Press, 1978), pp. 175-202. See also

Eric Golanty, "Fish Survival in Subfreezing Temperatures," *Oceans*, May–June 1977, p. 53.

105. "U.S., Japanese scientists find more meteorites on ice sheet," *Antarctic Journal*, June 1979, p. 16.

106. Recently, two very "young" meteorites were found in Antarctica—a mere 1.2 billion years old—leading scientists to speculate that they came from Mars. The theory is that a large meteorite crashed into Mars, spraying pieces of its surface into space. (NSF news release, June 26, 1980.)

107. "From Eternity to Here," *Natural History* 90, no. 4 (April 1981), p. 54.

108. Susan West, "Early life turns up on Earth and in Space," *New Scientist*, October 4, 1979, p. 4; and "Amino Acids in an Antarctic Carbonaceous Chondrite," *Science*, October 19, 1979, p. 335.

109. Cyril Ponnamperuma, "Message in the Rocks," NOVA broadcast on PBS, January 20, 1980 (Boston: WGBH Transcripts), p. 6.

110. Brian Mason, "A Lode of Meteorites," *Natural History* 90, no. 4 (April 1981), pp. 62–66.

111. E. Paul McClain, "Environmental Satellites," *McGraw-Hill Encyclopedia of Environmental Science* (New York: McGraw-Hill, 1980); and Donald R. Wiesnet, Craig P. Berg, and Glenn C. Rosenberger, "High Resolution Picture Transmission Satellite Receiver at McMurdo Station: The Antarctic Mosaic Project," *Polar Record*, January 1981, pp. 365–70.

The scope of Antarctic research has only been suggested here. For the U.S. program, see a special undated issue of *Antarctic Journal* (vol. 15, no. 5) that appeared in April 1981 with summary articles on about two hundred projects through the 1979–80 season. A number of substantial, wide-ranging anthologies are available, although they are somewhat dated: Quam, ed., *Research in Antarctica* has already been cited. There are also Trevor Hatherton, ed., in cooperation with the New Zealand Antarctic Society, *Antarctica* (New York: Praeger, 1965); Sir Raymond Priestley, Raymond J. Adie, G. de Q. Robin, eds. *Antarctic Research: A Review of British Scientific Achievement in Antarctica* (London: Buttersworth, 1964); M. W. Holdgate, ed., *Antarctic Ecology* (London: Academic Press, 1970), published for SCAR; and Mary A. McWhinnie, ed., *Polar Research: To the Present, and the Future* (Boulder, CO: Westview Press, 1978). In addition, there is Vivian C. Bushnell, ed., *Antarctic Map Folio Series* (New York: American Geographical Society). This remarkable series consists of nineteen folios published from 1964 to 1975, covering almost every polar scientific discipline. Besides hundreds of maps, there are scores of thousands of words of descriptive material and exhaustive bibliographies. Inevitably, some of the folios are slightly dated. More recently, the chairman of the Polar Research Board tried somewhat unsuccessfully to summarize polar research in a brief journal article with 113 footnote citations. See A. L. Washburn, "Focus on Polar Research," *Science*, August 8, 1980, pp. 643–52. The extent of current U.S. research is conveyed in Polar Research Board, National Academy of Sciences, *Report on United States Antarctic Research Activities, 1979–1980, and Activities Planned for 1980–1981*, Report no. 22 to SCAR. See also the 1979 *Annual Report* of the Polar Research Board.

112. The Marine Mammal Commission is a small, independent agency of the

executive branch created by the Marine Mammal Protection Act of 1972 (Public Law 92-522). Operating on a budget of under a million dollars, the commission serves as a whistleblower, a prod, legislative critic, and commissioner of relevant studies. (*Annual Report of the Marine Mammal Commission, Calendar Year 1980: A Report to Congress.*)

113. Todd, *Program Report*, pp. 11–12.

114. James H. Zumberge, address at the 1979 Orientation Session (for people going to Antarctica), Alexandria, VA, September 16, 1979. Zumberge, who has been heavily involved with Antarctica since the IGY, is president of the University of Southern California.

115. Gerald S. Schatz, "Polar Research: Emphasis on Understanding World Climate," *News Report*, National Research Council, June–July 1974, p. 1.

116. See testimony by John B. Slaughter, 95th Cong., 2nd sess., in U.S. Congress, Senate Subcommittee on Arms Control, Oceans and International Environment, *Exploitation of Antarctic Resources*, February 6, 1978, p. 48. At the time, Dr. Slaughter was assistant director for Astronomical, Atmospheric, Earth and Oceans Sciences.

117. See, for example, pp. 1–11.

118. Interview with Captain R. J. Smith, Washington, DC, July 22, 1980.

119. "The Long Look Ahead," in *Frozen Future*, pp. 304–19. This was the concluding article in the December 1970 issue of the *Bulletin of the Atomic Scientists*, which forms the first half of *Frozen Future*, frequently cited above.

120. *Ibid.*, pp. 308–309.

CHAPTER III

1. An impressive number of surveys of the scientific literature on the Southern Ocean, and especially on krill, have been produced in recent years. The most comprehensive is Inigo Everson, *The Living Resources of the Southern Ocean*, Southern Ocean Fisheries Survey Programme (GLO/SO/77/1) United Nations Development Program/Food and Agriculture Organization, Rome, 1977. Two companion volumes produced by the same FAO survey are G. C. Eddie, *The Harvesting of Krill* (GLO/SO/77/2), and G. J. Grantham, *The Utilization of Krill* (GLO/SO/77/3). John L. Bengtson, *Review of Information Regarding the Conservation of Living Resources of the Antarctic Marine Ecosystem*, prepared for the U.S. Marine Mammal Commission, July 1978, is excellent. The late Mary A. McWhinnie, with the assistance of Charlene J. Denys, performed a comparable feat for the National Science Foundation, but her report *Antarctic Marine Living Resources with Special Reference to Krill, Euphausia Superba: Assessment of Adequacy of Present Knowledge*, December 1978 (hereafter cited as *McWhinnie NSF Report*), is virtually unobtainable. Alternatively, a shorter but still useful treatment by McWhinnie, herself an outstanding marine biologist, is "Potential Impact of Harvesting Zooplankton on the South Circumpolar Ecosystem," in *Environmental Impact in Antarctica*, Bruce C. Parker and Mary C. Holliman, eds. (Blacksburg, VA: Virginia Polytechnic Institute and State University, 1978). And, again with Charlene J. Denys,

"The High Importance of the Lowly Krill," *Natural History,* March 1980, p. 66. The *Final Environmental Impact Statement for a Possible Regime for Conservation of Antarctic Living Marine Resources,* Washington, DC, Office of Environmental Affairs, Department of State, June 1978 (hereafter cited as *Marine Regime FEIS*), itself constitutes a competent survey. For its data on krill, it relies primarily on Katherine A. Green, whose "Role of Krill in the Antarctic Marine Ecosystem," Final Report to the Department of State, December 1977, is appended to the impact statement. The Department of State also commissioned *The Antarctic Krill Resource: Prospects for Commercial Exploitation,* Tetra Tech Report TC-903, February 1978, which summarizes masses of data but does not answer the implied question. See also G. A. Llano, ed., *Adaptations Within Antarctic Ecosystems* (Houston: Gulf Publishing Company, 1977), 1,252 pp., a formidable symposium; and within it especially R. M. Laws, "The Significance of Vertebrates in the Antarctic Marine Ecosystem," pp. 411-38.

2. *The Global 2000 Report to the President: Entering the Twenty-first Century,* A Report Prepared by the Council on Environmental Quality and the Department of State, Washington, DC: 1980, p. 21. According to a recent FAO report: "The present state of exploitation of the world fish stocks is such that it is unreasonable to expect much increase in the total catch of the familiar stocks, and the continued productivity of these stocks is threatened by the existence of a world fleet that is probably, taken as a whole, well in excess of what is desirable on economic grounds." See *Report of the ACMRR Working Party on the Scientific Basis of Determining Management Measures,* Hong Kong, December 10–15, 1979, FAO Fisheries Report no. 236, Rome, 1980, p. 41; and Richard C. Hennemuth, "Marine Fisheries: Food for the Future?" *Oceanus* vol. 2, no. 1 (Spring 1979), p. 12.

3. Everson, *The Living Resources,* p. 75.

4. *McWhinnie NSF Report,* p. 69.

5. *NSF News* (PR81–25), March 24, 1981.

6. *McWhinnie NSF Report,* p. 13. Since all scientific and technical literature uses the metric system, it seems artificial to convert all figures in this chapter. For reference: 1 meter = 39.4 inches; 1 cubic meter = 1.3 cubic yards; 1 kilogram = 2.2 pounds.

7. Eddie, *The Harvesting of Krill,* pp. 30–31.

8. G. E. R. Deacon, "Antarctic Water Masses and Circulation," in *Polar Oceans,* M. J. Dunbar, ed. (proceedings of the Polar Oceans Conference sponsored by the Scientific Committee on Oceanic Research and the Scientific Committee on Antarctic Research in May 1974 at McGill University, Montreal, Canada, 1977). The theory that the Southern Ocean is incomparably rich throughout its expanse is now being questioned. See S. Z. El-Sayed and J. T. Turner, "Productivity of the Antarctic and Tropic/Subtropic Regions: A Comparative Study," also in *Polar Oceans,* p. 463. Until recently it was believed that krill was exclusively herbivorous, but it is now known to be "an opportunistic omnivore," eating almost anything, including its own kind. See McWhinnie and Denys in *Natural History,* pp. 72–73.

9. See testimony by John R. Twiss in U.S. Congress, Senate Committee on Commerce, Science, and Transportation, *Antarctic Living Marine Resources*

Negotiations, National Ocean Policy Study, 95th Cong., 2nd sess., June 14, 1978, p. 14. Twiss is executive director of the Marine Mammal Commission.

10. *How* krill manage to swarm may be explained by their capacity to emit tiny blue-green lights, in flashes or for several minutes at a time.

11. McWhinnie and Denys in *Natural History,* p. 72.

12. James W. S. Marr, *The Natural History and Geography of the Antarctic Krill,* in vol. 32 of *Discovery Reports* (Cambridge, England: Cambridge University Press, 1962), pp. 33–464.

13. M. A. McWhinnie *et al., Euphausiacea Bibliography: A World Literature Survey* (Elmsford, NY: Pergamon Press, 1981).

14. See testimony by Ariel Lugo, in *Antarctic Living Marine Resources Negotiations,* pp. 25–26.

15. *McWhinnie NSF Report,* pp. 4–5.

16. Natural Environment Research Council, *British Antarctic Survey Annual Report, 1978–79,* Cambridge, England, 1980, p. 52.

17. John P. Croxall and Peter A. Prince, "Antarctic Seabird and Seal Monitoring Studies," *Polar Record,* vol. 19, no. 123, p. 590.

18. *McWhinnie NSF Report,* p. 34. As might be expected, the data for whales are more reliable than for other species. The figure for total consumption of krill is higher than some estimates but is well below the 443 mmt reached by averaging the highest estimate for krill consumption. Marine biologists generally interpret "abundance" and "population size" to mean not numbers of individuals but their total biomass, which is more relevant in estimating consumption, but somewhat confusing to laymen.

19. Green, "Role of Krill in the Antarctic," p. 26.

20. Roald Amundsen, *The South Pole: An Account of the Norwegian Antarctic Expedition in the "Fram," 1910–1912* (New York: Harper & Row, Barnes & Noble Division, 1976), vol. 2, p. 276.

21. Nevertheless, Brian Roberts, then of the Scott Polar Research Institute, considered crabeaters "vulnerable to commercial exploitation." See B. B. Roberts, "Conservation in the Antarctic," *Transactions of the Royal Society,* 1977, p. 99.

22. At a time of unsurpassed public concern for marine mammals, it may be worth noting that they are estimated to consume five to ten times as much fish as is taken by man. See Jim Larison, "Life Itself," *Sea Grant Today,* March/April 1980, p. 6. For the distribution of Antarctic mammals, see S. G. Brown *et al.,* "Antarctic Mammals," *Antarctic Map Folio Series,* Folio 18 (New York: American Geographical Society, 1974).

23. "Antarctica: Gold Mine or Landmine?" *IUCN Bulletin,* April 1978, p. 22.

24. "Report on Informal Consultation on Antarctic Krill," Rome, October 14, 1974, FAO Fisheries Reports, no. 153, p. 1. This was by no means a "low" figure. A 1975 FAO document, speculating on an ultimate limit of 100 mmt of "conventional" fish annually, reported that Antarctic krill could "quite possibly" produce "several times as much" (C 75/19, July 1975, para. 20). As late as 1979 it was said in a responsible journal that "some" believe a harvest of 270 mmt is possible. See Kurt Fleischmann, "The Antarctic Ocean— Empty, But International," *Impact of Science on Society* 29, no. 2 (April–June 1979), pp. 175–82.

25. Green, "Role of Krill in the Antarctic," p. 26.
26. See especially Robert M. May, *et al.*, "Management of Multispecies Fisheries," *Science*, July 20, 1979, pp. 267–77.
27. See, for example, "IUCN Statement on Southern Ocean Management," *IUCN Bulletin*, April 1979, p. 29.
28. SCAR/SCOR Group of Specialists in Living Resources of the Southern Ocean (SCOR Working Group 54), *Biological Investigations of Marine Antarctic Systems and Stocks (BIOMASS)*, vol. I: *Research Proposals*, Cambridge, England, August 1977 (hereafter, *BIOMASS Research Proposals*). (Reprinted as Appendix H in *Marine Regime FEIS*.)
29. *BIOMASS Newsletter*, March, July, and December 1980; Terry L. Leitzell, internal NOAA memorandum to Richard A. Frank, dated October 3, 1979, recommending participation in FIBEX.
30. Sayed Z. El-Sayed, ed., *Contributions of U.S. to the International BIOMASS Program*, November 1977, p. 76.
31. Committee to Evaluate Antarctic Marine Ecosystem Research, National Research Council, *An Evaluation of Antarctic Marine Ecosystem Research* (Washington, DC: 1981), pp. 2, 53.
32. G. C. L. Bertram and J. D. M. Blyth, "The Fisheries of Antarctica," *Fisheries Bulletin* (Rome: FAO), April/June 1956, p. 84.
33. *1979 Yearbook of Fishery Statistics: Catches and Landings* (Rome: FAO, 1980), Table B-46, p. 184. The figures for 1980 are even higher, by about 16 percent.
34. Inigo Everson, "Antarctic Fisheries," *Polar Record* 19, 120 (1978), pp. 236 and 238.
35. See, for example, D. L. Cram, "South African Research into Antarctic Krill," *The South African Shipping News and Fishing Industry Review*, July 1978, pp. 39–43.
36. W. A. Hovis, D. K. Clark, *et al.*, "Nimbus-7 Coastal Zone Color Scanner: System Description and Initial Imagery," *Science* 210 (October 3, 1980), pp. 60–63.
37. This is puzzling because fish meal of any kind is normally withheld for about two weeks before slaughter—by which time any fishy taste should have departed. And if the Soviets do not like krill, what did they do with 326,000 tons of it in 1979?
38. *McWhinnie NSF Report*, p. 184.
39. *Ibid.*, p. 183.
40. Stephanie Yanchinski, "No Cheap Krill for Fishermen," *New Scientist* 85 (February 28, 1980), p. 638. The organization referred to is the International Institute for Environment and Development, based in London.
41. "World Report," *Ceres*, March–April 1978, p. 6.
42. T. Soevik and O. R. Braekkan, "Fluoride in Antarctic Krill," *Journal of Fish Resources Board of Canada* 36 (1979), p. 1416.
43. "Developments in the Regime of the Sea and Their Implications for Fisheries," Item 9 of the Provisional Agenda, FAO Conference, Nineteenth Session, Rome, November 12–December 1, 1977 (C 77/21), para. 24.
44. Despite its 1974 date, N. A. Wright and P. L. Williams, eds., *Mineral Resources of Antarctica*, Geological Survey Circular 705 (Reston, VA: U.S. Geological Survey, 1974) has not been superseded as a basic source. James

H. Zumberge, ed., *Possible Environmental Effects of Mineral Exploration and Exploitation in Antarctica*, published by the Scientific Committee on Antarctic Research, Cambridge, England, March 1979, is, in effect, the final version of the report by the Group of Specialists on the Environmental Impact Assessment of Mineral Resource Exploration and Exploitation in Antarctica (EAMREA), convened by SCAR and originally produced in 1977. The *Report of the Group of Experts on Mineral Exploration and Exploitation*, Annex 5 of the *Report of the Ninth Antarctic Treaty Consultative Meeting*, London, September 1977, had similar origins and purposes and reached quite similar conclusions. *Antarctic Resources*—report from the Meeting of Experts at the Fridtjof Nansen Foundation at Polhogda, May 30–June 10, 1973, U.S. Congress, Senate Subcommittee on Oceans and International Environment (reprinted in *U.S. Antarctic Policy*, 94th Cong., 1st sess., May 15, 1975, pp. 68–85) —contains data not available elsewhere and reflects scientists' attitudes. "Antarctic Mineral Resources," a document presented by the U.S. delegation to the special meeting of the Antarctic Treaty Powers, 1976, is officially described as an "informal assessment prepared for use within the U.S. Government"; it is reprinted in U.S. Congress, Senate Committee on Energy and Natural Resources, *U.S. Activities in Antarctica*, 96th Cong., 1st sess., April 23, 1979 (Publication No. 96-21). pp. 20–24. D. H. Elliot, *A Framework for Assessing Environmental Impacts of Possible Antarctic Mineral Development* (Ohio State University, Institute of Polar Studies, 1976), which was prepared for the Department of State, is notable for its hypothetical case studies based on the scant knowledge available. M. W. Holdgate and Jon Tinker, *Oil and Other Minerals in the Antarctic* (report of a workshop held at Bellagio, Italy, March 1979, Cambridge, England: SCAR, 1979), is useful in framing questions and defining research needs; it is surprisingly sanguine regarding environmental implications.

45. Walter Sullivan, reporting from Leningrad, *The New York Times*, September 4, 1960, p. 9.

46. Edward J. Zeller, "Uranium Resource Evaluation in Antarctica" (paper delivered at an International Symposium on Uranium Evaluation and Mining Techniques, Buenos Aires, October 1–4, 1979).

47. See Campbell Craddock, "Antarctic Geology and Gondwanaland," in *Frozen Future: A Prophetic Report from Antarctica*, Richard S. Lewis and Philip M. Smith, eds. (New York: Quadrangle Books, 1973), pp. 101–21; Sir Edward Bullard, "The Origin of the Oceans," *Scientific American*, vol. 221, no. 3, October 1969, pp. 66–75; and "The Earth Beneath the Poles," *Mosaic* (published by the NSF) 9, no. 5 (September/October 1978), pp. 4–14.

48. Robert Muir Wood, "Coming Apart at the Seams," *New Scientist 85* (January 24, 1980), pp. 252–54.

49. John A. McPhee, *Basin and Range* (New York: Farrar, Straus & Giroux, 1981), p. 177.

50. It is not accepted in the Soviet Union, perhaps because of the inordinate influence of V. V. Belloussov, director of the department of geodynamics in the Institute of Earth Physics of the Academy of Sciences and Vice-President of the IGY in 1957, who ridicules the theory. See Robert Muir Wood,

"Geology versus Dogma: The Russian Rift," *New Scientist* 86 (June 12, 1980), pp. 234–37.

51. James Jackson and Robert Muir Wood, "The Earth Flexes Its Muscles," *New Scientist*, December 11, 1980, p. 718.

52. It should be noted that it was the limits of the continental shelves or margins that interlocked, not the present continents themselves; hence the apparent imperfections in the match.

53. Elliot, *A Framework for Assessing Environmental Impacts*, p. III-6.

54. Wright and Williams, *Mineral Resources*, p. 23.

55. James H. Zumberge, "Potential Mineral Resource Availability and Possible Environmental Problems in Antarctica," in *The New Nationalism and the Use of Common Spaces: Issues in Marine Pollution and the Exploitation of Antarctica*, Jonathan I. Charney, ed. (Montclair, NJ: Allanheld, Osmun; in press [hereafter cited as *The New Nationalism*]).

56. William J. Broad, "Resource Wars: The Lure of South Africa," *Science* 210 (December 5, 1980), p. 1099.

57. Constance Holden, "Getting Serious About Strategic Minerals," *Science* 212 (April 17, 1981), p. 305.

58. Elliot, *A Framework for Assessing Environmental Impacts*, pp. V-8–11 and VI-2–9.

59. The purity of the Antarctic environment can be exaggerated. Apart from manmade pollution, Mt. Erebus regularly spews gases into the atmosphere.

60. Elliot, *A Framework for Assessing Environmental Impacts*, pp. VI-2–9.

61. See Giulio Pontecorvo, "The Economics of the Mineral Resources of Antarctica," in *The New Nationalism*.

62. Jonathan Spivak, "Frozen Assets," *Wall Street Journal*, February 21, 1974.

63. Deborah Shapley, "Antarctica: World Hunger for Oil Spurs Security Council Review," *Science*, May 17, 1974, p. 777.

64. The most detailed account of this extended and somewhat bizarre episode was given by Gerald S. Schatz of the National Academy of Sciences in an unpublished lecture, "Antarctic Myths and the Quality of Policy Discourse," at Northern Illinois University, September 28, 1977.

65. NSDM 263, July 1974.

66. Zumberge in *The New Nationalism*.

67. To be "locked in" is not, of course, to be stationary but to circulate at the whim of the moving ice, perhaps several hundred miles in a season.

68. See Allen R. Milne and Richard H. Herlinveaux, *Crude Oil in Cold Water*, The Beaufort Sea Project (Ottawa: Minister of Supply and Services); Allen Milne, *Oil, Ice and Climate Change*, Beaufort Sea Project (Ottawa: Department of Fisheries and Oceans). These undated studies occurred between 1973 and 1976. They are available from the Institute of Ocean Sciences, Department of Fisheries and Oceans, P.O. Box 6000, Sidney, B.C., Canada V8L 4B2.

69. Holdgate and Tinker, *Oil and Other Minerals*, para. 111.

70. Zumberge, *The New Nationalism*.

71. Milne, *Oil, Ice and Climate Change*, p. 23.

72. John A. Dugger, "Exploiting Antarctic Mineral Resources—Technology, Economics, and the Environment," *University of Miami Law Review* 33, no. 2 (December 1978), p. 337.

73. Neal Potter, *Natural Resources Potentials of the Antarctic, A Resources for the Future Study* (New York: The American Geographical Society, 1969), p. 9.
74. Joseph M. Dukert, *This is Antarctica* (New York: Coward-McCann, 1965), p. 184.
75. Richard S. Lewis, *A Continent for Science* (New York: Viking Press, 1965), p. 195.
76. Frank Debenham, *Antartica: The Story of a Continent* (New York: Macmillan, 1961), p. 223.
77. There are only two comprehensive sources of information in English on Antarctic tourism. One is Rosamunde J. Reich, "The Development of Antarctic Tourism," *Polar Record* 20, no. 26 (September 1980), pp. 203–14; the second is Patricia J. Scharlin, "Antarctic Tourism—Trends and Impact," a background paper prepared for the Division of Polar Programs of the National Science Foundation, 1979 (39 typescript pages plus appendices). Both authors acknowledge the incompleteness of their data. Reich is a graduate student at Cambridge University. Scharlin is director of the Sierra Club Earthcare Center in New York.
78. Brian Lee, "Antarctica Falls to Tourism," *New Scientist* 78 (June 15, 1978), p. 764.
79. Katherine Bouton, "South of 60 Degrees South," *The New Yorker*, March 23, 1981, p. 105.
80. *The New York Times*, November 29 and December 3, 1979.
81. Scharlin, "Antarctic Tourism," pp. 9 and 10.
82. Reich, "The Development of Antarctic Tourism," p. 210.
83. Recommendation X-8 of the treaty parties. See Chapter V, below.
84. Jere H. Lipps, "Man's Impact Along the Antarctic Peninsula," in *Environmental Impact in Antarctica*, p. 357.
85. Reich, "The Development of Antarctic Tourism," p. 212.
86. "Private Research Expeditions to Antarctica, 1977–78," *Polar Record*, January 1979, p. 378.
87. Scharlin, "Antarctic Tourism," p. 13.
88. Articles written by the expedition leader, Sir Ranulph Fiennes, appeared periodically through 1980 and early 1981 in *The Observer* (London), which had exclusive rights.
89. *Antarctic Policy Group*—67-2. The "conditions" referred to in the first paragraph were spelled out in considerable detail in a separate statement.
90. Professor McWhinnie is reputed to have asked rhetorically: "What right does any non-scientist have to be involved in Antarctica?"
91. The Institute on Man and Science and the Western Australia and Overseas Development Corporation had co-sponsored a conference on the topic in February 1974. See *Transporting Icebergs as a Fresh Water Source*, a seminar held at the Institute of Man and Science, Rensselaerville, New York, February 1–3, 1974. A small meeting of experts was held in Paris in the summer of 1977. See below.
92. Actually, the NSF had been funding research on a small scale for years, but without publicity. See J. L. Hult and N. C. Ostrander, *Antarctic Icebergs as a Global Fresh Water Resource*, prepared for the National Science Foundation, October 1973 (R-1255-NSF).

93. Respectively, foreign secretary of the National Academy of Sciences, former director of the National Science Foundation, and Harvard's Man for All Sciences; each, of course, wears many hats.

94. A. A. Husseiny, ed., *Iceberg Utilization* (Elmsford, NY: Pergamon Press, 1978).

95. "Icebergs for the Desert: Cool Calculations," *Science News* 112 (October 15, 1977), p. 244.

96. Youssef M. Ibrahim, "Saudi Will Deliver Icebergs—at a Price," *The New York Times*, April 15, 1978. Faisal's optimism was based primarily on an engineering and economic study by French consultants, CICERO. The Paris meeting mentioned in note 91 was called to discuss their proposal, which proved very unrealistic. It is described in Anil Agarwal, "Will Saudi Arabia Drink Icebergs?" *New Scientist*, July 7, 1977, p. 11.

97. *Science News*, May 26, 1973, p. 338.

98. Charles Swithinbank, Paul McClain, and Patricia Little, "Drift Tracks of Antarctic Icebergs," *Polar Record*, May 1977, p. 495. See also Kendrick Frazier, "Is There an Iceberg in Your Future?" *Science News* 112 (November 5, 1977), p. 298.

99. Constance Holden, "Experts Ponder Icebergs as Relief for World Water Dilemma," *Science* 198 (October 21, 1977), p. 275.

100. C. Brent Cluff, "Use of Floating Solar Collectors in Processing Iceberg Water," in *Iceberg Utilization*, p. 477.

101. "Icing Up for Energy," *New Scientist*, September 27, 1979, p. 975.

102. John D. Isaacs and Walter R. Schmitt, "Ocean Energy: Forms and Prospects," *Science* 207 (January 18, 1980), p. 273. It was Isaacs who first suggested the use of *Arctic* icebergs for fresh water in the 1940s, although he never published his concept (Holden, "Experts Ponder Icebergs," p. 274). The idea of tapping Greenland icebergs as a water source was revived during the severe drought in Europe in the summer of 1976 (Ernst Berens, "Greenland's Ice Might Solve Europe's Drinking Water Shortage," *Suddeutche Zeitung*, July 22, 1976. Translated in *The German Tribune*, August 8, 1976). If the Rhine becomes any more polluted, the idea may still become viable.

103. Lowell Ponte, "Alien Ice: An Evaluation of Some Subsidiary Effects and Concomitant Problems of Iceberg Utilization," in *Iceberg Utilization*, p. 16.

104. Charles R. Goldman, "Ecological Aspects of Iceberg Transport from Antarctic Waters," in *Iceberg Utilization*, p. 642.

105. Herbert E. Huppert, "Icebergs: Technology for the Future," *Nature* 285 (May 8, 1980), pp. 67–68.

106. *Ibid.*, p. 67.

107. Quoted in "The Disposal of Radioactive Wastes in the Antarctic Ice Sheet," IUUG *Chronicle*, Paris, June 1975, p. 163. The International Union of Geodesy and Geophysics believes that the ice-sheet disposal scheme deserves careful study.

108. See especially E. J. Zeller and E. E. Angino, "The Disposal of Radioactive Wastes in the Antarctic Ice Sheet: An Environmental Impact Assessment," in *Environmental Impact in Antarctica*, pp. 279–94. See also by the same

authors, with D. F. Sanders, "Putting Radioactive Wastes on Ice," *Bulletin of the Atomic Scientists*, January 1973.

109. Zumberge in *The New Nationalism*.

110. Debenham, *Antarctica*, p. 225.

111. NSF news release, September 6, 1981.

112. Papers of Admiral George Dufek, George Arents Research Library, Syracuse University.

113. There was an additional reason why a U.S. investment of several hundred million dollars in this commercial enterprise seemed a questionable idea. The most desirable, ice-free site was in territory claimed by New Zealand. See next chapter.

114. See Potter, *Natural Resource Potentials*, pp. 48–51.

CHAPTER IV

1. The letters patent of 1908 and 1917 are reprinted in *Polar Record* 5, nos. 35/36, pp. 241–43.

2. Frank Debenham, *Antarctica: The Story of a Continent* (New York: Macmillan, 1961), pp. 230–31.

3. J. S. Reeves, "George V Land," *American Journal of International Law* 28 (1934), p. 118.

4. J. Daniel, "Conflict of Sovereignties in the Antarctic," *Yearbook of World Affairs* (London), vol. 3, 1949, p. 258. Earlier, in 1928, Norway had annexed Bouvet Island and, in 1931, Peter I Island "to give the Norwegian whaling industry in that region points of support and to guard it against possible encroachment on the part of foreign Powers" (Quoted in J. S. Reeves, "Antarctic Sectors," *American Journal of International Law* 33, no. 3 [July 1939], p. 520).

5. Japan had threatened all through the 1930s to stake a claim on the basis of one abortive expedition in 1911–12, but after World War II surrendered any right to do so under the terms of the 1952 peace treaty.

6. One of the earliest comprehensive discussions of Antarctic claims, and still a classic, is Gustav Smedal, *Acquisition of Sovereignty Over Polar Areas*, Skrifter Om Svalbard Og Ishavet nr. 36, Chr. Meyer, trans. (Oslo: Det Kongelige Department for Handel, Sjøfart, Industri, Handverk Og Fiskeri, 1931), 143 pp. For a general perspective on the relevant law, there is L. Oppenheim, *International Law: A Treatise*, 8th ed., H. Lauterpacht, ed. (London: Longmans, Green, 1955), a massive two-volume work first published in 1905–06 and kept up to date for thirty-five years after the author's death; see especially vol. 1, pp. 554–63. See also F. A. F. von der Heydte, "Discovery, Symbolic Annexation and Virtual Effectiveness in International Law," *American Journal of International Law*, July 1935, pp. 448–71; and Philip C. Jessup and Howard J. Taubenfeld, *Controls for Outer Space and the Antarctic Analogy* (New York: Columbia University Press, 1959), pp. 137–59. The Polar Area Series written by John Hanessian, Jr., for the American Universities Field Staff (Hanover, NH) is an unequaled source of information on the participants in Antarctica up to 1962; see especially the three-part "National

Activities and Interests in Antarctica," September 1962. On the British/Argentine/Chilean dispute, the best sources are E. W. Hunter Christie, *The Antarctic Problem: An Historical and Political Study* (London: Allen & Unwin, 1951); and Robert D. Hayton, "The 'American' Antarctic," *American Journal of International Law* 50 (July 1956), pp. 583–610. Both authors have excellent command of South American sources. The only comprehensive statement of the Latin claim available in English is Oscar Pinochet de la Barra, *Chilean Sovereignty in Antarctica* (Santiago: Editorial del Pacifico, 1955), 59 pp. An informed overview by a scholar in the U.S. Department of State is J. Peter A. Bernhardt, "Sovereignty in Antarctica," *California Western International Law Journal* (1975), reprinted in *U.S. Antarctic Policy*, Hearing Before the Senate Subcommittee on Oceans and International Environment, May 15, 1975 (made public July 6, 1975). (Note references are to reprint.) An exhaustive study from a Communist perspective is Jacek Machowski, *The Status of Antarctica in the Light of International Law*, 150 pp., which was published in Poland in 1968 but was published in English for the (U.S.) Division of Polar Programs and the National Science Foundation only in 1977.

7. Quoted in Pinochet, *Chilean Sovereignty*, p. 10.
8. On hearing of the pope's division of the world between Spain and Portugal, the king of France demanded to see "the will of Adam" to ascertain whether it deprived Frenchmen of the right to acquire American territory (Daniel, "Conflict of Sovereignties," pp. 249–50).
9. Treaty of Peace and Friendship between Great Britain and Spain, signed in Madrid, July 18, 1670, *British and Foreign State Papers*, London, 1841, vol. I, pp. 608–11. The operative language suggests that it was drafted by the English: "[I]t is agreed that the Most Serene King of Great Britain, his Heirs and Successors, shall have, hold, keep and enjoy for ever, with plenary rights of Sovereignty, Dominion, Possession and Propriety, all those Lands, Regions, Islands, Colonies, and places whatsoever, being or situated in the West Indies, or in any part of America, which said King of Great Britain and his subjects do at present hold and possess. . . ." By comparison, Spain's benefit under the treaty is put straightforwardly: "[T]he Subjects of the King of Great Britain shall not sail unto and trade in the Havens and places which the Catholic King holdeth in the said Indies." The word "holdeth" is obviously interpreted differently by the two parties.
10. Pinochet, *Chilean Sovereignty*, p. 14.
11. *Ibid.*, p. 15.
12. Daniel, "Conflict of Sovereignties," pp. 262 and 267; Pinochet, pp. 27–29.
13. Edward E. Honnold, "Thaw in International Law? Rights in Antarctica under Law of Common Spaces," *The Yale Law Journal* 87, no. 4 (March 1978), p. 814.
14. Examples are French scholars Daniel, "Conflict of Sovereignties"; M. Gilbert Gidel, *Aspects Juridique de la Lutte pour l'Antarctique*, Paris, 1948; and René-Jean Dupuy, "Le Statut de l'Antarctique," *1958 Annuaire Français de Droit Internationale*, pp. 208–14.
15. Robert D. Hayton, "Polar Problems and International Law," *American Journal of International Law*, October 1958, p. 746. See also James Nelson Goodsell, "Antarctic 'State Visit' Irks Chile's Neighbors," *The Christian Science Monitor*, January 28, 1977.

16. Reeves, "Antarctic Sectors," p. 521.
17. *The Antarctic Treaty,* Hearings before the Senate Foreign Relations Committee, June 14, 1960, p. 47.
18. Pinochet, *Chilean Sovereignty,* p. 46.
19. *The New York Times,* June 11, 1961.
20. *The Christian Science Monitor,* January 28, 1977.
21. *The New York Times,* January 9, 1978.
22. The first pregnancy in Antarctica was that of an American, Mrs. Harry Darlington, who was honeymooning with her husband on the Finn Ronne expedition in 1947–48. (Mrs. Ronne was also along.) Only rescue by U.S. icebreakers prevented Antarctica's firstborn from being an American. (Walter Sullivan, *Quest for a Continent* [New York: McGraw-Hill, 1957], p. 273.)
23. Hayton, "The 'American' Antarctic," p. 586.
24. The implications of the Rio Treaty for Antarctic claims are discussed in the *Polar Record* 6, no. 43 (January 1952), pp. 405–7.
25. Quoted in Bernhardt, "Sovereignty in Antarctica," p. 97.
26. Quoted in von der Heydte, "Discovery, Symbolic Annexation," p. 464.
27. For the English, it is somewhat galling that the Argentines took no initiative in establishing the weather station and that it was handed to them by a Scotsman! (See Chapter I.)
28. To those stationed closer to the South Pole, the peninsula is known as the Banana Belt because mean temperatures are vastly warmer—approximately the relative difference between south Florida and northern Minnesota. Thus, effective occupation in the usual sense is more nearly practicable at the tip of the peninsula than elsewhere on the continent. However, the heavy concentration of stations on the peninsula eliminates one requirement of effective occupation: that it be exclusive. (David Winston Heron, "Antarctic Claims," *Foreign Affairs* 32 [July 1954], p. 667.)
29. Christie, *The Antarctic Problem,* pp. 41–71.
30. Hugo Grotius, *The Freedom of the Seas* (New York: Oxford University Press, 1916), pp. 11–12. First published anonymously in 1608 in Latin, *Mare Liberum* was written to refute claims of Spain and Portugal to the high seas. The edition cited here was prepared by the Carnegie Endowment for International Peace.
31. Again, in the *East Greenland* case, decided April 5, 1933, it has been said that the "Court attached considerable importance to the fact that up to 1931 there had been no claim by any power other than Denmark. . . ." (Oppenheim, *International Law,* vol. I, p. 561). Of course, Argentina and Chile insist it would be absurd to declare sovereignty over what one already possesses.
32. Brian Roberts, "International Cooperation for Antarctic Development: The Test for the Antarctic Treaty," *Polar Record* 19, no. 119 (1978), p. 355.
33. Sir Vivian Fuchs, "Evolution of a Venture in Antarctic Science—Operation Tabarin and the British Antarctic Survey," in *Frozen Future: A Prophetic Report from Antarctica,* Richard S. Lewis and Philip M. Smith, eds. (New York: Quadrangle Books, 1973), p. 234.
34. Christie, *The Antarctic Problem,* p. 247; *Polar Record,* July 1946, p. 402.
35. *Application Instituting Proceedings Filed in the Registry of the International Court of Justice,* May 4, 1955 (General List, nos. 26 and 27). This contains the most

comprehensive statement of Britain's case for its Antarctic claim. See also "Letter from the Minister of Chile at The Hague to the Registrar of the International Court of Justice" declining the British offer to submit the case to the World Court (*Polar Record*, 8/52, January 1956): ". . . Chile exercises full and absolute sovereignty in virtue of unimpeachable titles of a juridical, political, historical, geographical, diplomatic and administrative character" (p. 49).

36. The extensive diplomatic exchanges of these years among Britain, Argentina, and Chile can be found in the *Polar Record* 5, nos. 34/35, pp. 228–40; 6, no. 43, pp. 413–18; and 7, no. 48, pp. 212–26.

37. Hayton, "The 'American' Antarctic," p. 588.

38. The Argentine name for the Falklands is derived from the French, Isles Malouines, a curious admission that the Spanish were not there first.

39. Evidence that the Argentines felt strongly included repeated stoning of the British Embassy, a plane hijacked to publicize nationalist demands, and occupation of an uninhabited outer island by Argentine civilians.

40. See, for example, Ian F. Strange, *The Falkland Islands* (Harrisburg: Stackpole Books, 1972); Christie, *The Antarctic Problem*; and "Britain's Antarctic Outpost," *The Economist*, March 26, 1960, p. 1225.

41. The understanding is said to be contained in an unwritten clause of the Webster-Ashburton Treaty in 1842, "the historic beginning of the Anglo-American *entente*." (*The Economist*, March 26, 1960, p. 1225.)

42. The Vergara/La Rosa Declaration of March 4, 1948, quoted in Hayton, "The 'American' Antarctic," p. 591. Putting the best face on this agreement to disagree, Oscar Pinochet de la Barra more recently referred to these overlapping claims as "a *de facto* condominium." ("Political and Juridical Evolution of the Antarctic Problem," an address to the Chilean International Law Society, May 29, 1980.)

43. Chileans and Argentines never refer to the Southern Ocean (singular), as others do, but always say "Southern Oceans."

44. *Beagle Channel Arbitration between the Republic of Argentina and the Republic of Chile: Report and Decision of the Court of Arbitration*, London, H.M.S.O., 1977, pp. 107–8. The Court of Arbitration consisted of a British chairman (Sir Gerald Fitzmaurice), a Frenchman, a Nigerian, a Swede, and an American (Hardy C. Dillard), all appointed by the British government. The more frequently cited May 2, 1977, is the date the award was communicated to the parties, after ratification by Her Majesty's government.

45. Note delivered by the Ministry of Foreign Affairs of the Republic of Argentina to the ambassador of Chile, January 25, 1978 (signed by Oscar Antonio Montes, vice-admiral).

46. *Latin America Political Report*, January 20, 1978, p. 19; July 21, 1978, p. 218; August 25, 1978, pp. 260–61.

47. Edward Schumacher, "Papal Solution to Boundary Quarrel Vexes Argentina," *The New York Times*, January 21, 1981. At the time that Chile and Argentina accepted their treaty obligation to compulsory arbitration, they agreed that hereafter they would apply for dispute settlement to the Court of International Justice rather than to the British Crown, with which Argentina is in perpetual battle over the Falkland Islands. However, the agreement

must be renewed every ten years. In any event, Argentina cannot seriously hope for a more favorable decision from the World Court.

48. Reeves, "George V Land," p. 118.
49. *Current Antarctic Literature,* prepared by the Library of Congress for the Division of Polar Programs of the National Science Foundation, no. 87, November 1979, pp. 20–21.
50. F. M. Auburn, "Dispute Settlement by Treaty: New Zealand and the Antarctic," *Recent Law,* August 1975, p. 252. Professor Auburn of the University of Auckland law faculty has written extensively on Antarctica and has been consistently critical of the government for failure to perfect New Zealand's claim and for frequently weakening it.
51. "How Strong Is New Zealand's Claim to the Ross Dependency?" *The New Zealand Law Journal,* March 4, 1980, pp. 76–77.
52. See, for example, Machowski, *The Status of Antarctica,* chapter IV; Bernhardt, "Sovereignty in Antarctica," section III; and Smedal, *Acquisition of Sovereignty,* pp. 27–32.
53. U.S. Department of State (Washington, DC), *Foreign Relations of the United States,* vol. 2, 1924, pp. 519–20.
54. Quoted in Laurence M. Gould, *Antarctica in World Affairs,* Foreign Policy Association, Headline Series no. 128, 1958, p. 21.
55. Quoted in Barry Merrill Plott, "The Development of United States Antarctic Policy" (Ph.D. dissertation, Fletcher School of Law and Diplomacy, 1969), p. 172.
56. *Foreign Relations,* vol. 2, 1928, pp. 1002 and 1004.
57. Paul A. Carter, *Little America: Town at the End of the World* (New York: Columbia University Press, 1979), pp. 136 and 138. The delay may have been due to the approaching London Naval Conference, which deterred the Department of State from its initial intention of contesting the British claim (Smedal, *Acquisition of Sovereignty,* p. 10). Even if a New Zealand claim were acknowledged, there would be some question whether it could include the Ross Ice Shelf, which floats on a vast bay.
58. Plott, "The Development of United States Antarctic Policy," pp. 32 and 33.
59. In a short note in *Foreign Affairs,* pegged to the Imperial Conference of 1926 at which British title to Antarctic territories was discussed, an American legal expert and former adviser to the Department of State concluded: "In no part of the globe are claims to sovereignty over land areas of as little apparent consequence as in the Antarctic" (David Hunter Miller, "National Rights in Antarctica," *Foreign Affairs,* April 1927, p. 510).
60. Senate Resolution 310, June 30, 1930, 71st Cong., 2nd sess.
61. File No. 800.014, Antarctic/28 and 32 (1930), National Archives. The file number designates Department of State papers.
62. Emphasis in the original note of March 29, 1935, File No. 800.014.
63. *Foreign Relations,* 1938, vol. 1, pp. 972–73.
64. *Ibid.,* pp. 973–74. The instructions on dropping proclamations from the air were quoted from a published article by Ellsworth's old friend and counselor, Sir Hubert Wilkins.
65. The consul general at Sydney (Wilson) to the secretary of state, February 22, 1938, in *Foreign Relations,* 1939, vol. 1, p. 975.

66. File No. 800.014, Antarctic/129A.

67. File No. 800.014, Antarctic/155A.

68. *Foreign Relations*, 1939, vol. 2, pp. 4–5.

69. *Ibid.*, p. 7.

70. *Ibid.*, p. 10.

71. Ernest Gruening, *Hearings on the Expedition to the Antarctic Regions*, House Committee on Appropriations, Subcommittee on Deficiencies, 76th Cong., 1st sess., June 2, 1939, p. 6. The committee was composed of representatives of the Departments of State, Treasury, Interior, and the Navy.

72. *Foreign Relations*, 1939, vol. 2, p. 13.

73. Quoted in Plott, "The Development of United States Antarctic Policy," p. 85.

74. *Ibid.*, p. 88.

75. See *Foreign Relations*, 1940, vol. 2, pp. 333–39, for reports to the Department of State from Ambassador Norman Armour in Buenos Aires and Ambassador Bowers in Santiago. See also Christie, *The Antarctic Problem*, pp. 268–69.

76. *Foreign Relations*, 1939, vol. 2, pp. 10 and 15.

77. Quoted in Walter Sullivan, "Antarctica in a Two-Power World," *Foreign Affairs*, October 1957, p. 174.

78. Quoted in Sullivan, *Quest for a Continent*, p. 300.

79. *Foreign Relations*, 1948, vol. I, pp. 980 and 982.

80. *Ibid.*, p. 981.

81. *Ibid.*, p. 992.

82. *Ibid.*, p. 985.

83. *Ibid.*, pp. 971–74.

84. *Ibid.*, p. 974.

85. *Ibid.*, p. 1000.

86. *Ibid.*, p. 1001.

87. "Discussions Asked on Territorial Problem of Antarctica," Department of State *Bulletin*, vol. 19, September 5, 1948, p. 301.

88. *Foreign Relations*, 1948, pp. 1008–1010.

89. Quoted in John Hanessian, Jr., "The Antarctic Treaty 1959," *The International and Comparative Law Quarterly*, July 1960, p. 439.

90. S. Wolk, "The Basis of Soviet Claims in the Antarctic," *Bulletin*, Institute for the Study of U.S.S.R., April 1958, pp. 47–48.

91. Peter A. Toma, "Soviet Attitudes Towards the Acquisition of Territorial Sovereignty in the Antarctic," *American Journal of International Law*, July 1956, p. 623.

92. *Ibid.*, pp. 624–26. In passing, the Soviet scholars perpetrated the canard that Captain Cook had "denied the existence of an Antarctic continent." See also Terence Armstrong, "Recent Soviet Interest in Bellingshausen's Antarctic Voyage of 1819–21," *Polar Record* 5, no. 39 (January 1950), pp. 475–78.

93. Except for Chile, with which the Soviet Union did not (and does not) have diplomatic relations.

94. The full text is appended to Toma, "Soviet Attitudes."

95. "National Claims and Development of U.S. Objectives in Antarctica," Background Paper no. 1, pp. 8–9. This undated summary, clearly intended as an internal document, may have been paraphrasing rather than quoting the NSC Memoranda, which the writer has not seen. It is interesting to note that

NSC Memorandum 5127 of July 1954 failed to mention natural resources—a matter that was corrected the following year.

96. Henry M. Dater, memorandum dated July 31, 1958, to the Department of State, Files of James E. Mooney, deputy in the U.S. Antarctic Projects Office, R.G. 330, Records of the Office of the Secretary of Defense, the Center for Polar Archives.

97. "Status of the Antarctic Region: Memorandum of the Department of State," March 30, 1956, *American Foreign Policy, 1950–1956* (Basic Documents, vol. I, Department of State Publication 6446, 1957), pp. 1430–31.

98. H. M. Dater, "Memorandum for the Record," meeting of July 9, 1957 (papers of Admiral George Dufek, George Arents Research Library, Syracuse University). These memoranda of Antarctic Working Group meetings were originally classified "secret."

99. *Ibid.*

100. Admiral Byrd's chief lieutenant, Paul Siple, contended that Americans had seen and mapped far more of the continent than all others combined, and in his book *90° South: The Story of the American South Pole Conquest* (New York: G. P. Putnam's & Sons, 1959), he published maps designed to prove it. He believed that if Highjump II had not been scrubbed in an economy drive, the United States would have been in a strong position to claim the entire continent (see pp. 81, 86, and 87).

101. Although in principle it would be hard to quarrel with a U.S. claim to this sector, in fact, there was a nice problem. If the 90° meridian were chosen as the eastern boundary, it could be interpreted as a recognition of the Chilean claim, which extends to 90°W. But if the United States took 80°W as its border, it would seem to be flouting the Chilean claim and accepting that of Great Britain, whose Antarctic territory reaches the 80° meridian.

102. Sullivan, "Antarctica in a Two-Power World," p. 165. Sullivan was probably mistaken with respect to the British. A reliable source in the Foreign Office states that the United Kingdom was instrumental in deterring the United States from making a claim in the 1950s.

103. L. F. E. Goldie, "International Relations in Antarctica," *Australian Quarterly,* March 1958, pp. 24–29; John Andrews, "Antarctic Geopolitics," *The Australian Outlook,* September 1957, p. 6; see also Siple, *90° South,* p. 363, where he testifies that he sensed a desire for merger "in semi-official quarters in both countries in 1947 and again in 1955 and 1956."

104. F. M. Auburn, *The Ross Dependency* (The Hague: Martinus Nijhoff, 1972), p. 82.

105. Quoted in Laurence M. Gould, "The Polar Regions in Their Relation to Human Affairs," Bowman Memorial Lectures (New York: The American Geographical Society, 1958), p. 32. Gould himself regretted that the United States did not make a claim, believing that at one time it might have claimed more than half the continent without objection. But by the time of the IGY, when he was speaking, he felt it was too late (Gould, *Antarctica in World Affairs,* p. 48).

106. Goldie, "International Relations in Antarctica," p. 23.

107. Memo to the Office of Secretary of Defense, April 17, 1957, Mooney file (R.G. 330); Siple, *90° South,* pp. 362–63.

108. Dater memo of July 31, 1958.

109. In 1965, a dissertation written by a lieutenant commander at the Naval War College was being handed around Washington with some approval. In addition to stating that "a declaration of United States sovereignty in Antarctica is imperative and long overdue" (although this was by then prohibited by the Antarctic Treaty), the author wrote: "A review of United States [Antarctic] policy from the end of World War II to 1959 reveals that it is one of indecision, repeated complete reversals of policy, a lack of coordination between government agencies and often damaging petty quarrels among government officials. This lack of consistent policy could not have occurred at a worse time; for the Soviet Union took advantage of this situation and commenced its move into Antarctica" (Joseph R. Morgan, U.S.N., "Strategy of the United States in Antarctica During and After the Thirty-Year Freeze," dissertation, Naval War College, Newport, RI, 1965, pp. 32–33 and 52). This is an exaggeration, but it has considerable validity for the period 1950–58.

110. It will be remembered that Norway refrained from extending its claim to the pole and left the southern boundary undefined. See, for example, Finn Sollie, "The New Development in the Polar Regions," *Cooperation & Conflict*, 1974: 2/3.

CHAPTER V

1. *The Times* (London), February 7, 1957. The Australian minister of external affairs was later to say, with that illogic nurtured by diplomacy: "One of the primary objectives of the Treaty must be to eliminate suspicions in the Antarctic. I do not wish to imply that at the present time there are such suspicions." (U.S. Department of State, *The Conference on Antarctica, Washington, October 15–December 1, 1959,* Washington, DC, September 1960 [hereafter, *Conf. Docs.*], p. 26.) At that time, all the Soviet stations were in the claimed territory of Australia.

2. Personal communication (November 6, 1979) from Daniels, who is frequently referred to as the chief architect of the treaty. The writer also interviewed Daniels at his home in Lakeville, Connecticut, October 16 and 17, 1979, and again on July 30, 1980. The best descriptions and analyses of the treaty are Robert D. Hayton, "The Antarctic Settlement of 1959," *American Journal of International Law* 54, no. 2 (April 1960), pp. 349–71; John Hanessian, Jr., "The Antarctic Treaty 1959," *International and Comparative Law Quarterly* 9 (July 1960); and Howard J. Taubenfeld, "A Treaty for Antarctica," *International Conciliation,* Carnegie Endowment for International Peace, New York, January 1961. See also Bernard H. Oxman, "The Antarctic Regime: An Introduction," *University of Miami Law Review* 33, no. 2 (December 1978), pp. 285–97; Finn Sollie, "The Political Experiment in Antarctica," in *Frozen Future: A Prophetic Report from Antarctica,* Richard S. Lewis and Philip M. Smith, eds. (New York: Quadrangle Books, 1973); and Christopher Beeby, "The Antarctic Treaty," New Zealand Institute of International Affairs, Wellington, 1972. An atypical Chilean view is given by Roberto E. Guyer, "The Antarctic System," in *Recueil des Cours* 2 (1973), pp. 153–226 (extracted and printed for the Academy of International Law by A. W. Sijthoff, Leyden).

3. Quoted in Hanessian, "The Antarctic Treaty 1959," pp. 25–26; see also Robert D. Hayton, "Polar Problems and International Law," *American Journal of International Law*, October 1958, p. 755.
4. *The Times*, February 12, 1958.
5. "U.S. Proposes Conference on Antarctica," Department of State *Bulletin* 38, no. 988 (June 2, 1958), pp. 910–12. The full text of the note as well as the president's announcement were also printed in *The New York Times*, May 4, 1958.
6. The Center for Polar Archives, R.G. 330, Records of the Office of the Secretary of Defense (formerly classified documents, group A).
7. *The New York Times*, October 26, 1959.
8. "Issues Before the Eleventh General Assembly," *International Conciliation*, no. 510, November 1956, Carnegie Endowment for International Peace, p. 136. See also Philip C. Jessup and Howard J. Taubenfeld, *Controls for Outer Space and the Antarctic Analogy* (New York: Columbia University Press, 1959), pp. 160–64.
9. Papers of Admiral George Dufek, George Arents Research Library, Syracuse University.
10. Memorandum of a March 10, 1959, meeting made by James E. Mooney, deputy U.S. Antarctic projects officer, Department of Defense, in the Center for Polar Archives, R.G. 330. Much later, when the treaty was being debated on the floor of the Senate, opponents would consistently ignore these preparatory meetings and contend that anything the Soviet Union agreed to in six weeks must be bad for the United States (*Congressional Record*, August 8, 9, and 10, 1960).
11. This may account for *The New York Times* reporting somewhat prematurely, in a story filed from Washington on March 31, that "the future of the United States in Antarctica will probably be decided here within the next two days" (April 1, 1959, p. 16). However, the very short item apparently referred to a forthcoming meeting of the National Security Council rather than to the preparatory talks. The timing of Daniels' luncheon meeting with Ambassador Menshikov is according to Daniels' recollection and has not been confirmed.
12. Quoted in James Simsarian, "Inspection Experience under the Antarctic Treaty and the International Atomic Energy Agency," *American Journal of International Law*, July 1966, p. 509.
13. Central Intelligence Agency, *Polar Regions Atlas*, Washington, DC, 1978, p. 44. All dates are for January even if inspection began in December of the previous year.
14. Interview, Washington, DC, June 17, 1980.
15. Interview, Washington, DC, September 19, 1979. Indirect evidence that the final negotiations were more difficult than expected is provided by a news story filed by Walter Sullivan on November 3, in which he anticipated signing of a treaty before the middle of the month. (*The New York Times*, November 4, 1959, p. 37.) In fact the treaty was not signed until December 1.
16. Opening statement by Mr. McIntosh, *Conf. Docs.*, pp. 10–11.
17. Opening statement by Mr. Mora, *ibid.*, pp. 17–18.
18. Opening statement by Mr. Scilingo, *ibid.*, p. 31.

19. The reference to "any State which is a Member of the United Nations" was designed to avoid controversy over the two Germanys and to exclude "Red" China—a provision that the Department of State considered essential for ratification by the U.S. Senate.

20. U.S. Department of State, *Handbook of Measures in Furtherance of the Principles and Objectives of the Antarctic Treaty*, 2nd ed., Washington, DC, September 1979, p. xiv.

21. See, for example, Gunnar Skagestad, "The Frozen Frontier: Models for International Cooperation," *Cooperation and Conflict*, July 1975, p. 180.

22. *The Antarctic Treaty*, Hearings before the Senate Committee on Foreign Relations, June 14, 1960 (hereafter, *Treaty Hearings*), p. 62. The head of the U.S. delegation to the Washington Conference was Herman Phleger, former legal adviser to the Department of State, who was called out of retirement at the last minute and placed over Ambassador Daniels. The action was attributed to pressure from the Far Eastern Desk and the China Lobby, which were unhappy with language in the preamble (still preserved) such as "the interest of all mankind" and "the progress of all mankind." From their point of view, Phleger was more reliable. Although an affront to Daniels, the arrangement had the advantage that, when Phleger was routinely elected chairman of the conference, Daniels, as acting head of the U.S. delegation, could participate in the debates far more freely than would have been possible if he were conference chairman. Also, Phleger probably had more influence in the Senate, an important consideration in obtaining ratification.

23. Richard B. Bilder, "Control of Criminal Conduct in Antarctica," *Virginia Law Review* 52 (March 1966), p. 260.

24. *Ibid.*, pp. 245–46.

25. Taubenfeld, "A Treaty for Antarctica," p. 288.

26. Sollie, "The Political Experiment," p. 61. For a more detailed examination of the issues, see Gerald S. Schatz, ed., *Science, Technology and Sovereignty in the Polar Region* (Lexington, MA: D.C. Heath, 1974), 215 pp.; Eric W. Johnson, "Quick, Before it Melts: Toward a Resolution of the Jurisdictional Morass in Antarctica," *Cornell International Law Journal* 10, no. 1 (December 1976), pp. 173–98; and Elizabeth K. Hook, "Criminal Jurisdiction in Antarctica," *University of Miami Law Review* 33, no. 2 (December 1978), pp. 489–514.

27. Charles Neider, *Edge of the World: Ross Island, Antarctica* (Garden City, NY: Doubleday, 1974), p. 77.

28. See Taubenfeld, "A Treaty for Antarctica," p. 291.

29. *Treaty Hearings*, p. 69.

30. Walter Sullivan, *Assault on the Unknown: The International Geophysical Year* (New York: McGraw-Hill, 1961), p. 414.

31. Walter Sullivan, *The New York Times*, September 22, 1963.

32. August 5, 1961.

33. William J. Fulbright, "The Antarctic Treaty," Report from the Committee on Foreign Relations, June 23, 1960. Fulbright, of course, was summarizing the arguments that had been raised against the treaty—not expressing his own opinion, which was highly favorable.

34. *Ibid.*

35. *Congressional Record—Senate*, August 9, 1960, p. 16061.

36. *Ibid.*, p. 16058.
37. *Ibid.*, p. 16065.
38. *Ibid.*, August 8, p. 15985.
39. *Ibid.*, p. 15982.
40. *Ibid.*, August 9, pp. 15986 and 16064.
41. *Ibid.*, p. 16067.
42. *The New York Times*, August 11, 1960.
43. *Congressional Quarterly Almanac*, vol. XVI, 1960, p. 512.
44. *The New York Times*, January 24, 1972.
45. *Hansard* 221, no. 40 (February 18, 1960), cols. 158–91.
46. Hayton, "The Antarctic Settlement," p. 364.
47. Taubenfeld, "A Treaty for Antarctica," p. 316.
48. Sollie, "The Political Experiment," p. 58.
49. New York: Columbia University Press, 1959. See also the same authors' "Outer Space, Antarctica, and the U.N.," *International Organization* 13, no. 3 (1959), pp. 363–79.
50. *Treaty Hearings*, p. 70.
51. The host country for each consultative meeting publishes a report that contains the recommendations, opening speeches, and sometimes other documents. Until recently, the texts of the recommendations have thus been difficult to obtain; but in conjunction with the Tenth Consultative Meeting in Washington in the autumn of 1979, the Department of State brought out a *Handbook of Measures in Furtherance of the Principles and Objectives of the Antarctic Treaty*, 2nd ed., carrying forward a similar document published by the British for the London meeting in 1977. This contains the recommendations of the first nine meetings, organized by subject. The report of the tenth meeting is also available from the Department of State.
52. These are huts and plaques and graves and cairns and the like, not one of which is American. The usual explanation is that all five Little Americas, the most likely site, have floated out to sea. But the Soviet Union, in the relatively brief time it has been in Antarctica, proposed half a dozen monuments that were accepted. That Richard Byrd's many friends in Congress have tolerated the United States alone being without any historical monument in the Antarctic is puzzling.
53. Confidential reports of the First and Second Consultative Meetings, dated August 11, 1961, and August 3, 1962, from T. O. Jones, director of the Antarctic Program and a member of the U.S. delegation, to Alan T. Waterman, director of the National Science Foundation. The Center for Polar Archives, RG 307, Records of the NSF, Box 29, 101.1.1 and Box 28, 102.1.2.
54. *Ibid.*, Box 29.
55. In an internal memorandum, expressing frustration more than fact, an officer of the National Science Foundation wrote his superior that the Specially Protected Areas are "ostensibly to protect the ecology but basically to keep each other out" (H. S. Francis to T. O. Jones, dated August 24, 1964, Center for Polar Archives, RG 307, Box 101/109).
56. For the text, see *Treaties and Other International Agreements on Fisheries, Oceanographic Resources, and Wildlife Involving the United States*, prepared for

the U.S. Senate Committee on Commerce, Science, and Transportation, October 31, 1977, pp. 136–44.

57. *Antarctic Conservation Act of 1978* (Public Law 95-541), with Regulations, Maps of Special Areas, Application Forms, Related Documents (Washington, DC: National Science Foundation, August 1979). For the regulations prepared by the NSF as directed by the act, see "Conservation of Antarctic Animals and Plants," *Federal Register,* June 7, 1979. (Also printed in *Antarctic Journal* 15, no. 2 [June 1979].)

58. Section 4, *Antarctic Conservation Act.*

59. Brian Roberts, "International Cooperation for Antarctic Development: The Test for the Antarctic Treaty," *Polar Record* 19, no. 119 (1978), p. 356. For a full discussion of this issue, see Johnson, "Quick, Before It Melts."

60. B. B. Roberts, "Conservation in the Antarctic," *Transactions of the Royal Society,* 1977, p. 116.

61. Interview, Washington, DC, October 4, 1979.

62. Oscar Pinochet de la Barra, "Political and Juridical Evolution of the Antarctic Problem," address to the Chilean International Law Society, May 29, 1980. Dr. Pinochet did not, of course, propose a surrender of sovereignty, for that is impermissible, but he hoped for the indefinite continuation of the status quo, which he called "a co-imperium."

63. Richard B. Bilder, "The Present Legal and Political Situation inAntarctica," in *The New Nationalism and the Use of Common Spaces: Issues in Marine Pollution and the Exploitation of Antarctica,* Jonathan I. Charney, ed. (Montclair, NJ: Allanheld, Osmun, in press).

CHAPTER VI

1. Trusteeship Council, Resolution 22 (II), December 1947, *U.N. Official Records,* T/179, p. 13.

2. *The New York Times,* April 16, 1947.

3. Commission to Study the Organization of the Peace, *Fifth Report,* June 1947, p. 22.

4. John Hanessian, Jr., "The Antarctic Treaty of 1959," *International and Comparative Law Quarterly* 9 (July 1960), pp. 448–49.

5. *U.N. World,* September 1949, p. 20. Shackleton weakened his case for internationalization of Antarctica under the United Nations by adding "with the possible exception of Graham Land (on which the British feel they have established claims by effective occupation)"; by this time, of course, all the present claimants had made their bids.

6. *Ibid.,* p. 21.

7. *Strengthening the United Nations,* Report of the Commission to Study the Organization of the Peace (New York: Harper & Bros., 1957).

8. *Ibid.,* p. 214. Although the authors of the report may not have been exactly in the political mainstream, they were an impressive group of businessmen as well as intellectuals, including Arthur Holcombe, chairman; Quincy Wright, chairman of the drafting committee; Clark Eichelberger; Philip Jessup;

Richard Gardner; Harding Bancroft; and Oscar de Lima, to name a few.

9. *Ibid.*, p. 216.
10. Hanessian, "The Antarctic Treaty," p. 450.
11. U.S. Department of State, *The Conference on Antarctica, Washington, October 15–December 1, 1959*, Washington, DC, September 1960 (hereafter, *Conf. Docs.*), pp. 10–12.
12. U.N. General Assembly, 11th sess., *The Question of Antarctica*, Doc. A/3118, February 21, 1956. Later he asked that the title be changed to "The Peaceful Utilization of Antarctica," Doc. A/3118/Add II, October 17, 1956.
13. U.N. General Assembly, 13th sess., *The Question of Antarctica*, Doc. A/3852, July 15, 1958.
14. *Ibid.*
15. K. Ahluwalia, "The Antarctic Treaty: Should India Become a Party to It?" *Indian Journal of International Law* 1, no. 4 (April 1961), p. 483.
16. Subash C. Jain, "Antarctica: Geopolitics and International Law," in *The Indian Year Book of International Affairs 1974*, T. S. Rama Rao, ed. (Madras, India: The Indian Study Group of International Law and Affairs, University of Madras, 1974), pp. 271, 277, and 278.
17. Patrick Armstrong, "Antarctica: The First World Territory?" *Pall Mall Quarterly* (London), Spring 1958, p. 38.
18. ECOSOC, E/C.7/5, January 25, 1971.
19. It is, of course, inconceivable that U Thant's successor could then or now have undertaken such an initiative.
20. "The Future of Antarctica," Earthscan Press Briefing Document No. 5 (undated), p. 31.
21. See "Report of the Eleventh Session of the Committee on Fisheries," Rome, April 19–26, 1977 (FAO Fisheries Reports, no. 196), p. 7. See also "Verbatim of Discussion" (April 21–22). The New International Economic Order was proclaimed by the U.N. General Assembly by Resolution 3201 (S-VI), May 1, 1974.
22. 30 U.N. GAOR, A/PV.2380, General Debate, October 8, 1975, pp. 13–16.
23. The reason for the constraint was that the government that Amerasinghe represented was voted out of office. He ceased to be head of the Sri Lankan delegation to the Law of the Sea Conference and therefore could not continue as conference president. After weeks of failure to agree on a successor, the conference arranged for Amerasinghe to become an official of the United Nations, and in that capacity he continued as president of the conference until his sudden death in December 1980. As a U.N. official he could not speak with the same candor and the subject of Antarctica was in any case becoming increasingly touchy. Repeated efforts by the author to interview Mr. Amerasinghe proved fruitless.
24. Quoted in Barbara Mitchell, "The Politics of Antarctica," *Environment*, January/February 1980, pp. 20–21. Mitchell, a research associate with IIED, is cited because her quotes are more complete than those in the original Earthscan releases.
25. *Ibid.*, p. 39.
26. Barbara Mitchell and Richard Sandbrook, *The Management of the Southern*

Ocean, International Institute for Environment and Development (London), 1980, pp. 25–28 (prepared under contract to the International Union for Conservation of Nature and Natural Resources). The IUCN did not endorse the study but summarized it with implicit approval in its *Bulletin*, July/ August 1980. See also Barbara Mitchell and Jon Tinker, *Antarctica and Its Resources*, An Earthscan Publication, International Institute for Environment and Development (London), January 1980, especially pp. 79–85; Jon Tinker, "Cold War over Antarctica Wealth," *New Scientist*, September 20, 1979, p. 867; and by the same author, "Antarctica: Towards a New Internationalism," *New Scientist* (London), September 13, 1979, pp. 799–801; Barbara Mitchell, "Antarctica: A Special Case?" *New Scientist*, January 13, 1977, pp. 64–66; and by the same author, "Antarctic Riches—For Whom?" *Mazingira*, no. 2, 1977, pp. 71–77. In its enthusiasm for Third World development, the IIED has frequently exaggerated the pressure from the oil industry for exploration rights and the machinations of the consultative parties to frustrate the will of the global community as expressed in U.N. agencies. For example, IIED authors have repeatedly suggested that the treaty powers were largely responsible for killing a ten-year, forty-five-million-dollar plan for FAO to survey the Southern Ocean. But officials in the Fisheries Division of FAO in Rome insist that they themselves had serious doubts whether the project, proposed by UNDP, was appropriate and that it fell of its own weight.

27. M. C. W. Pinto, "The International Community and Antarctica," *University of Miami Law Review* 33, no. 2 (December 1978), pp. 475–87.

28. *Ibid.*, pp. 480 and 483.

29. *Ibid.*, pp. 483 and 484.

30. In the Seabed Committee of the Law of the Sea Conference, "rational exploitation" became a code term that, translated, meant "retain checks on the amount of nodules that can be mined from the floor of the sea so as not to lower the world price of copper (and of other minerals contained in the nodules)."

31. Pinto, "The International Community," p. 487.

32. "Tactics, rather than negotiation, were the rule," wrote the heads of the U.S. delegation after the first (Caracas) session of the conference (John R. Stevenson and Barnard H. Oxman, "The Third United Nations Conference on the Law of the Sea: The 1974 Caracas Session," *The American Journal of International Law*, January 1975, p. 1).

33. "Development of Antarctica," *1979 Proceedings of the American Society of International Law* (Washington, DC), p. 294. The point was made in discussion by John Dugger of the U.S. Department of Energy.

34. *Draft Convention on the Law of the Sea* (Informal Text), A/Conf.62/WP.10/Rev.3, September 22, 1980, Parts V and VI. The final text of the convention, containing 320 articles and 9 annexes, will not be available until the autumn of 1982, but the articles cited here are not expected to be altered.

35. "Draft U.N. Convention on the International Seabed Area: U.S. Working Paper Submitted to U.N. Seabeds Committee," Department of State *Bulletin*, August 24, 1970, p. 209. The continental margin consists of the continental *shelf*, where the gradient is normally very slight, bordered by the much

narrower and steeper continental *slope,* and finally the continental *rise,* composed largely of sediment accumulated over the ages at the edge of the abyssal plain or ocean bottom.

36. John R. Stevenson and Bernard H. Oxman, "The Preparations for the Law of the Sea Conference," *The American Journal of International Law,* January 1974, p. 19.

37. As late as December 1975, a task force of the Trilateral Commission, consisting of unofficial leaders of developed countries in the Northern Hemisphere, recommended that wealthy coastal states contribute half their royalties from their two-hundred-mile zones "for international purposes" (Michael Hardy *et al., A New Regime for the Oceans* [New York: The Trilateral Commission, 1976], p. 46).

38. Articles 69 and 70.

39. Article 62.

40. Article 82.

41. The fishing estimate is from John Gulland, "Developing Countries and the New Law of the Sea," *Oceanus* 2, no. 1 (Spring 1979), p. 36: "Present catches beyond 200 miles (mostly tuna) are about 1 percent of the total world catch of marine fish."

42. Richard G. Darman, "The Law of the Sea: Rethinking U.S. Interests," *Foreign Affairs,* January 1978, p. 383. It is worth noting that the events leading to this conclusion began in 1945, when President Truman, under pressure from the oil industry, unilaterally proclaimed the exclusive right of the United States to explore and exploit the mineral resources of its continental shelf beyond the territorial sea, which then was three miles. Other countries followed suit, often claiming—as in the case of Chile—jurisdiction to two hundred miles. It was to establish order out of this impending chaos that the First United Nations Law of the Sea Conference was called in 1958. The convention adopted then, as it pertained to offshore oil drilling, was outdated by technology almost as soon as it was ratified. A second effort in 1960 failed. By the time the Third Law of the Sea Conference began in 1973, nearly a hundred countries had claimed jurisdiction of varying distances beyond the customary territorial sea. See John Temple Swing, "Who Will Own the Oceans?" *Foreign Affairs,* April 1976, pp. 527–31; and John A. Knauss, *Factors Influencing a U.S. Position in a Future Law of the Sea Conference,* Law of the Sea Institute, University of Rhode Island, Occasional Paper no. 10, April 1971, p. 12.

43. Fernando Zegers Santa Cruz, "El Sistema Antartico Y La Utilizacion De Los Recursos" ("The Antarctic System and the Utilization of Resources"), *University of Miami Law Review* (in both Spanish and English) 33, no. 2 (December 1978), pp. 459 and 461.

44. Statement in the Australian Parliament, September 25, 1979, by the minister for primary industry and acting minister for foreign affairs, Mr. Sinclair (typescript).

45. *Territorial Sea and Exclusive Economic Zone Act, 1977,* Wellington, New Zealand, para. 9 (3).

46. *Report of the Tenth Antarctic Treaty Consultative Meeting,* Washington, DC, September 17–October 5, 1979. Department of State, Washington, DC, p. 101.

47. Very few Americans know that it was President Lyndon Johnson who first enunciated the principle that the resources of the seabed should belong to all. The suggestion is generally attributed to Ambassador Arvid Pardo of Malta, speaking at the United Nations in 1967. But a year earlier at the launching of a new oceanographic research vessel from the Washington Navy Yard, President Johnson said: "Under no circumstances, we believe, must we ever allow the prospects of rich harvest and mineral wealth to create a new form of colonial competition among maritime nations. We must be careful to avoid a race to grab and hold the lands under the high seas. We must ensure that the deep seas and the ocean bottoms, are, and remain, the legacy of all human beings" *(The New York Times,* July 14, 1966, p. 10). Four years later, on December 17, 1970, the U.N. General Assembly, by a vote of 108 to 0 with 14 abstentions, declared the resources of the seabed to be "the common heritage of mankind" (Resolution 2749 [XXV]). By this time, preparations for the Third Law of the Sea Conference had already begun.

48. *The New York Times,* December 4, 1959.

49. *Treaty on Principles Governing the Activities of States in the Exploration and Use of Outer Space, including the Moon and Other Celestial Bodies,* No. 8843 United Nations Treaty Series, vol. 610, 1967, p. 207. (Also in Department of State *Bulletin,* December 26, 1966, pp. 953–55.)

50. *Agreement Governing the Activities of States on the Moon and Other Celestial Bodies* (A/SPC/34/L.12), adopted by the U.N. General Assembly, December 5, 1979.

51. Frank Church and Jacob K. Javits, letter of October 30, 1979, to Secretary of State Cyrus R. Vance.

52. One of the most extended and well noted of these was Philip C. Jessup and Howard J. Taubenfeld, *Controls for Outer Space and the Antarctic Analogy* (New York: Columbia University Press, 1959), published the same year the Antarctic Treaty was signed.

53. William J. Broad, "Earthlings at Odds Over Moon Treaty," *Science,* November 23, 1979, p. 915.

54. *Ibid.*

55. Quoted in *ibid.,* p. 916.

56. *Washington Post,* February 14, 1980.

57. Although for our purposes the attitudes reflected by L-5 and industrial interests are of more concern than the substance of the argument, the following points should be made: (1) The common heritage and "equitable sharing" provisions of the Moon Treaty were proposed by the United States; (2) parties to the treaty merely agree "to establish an international regime" to govern the exploitation of natural resources in space at some future time when exploitation becomes feasible; (3) meanwhile, samples of "mineral and other substances" may be brought back from space for scientific purposes without restraint and there are no restrictions on scientific investigations in space (other than environmental protection); (4) other provisions simply

repeat or elaborate commitments already undertaken by virtue of the Space Treaty.

58. George H. Aldrich, "A Few Thoughts on the Concept of the 'Common Heritage of Mankind,'" unpublished, Summer 1980, pp. 1 and 2. Many believed it a serious inadvertence when, in January 1979, an executive order extending the application of the National Environmental Policy Act (NEPA) overseas stated that the rules would apply to "major Federal actions significantly affecting the environment of the global commons" such as "the oceans *or Antarctica*" (Executive Order 12114 of January 4, 1979, *Federal Register* 44, no. 6 [January 9, 1979], p. 1957; italics added). Perhaps it was intended, but the language could only have distressed some of our treaty partners.

59. Interview, Washington, DC, December 11, 1980. At the time Ambassador Aldrich was acting chairman of the U.S. delegation. In early March 1981, he was summarily dismissed (along with most of the senior members of the delegation) less than forty-eight hours before the Law of the Sea Conference was to resume. (*The New York Times*, March 9, 1981.)

60. For a supreme instance, see William Safire, "The Great Ripoff," *The New York Times*, March 19, 1981.

61. Some well-placed observers believe that the position of the mining companies in the Law of the Sea negotiations was designed primarily to win government subsidies for seabed mining.

62. Aldrich, "A Few Thoughts," p. 5.

63. A citizen of the Third World might have been interested in an article in the *Foreign Service Journal* (August 1975) entitled "Antarctica: The Land Belonging to All the People." But he would have had a sense of letdown when he read that Antarctica and its resources were often referred to as part of the " 'global patrimony,' rather like the world's oceans beyond territorial waters." For more on the common heritage and the commons by a legal scholar, see Richard B. Bilder, "The Present Legal and Political Situation in Antarctica," in *The New Nationalism and the Use of Common Spaces: Issues in Marine Pollution and the Exploitation of Antarctica*, Jonathan I. Charney, ed. (Montclair, NJ: Allanheld, Osmun, in press). A scientist, writing on one aspect of this subject, has summarized these dichotomous views very effectively: See George Cadwalader, "Freedom for Science in the Oceans," *Science*, October 5, 1973, p. 17.

64. James N. Barnes, "The Emerging Convention on the Conservation of Antarctic Marine Living Resources: Meeting the New Realities of Resource Exploitation in the Southern Ocean," in *The New Nationalism*.

65. See Chapter VII.

66. K. D. Suter, *Antarctica: World Law and the Last Wilderness* (Sydney, Australia: Friends of the Earth, 1979), p. 48.

67. The text reads:

5. ESTABLISHMENT OF ANTARCTICA AS A WORLD PARK UNDER UNITED NATIONS AUSPICES

Recognizing the great scientific and esthetic value of the unaltered natural ecosystem of the Antarctic Continent and the seas surrounding it;
Recognizing that the Antarctic Treaty provides, to an unprecedented degree, protection to these ecosystems;
Believing that, in this second century of the national park movement, the concept of world parks should be promoted;
Considering that Antarctica offers special opportunities for the implementation of the concept;

The Second World Conference on National Parks, meeting at Grand Teton National Park, U.S.A., in September 1972:
Recommends that the nations party to the Antarctic Treaty should negotiate to establish the Antarctic Continent and the surrounding seas as the first world park, under the auspices of the United Nations.

"Establishment of Antarctica as a World Park under United Nations Auspices," Recommendation 5, *Second World Conference on National Parks,* IUCN, Gland. Switzerland, 1974, p. 443. Interestingly, the only national park in Antarctica was created by France in 1924 "pour la préservation des espèces de toutes sortes." It covers a number of islands only marginally within the Antarctic region and does not extend to the mainland. ("Décret du 30 Décembre 1924 créant un Parc National Antarctique Français," *Journal Officiel de la République Française,* 3 Janvier 1925, pp. 348–50.)

68. Barnes, "The Emerging Convention."
69. *The New York Times,* August 29, 1975, p. 28.
70. The letter, dated April 16, 1979, was drafted by James N. Barnes of the Center for Law and Social Policy, who was largely responsible for forming ASOC, the Antarctic and Southern Ocean Coalition. Among the signatories were such well-known people as Russell Train, David Brower, Russell Peterson, and Thomas L. Kimball.
71. Letter to Barnes dated October 2, 1980.
72. Quoted in personal communication from Tony Mence, July 25, 1979. Mence is senior executive in the Office of the Director General of IUCN.

CHAPTER VII

1. The most comprehensive account of the negotiations is James N. Barnes, "The Emerging Convention of the Conservation of Antarctic Marine Living Resources: Meeting the New Realities of Resource Exploitation in the Southern Ocean," in *The New Nationalism and the Use of Common Spaces: Issues in Marine Pollution and the Exploitation of Antarctica,* Jonathan I. Charney, ed. (Montclair, NJ: Allanheld, Osmun, in press). For an analysis of the convention by two of the principal British negotiators, see David M. Edwards and John A. Heap, "Convention on the Conservation of Antarctic Marine Living Resources: A Commentary," *Polar Record,* January 1981. The authors are respectively legal counselor and head of the Polar Regions Section of the British Foreign and Commonwealth Office.
2. It is said that exclusion was demanded not only because France wanted

uninhibited control over fishing in the islands but also because it intended to use the Kergúelen archipelago for atomic testing.

3. Some confusion was caused among nongovernmental groups because the convention was not formally signed at Canberra. As some delegates lacked full powers, only the so-called final act of the conference was signed in May. It was not until mid-September 1980 that all the participants formally signed the convention within a few days of one another.

4. However, conservationists are troubled by the ambiguity in paragraph 3(a). They point out that "it is not possible to maximize net annual increments of organisms at all levels of the food chain simultaneously" (*Report and Recommendations of the Southern Ocean Convention Workshop on Management of Antarctic Marine Living Organisms,* Washington, DC, March 31–April 2, 1980. The workshop had multiple sponsors). See also Barbara Mitchell and Richard Sandbrook, *The Management of the Southern Ocean,* International Institute for the Environment and Development (London), 1980, pp. 48–49. At the final meeting in Canberra, the United Kingdom tried to get paragraph 3(a) clarified but was unable to obtain sufficient support (R. Tucker Scully, "Report of the United States Delegation to the Conference on Antarctic Marine Living Resources," Washington, DC, July 29, 1980, p. 5). Nevertheless, as a statement of intent, Article II is without precedent among fishing conventions.

5. Keith Brennan of Australia, interview, Washington, DC, October 4, 1979.

6. Barnes, "The Emerging Convention," p. 71.

7. Edwards and Heap, "Convention on the Conservation of Antarctic Marine Living Resources," p. 358.

8. *Ibid.,* p. 359.

9. "Fifth, it should provide for effective enforcement arrangements to ensure compliance with conservation measures" (R. C. Brewster, chairman of the U.S. delegation, in his closing statement at the Ninth Consultative Meeting, London, 1977, *Report of the Ninth Consultative Meeting,* p. 41).

10. Cited in M. A. McWhinnie, with the assistance of C. J. Denys, *Antarctic Marine Living Resources with Special Reference to Krill, Euphausia Superba: Assessment of Adequacy of Present Knowledge,* A Report Submitted to the National Science Foundation, December 1978, pp. 32–33. However, another authority calculates that if "existing smaller fishing vessels" were redeployed to the Southern Ocean and supported by motherships and tankers, the annual krill catch might reach twenty million tons (Inigo Everson, "Antarctic Fisheries," *Polar Record* 19, no. 120 [1978], p. 248).

11. See John A. Gulland, "Fishery Management: New Strategies for New Conditions," *Transactions of the American Fisheries Society* 107, no. 1 (January 1978), especially p. 7.

12. Leonard C. Meeker, in *Exploitation of Antarctic Resources,* Hearing before the Senate Subcommittee on Arms Control, Oceans and International Environment, February 6, 1978, p. 89.

13. Inigo Everson, interview, Cambridge, England, October 8, 1980; and John A. Gulland, interview, FAO Rome, October 1 and 2, 1980.

14. A Polish leader of exploratory fishing expeditions in the Southern Ocean told the author, with considerable resentment, that the Soviets had withheld from

his government all the data they had gathered since the early 1960s—data that would have saved the Poles large amounts of time and money.

15. For the main provisions of this unpublished document, see Barnes, "The Emerging Convention."

16. *Ibid.*

17. Scully Report, p. 1.

18. West Germany had not then been elected to consultative status.

19. See, for example, Barbara Mitchell and Lee Kimball, "Conflict Over the Cold Continent," *Foreign Policy,* Summer 1979, pp. 136–37; and Jon Tinker, "Antarctica: Towards a New Internationalism," *New Scientist,* September 13, 1979.

20. John D. Negroponte in *U.S. Activities in Antarctica,* Hearing before the Senate Committee on Energy and Natural Resources (Publication No. 96-21), April 23, 1979, pp. 16–18.

21. *Environmental Policy and Law,* February 1979, pp. 58–62.

22. *Exploitation of Antarctic Resources,* Hearing before the Subcommittee on Arms Control, Oceans and International Environment of the Senate Committee on Foreign Relations, February 6, 1978, p. 22. In her carefully worded prepared statement, Secretary Mink said: "We believe that the initiative for the creation of such a convention should come from within the Antarctic Treaty system, consistent with the principles and purposes of the Treaty. We hold that the convention, however, should be concluded by a separate international conference with additional participation by non-Treaty Parties and international organizations with direct interests in the resources concerned" (*ibid.,* p. 19).

23. Mitchell and Sandbrook, *The Management of the Southern Ocean,* pp. 130–31.

24. Participants in the negotiations justify these provisions on the ground that "it is not unreasonable to expect [newly active] states to adhere to a regime such as the Antarctic Treaty system in order to avoid serious irregularities from developing between themselves and those states which have bound themselves to it" (Edwards and Heap, "Convention on the Conservation of Antarctic Marine Living Resources," p. 360). Perhaps so, but rather than demand that nations "adhere to a regime" to which they do not belong, it would have been preferable to restate the essential principles without reference to the Antarctic Treaty.

25. *Report of the Conference on the Conservation of Antarctic Seals,* February 3–11, 1972, Foreign and Commonwealth Office, London, 1972.

26. *Annual Report of the Marine Mammal Commission, Calendar Year 1979,* A Report to Congress, Washington, DC, p. 60.

27. Committee to Evaluate Antarctic Marine Ecosystem Research, National Research Council, *An Evaluation of Antarctic Marine Ecosystem Research* (Washington, DC: 1981), pp. 39–40 and 48.

28. For example, the Commission sponsored an ad hoc conference of scientists in August 1981 to address issues that should be discussed at the Hobart meeting, and commissioned a report by Katherine A. Green Hammond, *Antarctic Marine Living Resources Convention: Requirements for Effective Implementation* (Washington, DC, July 1981).

29. Letter from the Antarctic and Southern Ocean Coalition to heads of delega-

tions, Canberra, May 15, 1980. The letter was signed by representatives of ten organizations in behalf of the full membership.

30. Reviewing that period, the New Zealand foreign minister wrote of "a widespread concern that the research programmes of some countries were leaning progressively further in the direction of exploration for minerals on the continent itself" (B. E. Talboys, "New Zealand and the Antarctic Treaty," *New Zealand Foreign Affairs Review* 28, no. 3 [1978], p. 32).

31. Tucker Scully, in *U.S. Antarctic Program*, Hearings Before the Subcommittee on Science, Research and Technology of the House Committee on Science and Technology, May 1 and 3, 1979, p. 38.

32. Diplomats seem fond of the word "regime." It can mean anything and sounds as though it would be easier to negotiate than a treaty. Some of the participants in fact hope that the agreement will not have to take the form of a treaty; since only the consultative parties to the Antarctic Treaty are considered to be involved, a minerals regime could, in theory, be cast in a form comparable to the "Agreed Measures for the Conservation of Antarctic Fauna and Flora" (see Chapter V), which was simply one of many "Recommendations" to governments. It nonetheless required complex legislation in most countries to bring them into conformity. As to the policy of "voluntary restraint," it was widely reported in 1977 as a "moratorium," although the word was nowhere used officially. See, for example, Nigel Hawkes, "Science in Europe/Moratorium Set on Antarctic Oil at October Meeting," *Science*, November 18, 1977, pp. 709–12.

33. Recommendations IX-1.

34. *Report of the Tenth Antarctic Treaty Consultative Meeting*, Washington, DC, September 17–October 5, 1979, Department of State, Washington, DC, p. 101.

35. Joseph E. Bennett, interviews, Washington, DC, September 20, 1979, and May 15, 1981. Barbara Mitchell and Lee Kimball report that Texaco inquired in 1970 how to obtain a license for oil exploration on the Atlantic section of the Antarctic continental shelf ("Conflict over the Cold Continent," p. 130).

36. Jon Tinker, "Antarctica and the Third World," *Earthscan*, 1979, p. 2.

37. Interview, Washington, DC, October 4, 1979.

38. See, for example, Richard B. Bilder, "The Present Legal and Political Situation in Antarctica," in *The New Nationalism*.

39. See Fernando Zegers Santa Cruz, "The Antarctic System and the Utilization of Resources," *University of Miami Law Review* 33, no. 2 (1978), especially pp. 451–61. Ambassador Zegers has headed the Chilean delegation at many meetings of the treaty powers.

40. Brennan interview.

41. Law N. 21.778.

42. *Report of the Tenth Antarctic Treaty Consultative Meeting*, p. 70.

43. ANT/XI/34Add. 1, July 7, 1981, p. 3.

44. Bilder, "The Present Legal and Political Situation," p. 54.

CHAPTER VIII

1. Reprinted in *U.S. Antarctic Policy,* Hearing before the Subcommittee on Oceans and International Environment of the Senate Committee on Foreign Relations, May 15, 1975, p. 30.
2. O. N. Khlestov, *Report of the Ninth Antarctic Treaty Consultative Meeting,* London, September 19–October 7, 1977, Foreign and Commonwealth Office, London, p. 45.
3. U.S. Department of State, *The Conference on Antarctica, Washington, October 15–December 1, 1959,* Washington, DC, September 1960, p. 37.
4. *Report of the Ninth Antarctic Treaty Consultative Meeting,* p. 25.
5. C. Wilfred Jenks, "An International Regime for Antarctica," Chapter 8 in *The Common Law of Mankind* (New York: Praeger, 1958); see especially pp. 370–71 and 380.
6. *Ibid.,* p. 378.
7. Philip C. Jessup and Howard J. Taubenfeld, *Controls for Outer Space and the Antarctic Analogy* (New York: Columbia University Press, 1959), p. 187.
8. *Ibid.,* p. 188.
9. *Ibid.*
10. *Ibid.,* p. 189. See also Philip C. Jessup and Howard J. Taubenfeld, "Outer Space, Antarctica, and the U.N.," *International Organization* (Boston) 13, no. 3 (1959), pp. 374–75.
11. Edvard Hambro, "Some Notes on the Future of the Antarctic Treaty Collaboration," *American Journal of International Law* 68, no. 2 (April 1974), pp. 224–25. On the condominium idea, see also Julia Rose, "Antarctic Condominium: Building a New Legal Order for Commercial Interests," *Marine Technology Science Journal* 10, no. 1 (January 1976), pp. 25–27.
12. Brian Roberts, "International Co-operation for Antarctic Development: The Test for the Antarctic Treaty," *Polar Record* 19, no. 119 (1978), p. 343.
13. *Ibid.,* p. 342.
14. *Ibid.,* p. 343.
15. *Ibid.,* p. 344.
16. *Ibid.,* p. 355.
17. Steven J. Burton, "New Stresses on the Antarctic Treaty: Toward International Legal Institutions Governing Antarctic Resources," *Virginia Law Review* 65, no. 3 (April 1979), pp. 453, 458, and 474.
18. *Ibid.,* p. 470.
19. *Ibid.,* p. 495.
20. *Ibid.,* pp. 485–90.
21. *Ibid.,* pp. 497–510.
22. Frank C. Alexander, Jr., "A Recommended Approach to the Antarctic Resource Problem," *University of Miami Law Review* 33, no. 2 (December 1978), pp. 417–23. See also Gerald S. Schatz, "The Polar Regions in Human Welfare: Regimes for Environmental Protection," in *Earthcare: Global Protection of Natural Areas,* Edmund A. Schofield, ed. (Boulder, CO: Westview Press, 1978), p. 475.
23. Edward E. Honnold, "Thaw in International Law? Rights in Antarctica under

Law of Common Spaces," *The Yale Law Journal* 87, no. 4 (March 1978), pp. 848, 855, 857, and 859. For further discussion of a universal regime, see Jonathan I. Charney, "Future Strategies for an Antarctic Mineral Resource Regime —Can the Environment Be Protected?" in *The New Nationalism and the Use of Common Spaces: Issues in Marine Pollution and the Exploitation of Antarctica,* Jonathan I. Charney, ed. (Montclair, NJ: Allanheld, Osmun, in press). For proposals involving the United Nations in Antarctica, see Chapter VI, above.

24. *North-South: A Program for Survival,* The Report of the Independent Commission on International Development Issues (Cambridge, MA: MIT Press, 1980), pp. 244–47. While this is not the place to discuss the New International Economic Order, it must be said that Antarctica offers an opportunity for the treaty powers to indicate they take it seriously. The evidence is overwhelming that good-faith negotiations have not yet begun—more than seven years after the U.N. declaration. ("Declaration on the Establishment of a New International Economic Order," United Nations General Assembly Resolution 3201 [S-VI], May 1, 1974. Available in Richard P. Stebbins and Elaine P. Adam, eds., *American Foreign Relations 1974,* published for the Council on Foreign Relations by New York University Press, 1977, pp. 103–8.) See Ruth W. Arad, *et al., Sharing Global Resources,* 1980s Project/Council on Foreign Relations (New York: McGraw-Hill, 1979); Roger D. Hansen, *Can the North-South Impasse Be Overcome?,* Overseas Development Council, Washington, DC: 1979; and especially Mahbub ul Haq, "Negotiating the Future," *Foreign Affairs,* Winter 1980/81, pp. 398–417. Just the expectation of exploitable resources in Antarctica requires that it be a mentionable subject in the context of the New International Economic Order.

25. FAO has recently developed a program to help developing countries exploit the fisheries of their newly acquired exclusive economic zones. See *World Fisheries and the Law of the Sea: The FAO EEZ Programme,* Rome, 1979.

26. Poland's situation may be precarious. Its desperate economic circumstances have required a severe cutback in its Antarctic research program (V. Rich, "Poland Freezes Antarctic Research," *Nature,* 1/8, January 1981, p. 6).

27. It normally takes at least six years or three consultative meetings before a new proposal is formalized in a recommendation.

28. Of the eleven acceding states Brazil, Uruguay, Peru, and Papua New Guinea are members of the Group of 77. Czechoslovakia, East Germany, and Bulgaria would presumably follow the instruction of the Soviet Union; the Netherlands and Italy would likely follow the lead of the Western consultative parties, leaving Romania as a possible maverick.

29. *U.S. Antarctic Policy,* May 1975 hearing, p. 16.

30. *Ibid.,* p. 21.

31. *Ibid.,* p. 22.

32. James E. Heg, personal communication, March 5, 1981. Now retired from federal service, Heg worked on Antarctic affairs in the NSF and earlier in the Department of Defense.

33. Hearing before the Senate Committee on Foreign Relations on the Nomination of Thomas R. Pickering to be assistant secretary of state, Bureau of Oceans and International Environmental and Scientific Affairs, September 21, 1978, p. 5.

34. Heg communication.
35. Reference is to R. Tucker Scully, director of the Office of Oceans and Polar Affairs, who has now resigned from the Foreign Service in order to retain his post. The revolving deputy assistant secretaries: Robert C. Brewster, John D. Negroponte, Morris D. Busby, and Charles Horner.
36. The National Science Foundation has central power and responsibility in a lesser but important area. The Division of Polar Programs has well-nigh absolute authority to determine who gets to Antarctica. A decade or more ago, the Navy provided an alternative channel, especially for nonscientists, but now the Navy has no budget of its own. The mission of the NSF's Division of Polar Programs is to sponsor scientific research, so it rightly sends scientists to Antarctica. An exception is made each year for three or four journalists (out of scores of applications) who can ensure wide publicity for the NSF's polar research. They write one or two short pieces, and that is generally the end of it. True, the National Endowment for the Humanities has conducted a rather unsuccessful and inflexible program offering modest fellowships and an assured trip to Antarctica for which the Endowment reimburses the NSF. All concerned have been unhappy with the quality of the applicants and with what the chosen few have produced, whether as artists or writers or whatever. A serious student of Antarctica who is not a scientist and is not in government cannot get to Antarctica except on a commercial tour, which is too confining to be worth the high cost.

    What is needed is a flexible program for scholars and serious students, who are not scientists and cannot promise readership in six figures, to get to Antarctica on their own terms and, within reason, on their own schedule. Two or three grants a year, covering only the NSF's costs, would be sufficient to meet the demand of the most highly qualified—those who had devoted time to the study of some aspect of the Antarctic and demonstrated some capability. The administering body should be outside the NSF, small, and capable of making quick decisions. Interest in Antarctica is no longer exclusively scientific. It therefore seems inappropriate for the NSF to have a monopoly on deciding who can visit there.

Index

A

Adams, John Quincy, 13
Adélie Land, 14, 23, 112, 116, 131
Agreed Measures for the Con-
  servation of Antarctic Fauna and
  Flora, 148, 159–160, 195
Airglow, 52, 53
Aldrich, George H., 177–178
Alexander, Frank C., 207
Alexander I Land, 11
Amerasinghe, Shirley, 167–168
Amundsen, Roald, 1, 15, 20, 25–26,
  29, 42
Antarctic and Southern Ocean
  Coalition, 190, 193
Antarctic Conservation Act (1978),
  159–160
Antarctic Convergence, 37–38, 184
Antarctic Peninsula, 32, 97, 110, 115,
  130
Antarctic Policy Group, 195, 215
Antarctic Treaty, 1–3, 103, 143–147,
  149–150, 163, 180, 181, 204 (See
  also Consultive meetings;
  Consultive powers; Washington
  Conference (1959)); Article III,
  95, 191, 200; Article IV, 143–144,
  149–150, 173, 191, 196, 199;
  Article V, 56, 106–107, 148, 191;
  Article VI, 152; Article VII, 147;
  Article VIII, 150–152, 161; Article
  IX, 149, 150, 157, 161, 210;
  Article X, 152; Article XI, 152;
  Article XII, 153, 213; Article XIII,
  149; ratification, 151, 153–156:
  review, 4, 152–153, 162, 174,
  212–213, 216
Antarctic Working Group, 59, 138,
  140
Antarctica, myths about, 5–6
Arctowski, Henryk, 20
Argentina, 120, 143, 147, 158, 165,
  168, 217 (See also Expeditions,
  Argentine; Stations, Argentine;
  Territorial claims, Argentine);
  and the Antarctic Treaty, 145,
  148–149, 152, 156, 162, 212;
  claims vs. Chile, 113, 115, 123–
  124, 132, 133, 134; claims vs.
  Great Britain, 23, 113, 115, 117,
  119–123, 133, 134, 136
Atmospheric pollution, 53–54, 65–66
Atmospheric sciences, 49, 52–54, 60,
  62, 64 (See also Climate;
  Meteorology)